THE INFLUENCE OF AFFLUENCE

THE INFLUENCE OF AFFLUENCE

How the New Rich Are Changing America

RUSS ALAN PRINCE *and* LEWIS SCHIFF

BROADWAY BOOKS

NEW YORK

Previously published under the title *The Middle-Class Millionaire*

To Sandi, of course

—Russ Alan Prince

To Lynette and Jacob, my network

—Lewis Schiff

Published in the United States by Broadway Books, an imprint of The Crown Publishing Group, a division of Random House, Inc., New York.
www.crownpublishing.com

A hardcover edition of this book was originally published in 2008 by Currency Doubleday under the title *The Middle-Class Millionaire*.

Book design by Tina Henderson

Library of Congress Cataloging-in-Publication Data
Prince, Russ Alan, 1958–
The influence of affluence : How the new rich are changing America / Russ Alan Prince and Lewis Schiff.
p. cm.
Includes bibliographical references and index.
1. Rich people—United States. 2. Millionaires—United States. 3. United States—Economic conditions—2001– 4. Wealth—United States. I. Schiff, Lewis. II. Title.
HC110.W4P75 2008
305.5'2340973—dc22
2007046047
ISBN: 978-0-385-51928-1

PRINTED IN THE UNITED STATES OF AMERICA

1 3 5 7 9 10 8 6 4 2

First Paperback Edition

CONTENTS

ACKNOWLEDGMENTS

The idea for *The Influence of Affluence* occurred on April 22, 2005, during a lunchtime conversation between the two of us at one of New York City's finest restaurants, Per Se. We were the hired help that day, having spent the late morning in the private dining wing presenting data about recent changes in the financial industry to a room full of financial trade reporters. As the tables were being cleared, Russ and I drifted into a conversation about upcoming research projects. Russ, who is able to see stories, hopes, and dreams in a spreadsheet full of numbers, mentioned his recent "discovery" of a new demographic of millionaires. (This discovery process is described in the first chapter of this book.) He called them "middle-class millionaires." I was immediately struck by that contradiction in terms—as many others have been since. Having a million dollars sounds like a fantasy, conjuring up images of first-class status, luxury living, and perhaps most important, financial peace of mind. But for those working Americans who've reached the million-dollar mark and still find themselves with mortgage payments, tuition bills, and other expenses, it can be just a number—and not necessarily an address on Easy Street.

This book doesn't dwell on the financial contradictions of the world we live in—although that's a worthy topic. Rather, we set out to introduce you to the people who are at the heart of that contradiction—the substantial and increasing population of people who would call themselves "middle-class" but whose wealth, behavior, and attitudes have put them in a class all their own. Taking the exercise a step further, we've attempted to identify their unique attributes and contributions and explored how these can be harnessed by society at large as well as by the reader for personal and professional gain.

Spending the last two years analyzing a nascent demographic sometimes felt like a risky pursuit. What if, we worried, the Middle-Class Millionaire was really just a new coat of paint on an old car—a baby boomer in Burberry? We might have given in to these concerns, denying us the chance to learn about this important and influential body of people, had it not been for certain influential individuals in our lives who encouraged us to move forward. That list begins with our spouses, who, partly because we thought it was worthwhile, found it worthwhile, too. Sandi and Lynette provided more support and guidance than we deserve, and we are grateful for their patience, their love, and their willingness to discuss the topic of this book from nearly every conceivable perspective.

Mark Ganem provided a great deal of guidance that helped turn a vague notion into a fully fleshed-out concept. Mark was extremely generous with his time and extensive experience even before we had an inkling that there was something worth pursuing. And he continued to deliver good advice all the way to the last page. That kind of help is only offered out of friendship and deserves special recognition.

After we wrote an outline, it was time to sell it. The first hurdle was our savvy and knowledgeable literary agent, Robert Levine. Bob liked what he saw but asked us to hone the concept, guiding us through no fewer than ten drafts before finally declaring it "ready for market." Again, spouses proved to be essential business partners as Bob's wife, Suzanne Braun Levine, the author of *Inventing the Rest of Our Lives: Women in Second Adulthood* and a legendary magazine editor in her own right, added her own two cents at a pivotal juncture.

Eventually, the committed editors and staff at Random House's Doubleday Books, including Stephen Rubin, Roger Scholl, Talia Krohn, Meredith McGinnis, Louise Quayle, and Carolyn Pilkington, saw something they liked and convinced us that the book had an even bigger mission than we originally imagined. They thought that what we were writing about would be valuable to "people everywhere who are curious about the world they live in." For opening up a wider set of possibilities, we thank the team at Doubleday Books.

The original research that makes up the skeleton of this story required a survey of 3,714 American households. To do this we called upon the efforts of Russ's long-time research partner and collaborator, the talented Karen Maru. Many thanks to her and to those surveyed. Our gratitude also goes to the scores of people who sat for one-on-one interviews for the book. Because they shared their stories with us, we were able to add muscle and tissue to our skeleton of data, bringing this story to life.

Early on we found a writing coach—after all, coaches are used by the very best athletes and businesspeople, so why not us? We can string sentences together, but we believed this book would require the very best we had in us. So we asked Noel Weyrich to help bring it out. Noel's dedication to this book was more than we could have hoped for, and we are thrilled that he took the journey with us.

If this sounds like a lot of cooks in the kitchen, it wasn't. In fact, each person in our little army, from our spouses to our friends to our long-time associates to our new business partners, has made an invaluable contribution to this effort. Sentence by sentence, idea by idea, there was something important added by every member of the team. Our names may be on the cover, but they deserve much of the credit for helping bring this book to reality.

—Lewis Schiff

CHAPTER ONE

THE INFLUENCE OF AFFLUENCE

In 2004, the sales department at *Elite Traveler* magazine asked Russ Alan Prince to conduct a marketing survey of its readership. *Elite Traveler* is likely the most exclusive consumer magazine in the world. The magazine is distributed primarily on private jets, and it covers subjects such as how to book your own private island. Its reader demographics, with an average household income in the seven figures, eclipse those of its nearest competitor by more than sixfold. Russ's job, in part, was to measure how much influence the buying habits of these very affluent readers exert on others around them.

In the field of luxury marketing, purchasing decisions of high-net-worth individuals are assumed to exert a "downline influence" on people of the same or lesser means. *Elite Traveler* wanted to know if Russ could document a similar relationship between the purchasing decisions of the people who read *Elite Traveler* and other people who associate with them.

Russ has been studying the spending and investing habits of high-net-worth individuals for more than twenty years. He knew that carrying out a methodologically sound survey of very wealthy individuals would be a difficult and time-consuming task. To find 203 respondents willing to answer a long series of personal questions posed by a researcher in personal interviews, Prince had to network his way through lists of financial advisors and private jet services who served as go-betweens. Most of the survey subjects either accepted a $500 payment for their cooperation or directed that sum to one of their pet charities.

The survey results provided *Elite Traveler* with an unwelcome surprise. According to the survey, the buying decisions of very-high-net-worth individuals—those with wealth in excess of $10 million—exert very little influence on the people around them. Except for certain celebrities, wealthy people who are influential by almost every other measure don't serve as role models when they purchase goods and services. They are not "referentially influential." If they buy something for their home or office, they tend not to talk about it very much. In the case of more easily observable purchases, such as clothes, watches, and jewelry, they seldom interact with enough people on a day-to-day basis to exert any significant influence. And when it comes to providers of personal services—life coaches, personal trainers, financial advisors—the very rich can be very secretive. Express too much praise for your coach or trainer, after all, and he or she might get poached by someone else.

Russ had managed to measure in a meaningful way, perhaps for the first time, the profound insularity of the very wealthy. They don't have a very big impact on the rest of us. This conclusion was not terribly helpful to *Elite Traveler,* but Russ found himself intrigued by one small set of details buried in the data. The sample was too small for him to draw any concrete conclusions, but it seemed to him that a handful of the least affluent in this particular sample group reported behavior patterns that set them apart from the rest. They enjoyed making their opinions known, and they actively solicited opinions from others. They talked with a lot of people each day. Here was a subset of the multimillionaire cohort who didn't act like multimillionaires.

In a subsequent readership survey done for *The New Yorker* and *Registered Rep* magazines, Russ's researchers interviewed 1,417 people who declared a net worth between $1 million and $10 million, including the equity they hold in their primary residence. It was here that he discovered, as a sociological phenomenon, the Middle-Class Millionaire. Most are baby boomers, but some were born after the boom's end in 1964. They made, rather than inherited, their money, often through technology, real estate, entrepreneurship, or a mix of all three. And while Middle-Class Millionaires are found in just about every kind of community, they tend to congregate on the East and West Coasts.

Months later Russ compared survey responses from these self-identified working millionaires with a pilot study of ordinary middle-class individuals. Here he found measurable differences in areas closely related to financial success. The attitudes and beliefs of the Middle-Class Millionaires were significantly different from those of the broader middle class. Some behaviors were valued more highly than others or were practiced more rigorously. Knowing what those behaviors were might help others achieve similar success. For example, Middle-Class Millionaires worked much longer hours. They were more likely to focus on drawing financial gain from their work. They were less inclined to be discouraged by failure.

Above all, Russ found that the millionaires in his middle-class sample were measurably more influential than people who had not achieved millionaire status. Middle-Class Millionaires are networkers by nature. They reported seeking the advice of others—and offering advice—far more frequently than the other survey respondents. And they believe that the advice they offer is much more likely to be followed by others. In other words, as a group, Middle-Class Millionaires aren't merely talented professionals who happen to make a lot of money. Instead, their distinctive temperament and behavioral tendencies seem to be significant factors in the achievement of their wealth.

What was most interesting to Russ as a market researcher was how their knack for networking—for talking to people, for trading information—gives Middle-Class Millionaires an oversized impact on the middle class's aspirations, attitudes, and spending habits. Middle-Class Millionaires exert that strong "downline influence" that Russ could not detect among the ultra-rich. They are natural apostles for whatever products and services they find most useful, products and services that often make their way downstream over time and become available to a much broader population. Taking into account also the natural desire of middle-class people to emulate those more affluent than themselves, Russ could see how the working rich have begun to lead a transformation of middle-class life in America.

From the Ultra-Rich to the Middle-Class Millionaire

John Hutchins is one of the many entrepreneurs who more or less accidentally discovered the Middle-Class Millionaire over the last ten years. He began with a business plan designed to satisfy the needs of the ultra-wealthy. But eventually it led him to the birth of a company that depends upon a completely different clientele—one that has far more in common with the middle class than with the super-rich.

Hutchins is a veteran hospital administrator who moved overseas in the late 1970s to run the then-new Al Hada hospital in Taif, Saudi Arabia. That job, which sometimes required him to settle disputes over which Saudi prince had the larger hospital room, also helped Hutchins familiarize himself with Europe and Asia's network of top medical specialists. In 1985, when the world-renowned Cleveland Clinic was looking for a director to open its new International Center, Hutchins was picked for the position. The center represented a first for American hospitals, a unit within a hospital devoted solely to the highly profitable recruitment and care of rich and powerful overseas patients.

With a staff of a hundred, Hutchins set about catering to the Cleveland Clinic's VIP patients and their guests from the moment they were met at the airport and whisked into waiting limousines. A sheikh from the United Arab Emirates might arrive for two weeks of cardiology tests and bring with him an entourage of a hundred or more family members and personal attendants. Hutchins and his staff needed to tackle such logistical headaches as arranging for lavish lamb dinners, booking enough rooms at the Ritz-Carlton, and finding reliable translators. As many as sixty royal Arab family groups and their entourages would come through town in a single summer, but as Hutchins, now sixty-five, remembers it, only a few of these patients suffered from any ailments serious enough to require the Cleveland Clinic's high standard of care. "In the Middle East, when it's a hundred and thirty degrees in the summer," he says, "if someone has an ingrown toenail, the whole family likes to bail out."

Hutchins eventually moved to Baltimore to launch a similar program at Johns Hopkins. Under Hutchins's direction, Johns Hopkins spent millions renovating the exclusive Marburg Pavilion, a secluded unit of fifteen hospital rooms and suites designed to provide patients with all the comforts they might expect from a five-star hotel. Each room is furnished with Chippendale guest chairs, hardwood floors, and Oriental area rugs. Hutchins contracted with the Walt Disney Company for the staff's customer service training, and the Ritz-Carlton developed the program's management protocols. Each day, staff were required to familiarize themselves with an updated log of every VIP patient's personal likes and dislikes.

For all the pampering that Hutchins offered his patients at Johns Hopkins, however, he wasn't always happy about how their actual medical treatment was handled. For one thing, slotting appointments with the best doctors in certain specialties was extremely difficult. The hospital's culture seemed resistant to accommodating what he calls "large volumes of difficult patients." The second issue was this: Although Johns Hopkins regards itself as the best hospital on earth, Hutchins knew that not all of its departments were equally distinguished. When it comes to cardiac surgery, for instance, the Cleveland Clinic, which does a far greater volume of heart operations than Johns Hopkins, might be preferable. But while he was working for Johns Hopkins, Hutchins felt it wasn't his place to point out the merits of other institutions. Over time, he came to feel that his job "wasn't to care about the patient or the family. It was caring about the institution."

In 2001, Hutchins left Johns Hopkins to start a medical consulting business. As he pictured it, the new firm would allow him, at last, to consider his clients' well-being his sole obligation. He wanted to build a nationwide network of hospitals and physicians—including some of the world's most sought-after medical specialists—and then refer the wealthy and powerful to them via his medical contacts from around the globe. In essence, the firm would function like an HMO for the world's super-elite.

A funny thing happened, though, when Hutchins sought out a financial partner for the project. One day in January 2001, he sat down with a Baltimore-area businessman and serial entrepreneur named Bruce Spector. Then aged forty-nine, Spector had just successfully sold his third company, and now he was looking for a new challenge. As he listened to Hutchins go on about all the privileges that the super-wealthy clients of this new business would enjoy—an attentive staff monitoring each patient's medical needs, thorough "executive physicals," high-tech recordkeeping, expedited appointments with top specialists—he began to wonder just how rich you really need to be to afford such care.

Spector had done very well financially for himself and his family, but he had hardly achieved the level of wealth where he could afford to hire a full-time household physician, as so many of Hutchins's international patients had. Instead, he always felt stuck with the same frustrating indignities that the health care system dishes out to everyone: the interminable time wasted in waiting rooms, the jarring discontinuity in care among various specialists, the hassles with insurance reimbursements. The more Spector listened, the more certain he was that the germ of Hutchins's idea, with some modifications, would work not just for the jet set but also for Americans like himself—people with enough disposable income to pay extra for top-quality medical care and a better experience.

Seven years later, Hutchins and Spector work out of side-by-side cubicles in a downtown Baltimore office tower. Their health care advocacy company, PinnacleCare International, has sold about 1,000 memberships, which serve approximately 3,000 members and their dependents. More than 90 percent are American citizens. Most are corporate executives and owners of successful privately held businesses on the East Coast. The most popular family membership plan at PinnacleCare costs $8,000 per year, regardless of family size, and requires a one-time $7,000 setup fee. Other membership levels run the gamut from a $3,000 per year "just-in-case" plan, which provides PinnacleCare's help in the event of a medical emergency, all the way up to $20,000 per year for people with life-threatening conditions such as stage-four cancer. News stories about PinnacleCare usually peg the company as an exclusive club for the rich, but $8,000 is considerably less than the $9,641 that AAA estimates car owners pay each year to operate ordinary family sedans such as the Toyota Camry or the Chevy Impala.

PinnacleCare is not an insurance company, nor is it a health care provider. Instead, members pay to have their health looked after by an account representative, as if each member's medical record were a financial portfolio. A trained staff of health care advocates, most of whom are registered nurses and social workers, assess goals, draw up plans, monitor progress, and attend to crises. This team also assists members with diet and prescription reminders, accompanies them to medical appointments, hammers out problems with insurers, and consults with the company's staff physicians about second-opinion referrals. In a sense, the advocates serve the same function within the health care system as financial advisors do within the financial system.

Five years ago, no such service was available at any price. Now there are PinnacleCare members who can't imagine entering a hospital or a specialist's exam room without an advocate by their side to ask questions and look out for them. One PinnacleCare member who sprained an ankle getting out of a Manhattan cab tells the story of calling his PinnacleCare advocate from the street corner where he was hurt, and within forty-five minutes, he was being treated in the office of a Manhattan foot specialist, sparing him the experience that most out-of-towners would suffer—hours of waiting in an emergency room. PinnacleCare claims that, thanks in part to the relationships it has developed through its board of medical advisors, the company can accomplish "in days and weeks what it would take an individual weeks or months to do."

Doctors, for the most part, are glad to clear their schedules for PinnacleCare clients, largely because they are influenced by the perception of affluence. An ear, nose, and throat physician told *Departures* magazine in November 2004, "If Pinnacle calls me about someone with a specialized ear problem, I will often squeeze that person into my schedule. The advantage for me is that it's a wealthy clientele base. . . . My reputation would spread as they talk about the care they received from me."

This book examines the pivotal role of the Middle-Class Millionaire in shaping the world we live in: the 7.6 percent of American households headed by what some might call the "working rich." These 8.4 million households make up a new generation of millionaires who began to emerge from the middle class in the late twentieth century. Overwhelmingly, these millionaire households are headed by people raised in ordinary middle-class homes. They've achieved significant financial success, but their fortunes are not so secure that they can afford to stop working. As their wealth has grown, so have both the cost of maintaining their lifestyles and their need for products and services that make their lives run smoothly. Now, through the influence of their affluence, this group is helping to bring about momentous changes throughout American society.

Our own exhaustive research in this field shows the degree to which the working rich are different from the broader middle class. They are uniquely achievement-oriented. They tend to be high-earning and big-spending. Through their lifestyle choices and spending decisions, they wield influence in the overall economy in support of the same middle-class values and concerns they were raised with: security, health, self-betterment, family, and community. They have achieved the American dream the American way.

By some estimates, the number of millionaire families in America will increase by about half again over the next decade. *The Middle-Class Millionaire* explores how this burgeoning population is shaping our own attitudes while using its expanding wealth to influence spending and lifestyle choices throughout our economy and society. How will its growing influence affect the values we advance, the products we buy, the ways we live, and the communities we live in? How, in the coming decade, will this market grow as goods and services for the few are transformed into "scalable" enterprises and services such as PinnacleCare that promise to transform industries and change all of our lives? Will these trends widen the gap between the haves and the have-nots in our society? Or will they, as some predict, lead to improvements that find their way throughout the middle class and American society as a whole?

The growth of PinnacleCare's member base is a clear example of the Middle-Class Millionaire effect in action. The firm has no advertising budget. Its number one source of new subscribers is referrals from existing members. It is a company whose success relies on its clients talking about their experiences.

To be sure, only a certain type of PinnacleCare member contributes to the company's pool of prospects. PinnacleCare's executives assume that members with the highest net worth are least likely to tell friends about the company. To these people, health care arrangements are personal matters to be dealt with privately and with discretion. In fact, certain PinnacleCare members put such a high premium on privacy that they have asked the firm to arrange medical procedures far from home, in out-of-town hospitals where no one is likely to recognize them.

But then there's Richard Rossi. As the co-founder of an education firm in suburban Washington, D.C., the fifty-two-year-old Rossi fits our definition of the Middle-Class Millionaire in just about every respect.

Rossi likes PinnacleCare because it satisfies his desire to surround himself with what he calls his "360-degree circle of support": lawyers, financial advisors, personal trainers, home help, and now PinnacleCare. "I've kind of gotten to the point in my life where I'm pretty clear how I want to spend my time—with my family, my friends, my business, and with my own evolution as a person," he says. "I've really figured out I don't want to spend my time worrying about anything else, to the degree I can avoid it. And that's what my circle of support is for."

And Rossi is happy to spread the wealth. He has single-handedly recruited more new PinnacleCare members than anyone else. "I tend to promote things I believe in, just because of my personality," he says. "It's a genuine desire to help people. If something has helped me or benefited me, I want others that I care about to be aware of it." He calls friends to tell them about PinnacleCare, and after he hangs up, he sends their contact information to John Hutchins for follow-up.

Rossi says he is shy by nature, except when it comes to letting friends and colleagues know what PinnacleCare has done for him. This is why, for instance, everyone who knows Richard Rossi also knows about his colonoscopy.

In preparing for what has become a middle-age rite of passage, Rossi says he reviewed his options with his PinnacleCare advocate and grew attracted to the idea of undergoing a virtual colonoscopy. By using a combination of X-rays and computer imaging, a virtual colonoscopy is safer and less invasive than the conventional procedure. The sole drawback is that if a virtual colonoscopy shows any abnormalities, the patient must return weeks later for a traditional colonoscopy. For most people, that means enduring the necessary twenty-four-hour fasting and cleansing process all over again.

"I said, 'This is ridiculous,'" Rossi recalls. "'I'm going to cleanse just once.'" He asked PinnacleCare to set up a virtual colonoscopy for him in the morning, and then to make an appointment for a conventional one later that day, just in case he needed it. As it turned out, his virtual scan at Johns Hopkins went well, and there was no need for the second session. PinnacleCare canceled his afternoon colonoscopy at a cost to Rossi of $300. "But it was worth it," he says now. "That's how you can bend the medical system to your will—if you have people to do the heavy lifting for you." Rossi's point reflects an important Middle-Class Millionaire attitude: that most problems can be solved with a mix of creative thinking, the right people, and an open wallet. It's an approach to life that they use in business, but it's also a testament to the influence they wield as consumers.

In the first few chapters of this book, we will describe the results from our survey of 3,714 households and explain how the distinct set of personality traits among Middle-Class Millionaires—hard work, networking, financial savvy, and persistence—contributes to something we call

Millionaire Intelligence. We will show how the spending habits of Middle-Class Millionaires are watched and imitated by others around them, which in turn prompts still more products and services with the Middle-Class Millionaire in mind—a process we've described as the Influence of Affluence.

The later chapters look at the particular ways in which Millionaire Intelligence and the Influence of Affluence converge to create what may be the world's most influential group of mass consumers. We'll explore how the values-driven spending habits of Middle-Class Millionaires are responsible for new and expanding modes of service, ownership, and community. Whether the concern is consumer-driven health care, professional coaching, personal security, or ways to enhance their children's education, we will show how the common thread of middle-class values helps to shape and influence them all.

Before we could begin our survey research, we needed to define "middle-class," a notoriously difficult thing to do. We started out by classifying Middle-Class Millionaire households as those with a net worth that fell between $1 million and $10 million—including the equity they maintain in their primary residence—and where the head of household's wealth was self-made (as opposed to inherited or acquired through divorce or other settlement). Then we decided that our sample population of middle-class respondents would be confined to heads of households with annual household incomes between $50,000 and $80,000 per year and with a net worth under $1 million. This income range is on the high end of the statistical middle in American household income. According to the latest census estimate, just 21 percent of U.S. households earn more than $80,000, while most households (55 percent) have earnings below $50,000. As we would later discover, almost 80 percent of the survey respondents in the $50,000-to-$80,000 income range consider themselves "middle-class," while 20 percent regard their social status as "upper-middle-class." Of course, $80,000 in one region of the country, such as the Midwest, can go a lot further than $80,000 in high-cost, high-tax states such as California or New York.

Our staff of professional researchers surveyed 586 Middle-Class Millionaire households and 3,128 households in the middle-class $50,000-to-$80,000 income range. All survey respondents were randomly contacted by phone, adhering to the most rigorous standards of social science research. The survey itself was designed with ninety-eight questions about a wide variety of attitudes, assessments, and behaviors related to working life, personal values, community life, and certain areas of consumer spending.

With a few very limited exceptions, we did not ask our survey respondents about what might be called "luxury" spending. This book is not about conspicuous consumption or high-tech bling. Luxury trends and similar cultural ephemera are interesting for other reasons, but they are not central to our discussion. Instead, we focus on the kinds of consumer choices that are informed and driven by common middle-class values. We believe these are the purchasing choices and behaviors that hold the greatest potential for influencing and transforming American society.

Take, for example, the growing acceptance over the past decade of OnStar, the automotive tracking and communications system offered by General Motors. Developed initially in the mid-1990s by a team at IBM, OnStar combines cell phone and GPS (global positioning satellite) technologies to provide drivers with twenty-four-hour access to any number of services, including roadside assistance and emergency calls for help, by simply pressing a button on the car's ceiling console. Over the years, GM has gradually expanded the range of services available through OnStar, and today the device can be used to make hotel reservations, receive turn-by-turn road directions, and even monitor tire pressure. Every month, 52,000 OnStar subscribers lock themselves out of their cars and use the system's remote door-lock activation to get back in. Since the system is alerted when a subscriber's airbag deploys,

OnStar notifies local 911 operators of about 12,000 traffic accidents a year. OnStar staff also track approximately 5,000 stolen subscriber cars annually.

Upon its introduction in 1996, OnStar cost more than $1,000 to purchase and custom-install. General Motors offered it as an option only in its highest-end production vehicles, including the Cadillac, as though it were a luxury accessory. The system's appeal as a safety feature was so profound, though, that GM soon made OnStar available in its family-friendly SUVs and minivans. Middle-Class Millionaire families originally drove that change; they were willing to pay a premium for a service that would offer them greater safety. Today, OnStar is standard equipment on all American-made GM vehicles, including the $13,790 Chevrolet Cobalt. Mercedes and other manufacturers have only begun to catch up in recent years with their own versions of OnStar; industry analysts say it is just a matter of time before such systems are standard equipment on all production vehicles.

OnStar's course of development is a perfect illustration of what we call the Influence of Affluence. Some privacy advocates have raised concerns about OnStar's new status as standard equipment, fearing that widespread access to travel data could turn OnStar into a Big Brother-like mass surveillance system. We have found, however, that abstract concerns about privacy have had little impact on our buying behavior when products are able to address more fundamental middle-class concerns, such as safety. Family safety is a crucial middle-class value, and Middle-Class Millionaires tend to use their purchasing power to express that value in as many ways as they can.

Our research suggests that the Influence of Affluence can help predict consumer appetites for other new technologies that respond to or are informed by such powerful middle-class values. For several years now, a number of small companies have been selling aftermarket tracking systems that use satellite technology similar to OnStar's in order to provide nervous parents with reports on their teenagers' driving behaviors. More advanced systems allow real-time tracking via PC. And now mobile phone providers have begun marketing GPS-enabled phones with similar capabilities at a cost of about $10 per month. Our survey shows that Middle-Class Millionaires are more than seven times as likely to purchase such devices compared with our sample of middle-class households. Among Middle-Class Millionaires, nearly 85 percent expect to acquire such devices within the next three years. Is this a feature that in the near future will be included on *all* new cell phone models, at little or no additional cost, as cell phone providers compete for that Middle-Class Millionaire market?

In Mexico today, a more elaborate and controversial variation on this child-tracking concept is already on the market. The kidnapping and ransoming of affluent children has become an epidemic in some parts of the country, and the Mexican distributor of a tiny implantable device already used to identify lost dogs and cats in America has begun marketing the same device for implants in small children. In a less crime-ridden country such as ours, that may seem extreme, but our research suggests that Middle-Class Millionaires are already considering such a tracking tool as a way to protect their children. For them, the ethical qualms about such technology are trumped by the nightmare of a child's disappearance. It's not so far-fetched to think that in the near future many more of our children will have some form of homing or tracking chip implanted in them—and that the children of Middle-Class Millionaires will have them first.

High End Today, Mass Market Tomorrow

Do companies such as PinnacleCare create a velvet rope that siphons off limited medical resources toward those who can afford to "jump the line"? PinnacleCare's many critics in the medical field complain that the company is exacerbating the health care system's chronic troubles by further dividing it into a two-tier system—one for the rich and one for everyone else. PinnacleCare founder Hutchins disagrees. Interviewed in early 2006, he told CNN with a fatherly grin, "I like two-tiered systems. I think they force necessary changes in various fields." As he sees it, PinnacleCare is making health care more responsive and consumer-oriented—the benefits will eventually have an impact on the entire industry and be enjoyed by families everywhere.

That may be marketing bravado, but one interesting effect PinnacleCare seems to have is that its members use the health care system less. There are countless stories of how the company's preventive health programs and taking of thorough medical histories have spared members unnecessary diagnostic tests and procedures they might otherwise have had to undergo. PinnacleCare members are paying out of pocket to spare their insurers expenditures.

Take the Biophysical250, a comprehensive annual blood-testing regimen developed by Texas-based Biophysical Corporation. The test uses a blood sample of just 30 cc to track the levels of 250 common and not-so-common disease markers in the bloodstream. The purpose of doing such a thorough test each year is the early detection of disease. Many serious illnesses, including a variety of cancers and heart ailments, betray themselves in blood tests long before they become symptomatic. By combining already-existing blood tests commonly used in twelve major medical specialties, the Biophysical250 can help physicians analyze your blood from year to year and track any changes that may indicate trouble.

The various blood tests that make up Biophysical250 would cost $35,000 or more if they were done individually. Biophysical is currently marketing its annual test for all 250 markers at just $3,400. "We've rolled it out at a fairly reasonable price, although it's still expensive for many people, obviously," says Craig Parks, a Biophysical vice president. "There's not widespread acceptance yet because the insurance industry doesn't cover it." This kind of test conflicts with the insurance industry's traditional approach in which it covers the statistically infrequent—although astronomical—expense of disease, rather than funding widespread early-detection measures. But the Biophysical250 test could potentially help doctors treat diseases early enough to save millions of lives and, at the same time, save the medical insurance industry money. PinnacleCare's medical staff was so impressed with Biophysical250 that in the summer of 2006 they decided to offer the annual test as a supplement to—or even as a convenient alternative for—their annual daylong executive physical.

Would you be willing to pay for such a test for yourself—or for your children? What if Biophysical Corporation were able to scale up its operations, thereby reducing the test's cost, as was once done with mammograms and colonoscopies? And how would the price be affected if other companies entered the market with competitive blood marker tests? If the price were reduced by half or three-quarters, at some point the advantages would soon outweigh the currently prohibitive cost for the rest of us. We and our families would receive more convenient and more thorough examinations, our doctors would spot potential problems earlier and be able to prevent illnesses before they start, and our health care and insurance costs would fall. Suddenly, the world has changed a little.

That's the Influence of Affluence.

CHAPTER TWO

MILLIONAIRE INTELLIGENCE

When Benjamin Franklin arrived in Philadelphia in 1723, he was a seventeen-year-old fugitive with three pennies in his pocket. Franklin had ended his formal schooling at ten, and since the age of twelve he had been apprenticed in Boston as a printer's assistant to his older brother James. The apprenticeship system in those days involved a contract of indentured servitude that in Benjamin's case made his brother his legal master for nine years. The younger Franklin, who had ambitions to be a great writer, chafed under James's supervision at the printing shop. Betting that his brother would not come after him, young Benjamin boarded a ship in Boston Harbor and sneaked away.

He couldn't have known it then, but Franklin was embarking on a career that would make him an American icon—and in many ways an American archetype as well. The fugitive apprentice found work soon enough in a Philadelphia print shop. For a young man with limited education and no family connections, this kind of steady employment in a respectable trade might have seemed like the best the world had to offer.

Franklin, however, wasn't satisfied. He accepted an offer by the governor of Pennsylvania to set him up in a printing business of his own. The governor sent Franklin to London with letters of credit in hand and instructions to return with new printing equipment. But the governor's letters of credit turned out to be worthless, and Franklin spent eighteen months working in London print shops. When he returned to Philadelphia, he took up work as a stock boy and bookkeeper in a dry goods store.

The ambitious young man wanted to return to the printing trade, but he was determined to be his own boss this time around. When he was just twenty-four, he and a group of friends started a social club in Philadelphia called the Junto. Through his connections within the Junto, it wasn't long before Franklin found a business partner and opened up an independent print shop. Within a year, Franklin had secured loans from two other members of the Junto, and he bought out his partner's share to become the sole owner of the business. It was from there that Franklin launched his career as editor and publisher of the *Pennsylvania Gazette* and *Poor Richard's Almanac*.

Franklin prospered in the printing business—an influential medium that might be considered the Internet of its day. He used his cash flow to set up other printers in shops of their own in other cities, taking a cut of their profits in return. By the age of forty-two, Franklin was ready to realize the goal he had set for himself years earlier: to retire from business and lead a "gentleman's life" of scientific inquiry and public service. He sold his ownership in the print shop to its foreman in exchange for half the business's profits over the next eighteen years. This income, plus that from his partnerships and other investments, made Franklin independently wealthy. Every great achievement for which Benjamin Franklin is remembered today took place in the latter half of his life, after the age of forty-two. Few appreciate today that none of those achievements would have been possible if Franklin hadn't spent the first twenty-five years of his adult life intensely focused on getting rich.

Despite his great wealth and fame, however, Franklin never put on the airs typical of an eighteenth-century gentleman. Unlike Washington, Jefferson, and most of the other Founding Fathers, Franklin never took to wearing the powdered wig that connoted high social status in the English colonies. To his dying day, Franklin socialized with all kinds of people, and throughout his life he signed his name "Benjamin Franklin, Printer." When he held forth on the subject of social class, he said he belonged to several classes at once: printing involved manual labor, his business interests placed him among ordinary tradesmen, and his scientific and political activities kept him in the company of the educated upper class. At his death in 1790, Benjamin Franklin was one of the wealthiest men in the new United States, and among only a few to have achieved their wealth through business.

Franklin's practical nature, profound curiosity, and egalitarian outlook all contribute to his place in history as an American icon. Some historians regard Franklin as the nation's first entrepreneur. Others, such as H. W. Brands in his Pulitzer Prize-finalist biography, have hailed him as *The First American*. But we see in Benjamin Franklin's life the very same character traits that our research has associated with today's Middle-Class Millionaires. Every turning point in the great man's life story required some deft combination of hard work, personal connections, perseverance in overcoming setbacks, and putting himself first in his financial dealings. Taken together, these traits add up to what we call Millionaire Intelligence. Benjamin Franklin's relentless exercise of his Millionaire Intelligence is largely why he grew rich and why he is remembered long after his death. You might say he was really the first Middle-Class Millionaire.

Surveying the Above-Average Universe

In November 2005, ICR Research of Media, Pennsylvania, conducted a telephone survey of 1,003 randomly selected American adults, and the results proved a crucial point about the science of survey research. Respondents were asked whether they considered themselves "at least slightly above average" in a variety of respects. Their collective response defied mathematical possibility. Based on this statistically significant sampling, 94 percent of Americans are above average in their honesty and trustworthiness. Between 86 and 89 percent are above average in intelligence, common sense, and friendliness. Even in physical appearance, 79 percent of Americans are above average. Only in the matter of health did the survey results begin to resemble harsh reality. Just 69 percent of respondents consider their health "above average."

This familiar phenomenon in survey research is called self-reporting bias. It is also known as the Lake Wobegon effect, named after the fictional town on the radio show *Prairie Home Companion* where "all the children are above average." Most survey respondents overrate their abilities when asked to rank themselves against others. A number of surveys have shown that about three-quarters of all automobile drivers believe they drive more safely than the average motorist. A 1997 study revealed that almost half of all college freshmen ranked their own academic and leadership skills among the top 10 percent of their peers.

The same problem has affected the numerous surveys that have sought to unlock the secrets of success. Many involved questionnaires that asked accomplished individuals to rank themselves on a variety of traits, and the results are often rife with self-reporting bias. It should be no surprise that most successful people claim that their achievements are the result of self-discipline, honesty, and hard work. The trouble is that these and other glowing self-evaluations are just as likely to be found among salaried middle-class people who are neither millionaires nor likely ever to become millionaires. Most people who have achieved some success in their respective fields—whether as wealthy financiers or not-so-wealthy finance professors—would probably respond with the same set of positive self-appraisals.

The method we used to avoid Lake Wobegon–type results was to construct a survey that sought answers on matters of specific behavior rather than generalized self-assessments. For instance, the question "Do you consider yourself a responsible car owner?" would likely draw the same overwhelmingly affirmative responses as "Do you consider yourself to be above average in honesty?" On the other hand, questions such as "How many times in the past year have you changed your motor oil?" and "How many times in the past six months have you washed your car?" are far more likely to identify those people who take a serious interest in caring for their cars. The method still relies on self-reporting, but people in general are more honest about their behaviors than they are about their beliefs—especially when those beliefs might not be popular. This helps make self-reported rates of behavior far more reliable than self-reported assessments of comparative abilities.

The chief focus of this chapter is to explore more fully the unique mind-set we call Millionaire Intelligence. Through our survey results and the stories we provide about the working lives of Middle-Class Millionaires, you will see the distinctive patterns of work life behaviors that set Middle-Class Millionaires apart from the rest of their middle-class peers. The four markers of Millionaire Intelligence—hard work, networking, persistence, and financial self-interest—come to life in this chapter, and in some surprising ways. For each aspect of Millionaire Intelligence, we also examine our two survey groups' corresponding beliefs, values, and attitudes—which are at times closely shared and at other times wildly divergent. Some of these results left us truly amazed. They play an important role in our overall analysis of how Middle-Class Millionaires can remain unmistakably members of the middle class and, at the same time, distinguish themselves as the middle class's most influential members.

1. Always "On"

The corner of 96th and Broadway on Manhattan's Upper West Side is hardly the best place in America to run a storefront postal and business service center. It's not even the best location in Manhattan. The midtown area, for instance, has many more small firms in need of shipping and mailing services, and the Upper East Side has a far higher median income. Despite being home to multimillion-dollar condominiums and a smattering of celebrities, the blocks around 96th and Broadway are also well known to police as a late-night bazaar for sex and drugs. And yet, for eight years, store #2992 at 96th and Broadway was one of the top revenue-producing franchise sites for MBE—the Mail Boxes Etc. chain. Only the MBE store in the tony art gallery district of Santa Barbara, California, was able to top #2992 with any consistency.

The list of reasons why MBE store #2992 became a revenue standout begins and ends with its owner, Greg Hund, a forty-four-year-old Ohio native with a brisk and courteous demeanor. As with all retail chains, MBE's product line doesn't vary that much from one store to another. So when one single outlet outperforms in a neighborhood with a demographic no more promising than many others, the crucial difference is almost always the hands-on owner who is willing to work long, hard hours.

"There's no such thing as a business that runs itself," Hund says by way of explanation. For three or four years, he estimates, he worked from 6:30 A.M. to 10 P.M. six or seven days a week. In 2001, when he stepped back from that punishing regime just a little to start investigating another business opportunity, revenues slipped, even though he'd done his best to find two great store managers whom he trained personally. Hund says that "expecting someone will run your business like you would is like expecting to find a babysitter who will care about your children the way you do. She may be great, but you know what? She'll never love your kid the way you do."

The love Greg Hund held for his business was expressed by the hours he devoted to its details. He wrote out a three-ring binder full of scripted responses to common customer complaints. Every employee was required to memorize it and practice using it. He personally selected the music played in the store, stocking the CD player with a mix of upbeat classic rock, easy listening, and movie soundtracks. All his employees were subject to an elaborate system of monthly bonuses and incentives that wouldn't kick in unless store #2992's revenues had beaten out those of the forty other MBE stores in Manhattan. They failed to win the race just a few times, but when they did win, everyone in the shop benefited from the victory.

The national office took notice. Hund became a poster child for just how far hard work and dedication could take an MBE franchise. When he attended franchisee conventions, MBE managers sought him out and asked him to speak to their new and prospective storeowners.

It was around that time that Hund started toying with the idea of taking on a second store, which was available some blocks away. Ultimately, he passed. He remembers how a fortuitous conversation with the founder of Pizza Hut had an impact on his thinking. "He said, 'You know, Greg, you have to accept that no matter how talented you are, as owner of the business, for every step back that you take, you're probably going to sacrifice a layer of performance.'" MBE told him that when successful MBE operators took on a second store, they sacrificed about 20 percent of their overall revenues. From that perspective, Hund saw that owning two stores might end up doubling the management headaches while paring back profits—a very bad bargain.

In March 2001, MBE was bought out by United Parcel Service. Hund learned that the long-term business plan included turning MBE into a chain of UPS retail outlets, which would likely reduce the size of the product line and along with that, he surmised, the profit margins. In March 2006, as the deadline requiring him to renew his franchise license and convert his MBE store into a UPS branch neared, Hund reached out to the long list of other franchisees who'd told him to call when he was ready to sell.

Within three days Hund had an offer. On the day he sold his store, he became a Middle-Class Millionaire and began looking forward to his next challenge.

Americans, in general, work longer hours than the populations in most other industrialized economies, and the effect continues to grow more pronounced. Sometime in 2005, this trend had an impact on the Metro-North commuter line in affluent Westchester County, New York. That's when the rail line began experiencing standing-room-only crowding on its earliest morning train, which pulled into Grand Central Station at 6 A.M. A subsequent survey of the railroad's ridership showed that a lot of commuters were eager to get into the city far earlier than was ever deemed necessary in the line's hundred-year history. In 1985, only one out of every sixty-eight riders arrived in Manhattan before 7 A.M. By 2005, it was one in thirteen. Riders were leaving Manhattan later, too. In the largest revamping of its schedules in twenty years, Metro-North expanded its service in the early morning and late evening, acknowledging that those are the two fastest-growing areas of ridership growth for the system.

Train lines on Long Island and in Chicago have had to make similar adjustments in recent years, and traffic reporters in other metro areas have noted how rush hour keeps steadily expanding, starting earlier in the morning and ending later at night. Part of this trend can be chalked up to suburban sprawl, but most of it appears to be related to the American appetite for hard work. And our findings show that Middle-Class Millionaires put in the most hours of all. The working rich are the hardworking rich.

Both Middle-Class Millionaires and the members of our middle-class survey sample share an almost unanimous belief in the virtue of hard work. Nine out of ten respondents in both groups consider the following statement either very accurate or extremely accurate: "Anyone can become a millionaire if he or she works hard enough." The people in our sample of 586 Middle-Class Millionaires, however, work on average 70 hours per week, versus 41 hours per week for the survey sample of 3,128 middle-class heads of households. Work hours for Middle-Class Millionaires are far more likely to spill over into nights and weekends than for our middle-class group. Middle-Class Millionaires are five times more likely to say they are always available for business by e-mail or phone (76 percent vs. 16 percent) and about three times more likely to say that they regularly have to deal with business issues "after hours" (86 percent vs. 29 percent). They are four times more likely to say they regularly work nights (51.5 percent vs. 12 percent) and three times more likely to say they regularly work weekends (67 percent vs. 21 percent). They even take fewer vacation days per year on average (12 days vs. 19.5 days).

The challenge that every Middle-Class Millionaire faces is common among entrepreneurs, managers, and professionals with large responsibilities: The work is never done. Tons of ink have been spilled in the media about how cell phones and e-mail are making twenty-four-hour access to the office both an opportunity and a nuisance.

"My mind-set is, don't dawdle on anything," says Lou Bivona, a sixty-year-old entrepreneur from Tenafly, New Jersey. "Get it off your plate as quick as it gets on your plate. I never want a message to go unanswered for more than a day." Bivona would rather avoid voice mail messages altogether. "If somebody calls me late in the day and I check my messages at nine o'clock, then I'm lying in bed all night thinking about my response. That's not what I want. Instead, I want to get it off my plate, move on to the next thing, and get a good night's sleep."

After his morning workout, Bivona takes two-hour bike rides each morning with a group of other affluent self-made businesspeople from his area. Even in that crowd, however, Bivona stands out because he's the only one who cycles while wearing his cell phone headset. He says with a laugh, "They bust my balls because I'll drift to the back and take the call if the phone rings." At any given time, Bivona is typically juggling five different business interests along with his active fund-raising for a national missing-children charity. "In a sense it's slot-machine management," he says of his phone habits. "It's like hitting a lot of slot machines looking for the next payout. If I'm in a meeting, I'll take your call, if only to say that I'll call you back. It's a little distracting for the people I'm with, but I try to dispose of it real quick."

Bivona realizes he'd probably make fewer mistakes if he focused on just a few projects, but he says it makes more sense for him to try to orchestrate the activities of his various business partners and let them do the focusing. "I'm trying to leverage other people who have talent," he explains. "Once I pass something off to those with an equity stake in the deal, they'll make it happen better than I could make it happen. They can think clearer and get it done." He admits that "I have a tendency to have too many balls in the air, and people decide, 'Lou's too busy, why bother him?' So it's dangerous. It's a two-edged sword. I just tell people, 'I want to be bothered. That's my life.' "

Add in the phenomenon of globalization, and twenty-four-hour access can look more like a necessity than an obsession. What was confined twenty years ago to the financial markets continues to spread throughout the economy: round-the-clock responsibilities. It's another one of the reasons the train systems in New York and Chicago have had to reset their schedules.

For Laura Goldenberg, vice president of Clinique's worldwide travel retail division, the sun literally never sets on her responsibilities, which involve a global network of duty-free shops selling Clinique cosmetics and fragrances. Her fastest-growing markets are in cities such as Dubai, Hong Kong, and Shanghai. "It's certainly the type of job that—between the travel and the communications and the time zones—*could* be all-consuming. Singapore is a twelve- or thirteen-hour time difference, so even if you want to be reasonable, you're either going to be on the phone late at night or very early in the morning, just to stay in touch with your key colleagues."

It all adds up to a set of job responsibilities that pull in every direction, twenty-four hours a day. Goldenberg oversees a team that handles merchandising, product-set development, promotions, and special events. Staying competitive in this fast-growing industry requires Goldenberg to put out dozens of new sets of attractively priced and packaged Clinique products, exclusive to the travel retail market, twice per year. At the same time she needs to stay in contact with the retailers at airports and other locations all around the world to ensure that the products she and her team have developed are selling.

"It's hard to strike the balance," says Goldenberg, forty-five. "I need to be here for my team, on the one hand, and I have to be here for my own personal humanity. But I also need to be out there to see and feel what's actually happening. Also, I'd gain credibility with the retailers in their location. On the other hand, there's no such thing as a one-week trip to Asia. It can't be done. You leave on a Friday, you get there on Sunday."

Compounding the challenges of travel retail is that the stores themselves, where products from Clinique and its competitors often sit side by side, don't capture cash-register data the way they do at U.S. department stores. "Relationships are critical everywhere," she says. "But there's so little data that it's a little more special."

So where is Goldenberg's time best spent? In the office or overseas? On the phone making international calls all night or in meetings all day? Welcome to the globalization treadmill. "It's the sort of job and the sort of industry that could easily fully consume and take away the ability to have a life outside of work," she says. "There are probably people who do that. That's not what I want, so I work on that balance. I'm willing to look at time in a different way. So if I'm home at ten-thirty at night talking to Singapore, that's what I need to do. I'm not going to be in the office at eleven at night."

To stay with this discipline, Goldenberg has engaged an executive coach—a private consultant who helps her sort out the day's priorities and remain faithful to the program she has set for herself. Later in the book we'll examine the enormous appeal that executive coaching—and other forms of expert-guided self-betterment—holds for the Middle-Class Millionaire. When long hours and hard work are the price of realizing opportunities, truly successful people seem more finely attuned than others to the value and finite nature of time itself. Maximizing its value can be the hardest work of all. In our search to discover just how Middle-Class Millionaires are transforming America, we saw how so many of their consumer and lifestyle choices are guided in some significant way by the value they place on their need to manage time.

2. It's Who You Know

When Richard Rossi, the PinnacleCare client from the previous chapter, was working as an aide to Connecticut senator Lowell Weicker in the late 1970s, a junior high school teacher from Ridgefield named Barbara Harris would call the office every year with a long list of requests for her class's spring field trip to Washington, D.C. "Everyone in the office avoided her except me," Rossi recalls.

Barbara Harris was a uniquely high-maintenance constituent. Whenever she arrived in D.C. with thirty-five students in tow, she wasn't content to lead them all around in a group. Instead, she insisted that each of those students have a tailor-made visit—and she expected her senator's staff to make it happen. "If your child wanted to be a physician," Rossi says, "Barbara wanted her to spend the day at the National Institutes of Health. If another child wanted to be an astronomer, Barbara wanted to arrange for him to go to the Goddard Space Flight Center for the day." It fell to Rossi to arrange most of what Harris wanted, because "no one says no to Barbara."

Despite her demanding nature, Richard Rossi came to like and admire Barbara Harris. Soon after Rossi left government in the early 1980s to start a small computer software company, Harris quit teaching and came to Washington seeking a career change. It was 1984, a presidential election year, and Harris hatched a moneymaking plan in which she and Rossi would bring four hundred children to the upcoming inaugural ceremony as a sort of Outward Bound experience in civics. Rossi's computer venture was struggling, so he jumped at the chance to work with Harris and start using all the skills and contacts he'd developed in his nine years on the Hill.

They had almost no money and little credibility, but they knew how to get things done in D.C. They sent out a letter to 535 members of Congress, inviting them to join the "honorary board of advisors to the Election 1984 Youth Inaugural Conference." Ninety-three members agreed to appear on their letterhead, solving their credibility issue. Pooling about $8,000, they sent a direct mail solicitation to several thousand high school principals asking them to nominate students for the "honor" of attending the inauguration and inaugural ball. It wasn't long before checks from parents started pouring in.

Only then did Rossi and Harris approach the inaugural committee and ask for four hundred passes to the ball. "They told us there were people dying for *two* tickets," Rossi remembers. "So we started making friends down there, and we kept begging and begging." Technically, there wasn't just one official inaugural ball that night. There were several on the First Family's schedule, and eventually Harris and Rossi got the four hundred passes they needed to one called the President's Youth Ball. Just as the solicitation letter promised, all the kids got to see the president and Mrs. Reagan dance at an inaugural ball.

Twenty-two years later, Rossi and Harris are partners in what has become a $75-million-a-year business called Envision EMI, which claims to be the "world's largest creator of leadership and success programs for high-achieving young people." It is a company built pretty much from the ground up through the power of networking in the nation's capital. It seems as though every important gatekeeper in the district knows Rossi, with his sunny disposition and bright, electric smile. Two weeks after the 9/11 terror attacks, when the whole Capitol area was still locked down, Rossi and some high school students composed the first public group that the sergeant-at-arms allowed to visit the floor of Congress. One Capitol cop told Rossi, "Seeing you guys here makes it feel like things are getting back to normal."

Rossi and Harris are people who take immense pleasure in working with others to get things done, and that trait has gone a long way toward making them Middle-Class Millionaires. In a word, Middle-Class Millionaires *network*. Many seem to do it compulsively, whether they realize it or not. For many Middle-Class Millionaires, networking is a natural means of getting what they want in life, even if, like Rossi and Harris, they don't have much money to begin with. To someone starting out with almost nothing, the most valuable, easily available, and cheaply attained resource to draw upon is other people.

Our survey shows that Middle-Class Millionaires are much more likely than those in our middle-class sample to mention "knowing many, many people" as something that is very or extremely important in achieving financial success (62 percent vs. 43 percent). They are nearly three times more likely than our middle-class sample to say they belong to a "formal or informal networking group" (43 percent vs. 16 percent). But even when compared to the minority in our middle-class sample who actually engage in networking, the Middle-Class Millionaires have a completely different take on where the value in networking arises. Middle-Class Millionaires are more than three times as likely to cite "it's a way for you to connect with people you can turn to for information" (83 percent vs. 29 percent). For the middle-class networker, the primary value to networking for about 66 percent of respondents is that "it enables you to keep abreast of significant changes in your personal or professional community." Just 32 percent of Middle-Class Millionaires considered this an important feature of networking.

When we talk to Middle-Class Millionaires about networking, sometimes we find resistance to the word itself, in part because it might imply manipulating or "using" people. "Most of us who are good at it hate the word because it's been bastardized by the smarmy, eye-darting, card-passing guys," says Keith Ferrazzi, a networking guru and author of the bestselling book *Never Eat Alone*. "That's why I had the word *networking* removed from my book." He favors the expressions "connecting" and "building relationships."

It's very likely that some of the best networkers do it unconsciously; for them, networking is a way of doing business and a way of life. As one Middle-Class Millionaire told us, "I don't think I give much thought to it. If I need to get to another company to do a business deal, it just takes a couple of phone calls and I'm connected. The other thing I do is take calls from people who come to me who are starting companies. They're looking for investors; they're looking to hire people. Sometimes they're investors looking for references.

"I don't *think* I network a lot, but I probably do, all day long."

3. Never Give Up

Robert Levitan was dining in a Manhattan restaurant in 2003 when out of the corner of his eye he saw Whoopi Goldberg being seated several tables away. Back in 1999, the comedian had signed on as a commercial spokesperson for Levitan's Internet start-up company, Flooz.com, with the bulk of her compensation coming in the form of stock options in the company. Flooz flew high for a time with Whoopi as its public face, and the online gift certificate firm had signed up 1 million accounts by the 2000 holiday season. But by the next summer Flooz filed for bankruptcy. The investors had lost $50 million, and Whoopi Goldberg's stock options were worthless.

Levitan hadn't seen Goldberg since the company had folded. He knew that it's not a good thing for celebrities to have their public image associated with failure, so he wasn't sure how she'd react to seeing him again. He was relieved and delighted when she greeted him with a giant hug. After a brief chat that included references to the criminal indictments at WorldCom and Enron in the news at the time, Goldberg said, "Hey, at least we weren't crooks! Let's do something else together sometime!"

Failure in the case of someone with Robert Levitan's high profile can be humiliating. CNET derided Flooz as one of the Top Ten busts of the dot-com era and wrote how the company was among "a handful of really terrible ideas . . . a perfect example of a 'what the heck were they thinking?' business."

Levitan says now that he went through periods of self-doubt after the Flooz collapse. "It was really difficult," he says. "But the more distance you get from it, you get a sense of what you accomplished." A lot of dot-com companies closed their doors so suddenly in 2000 and 2001 that employees were frequently stiffed for weeks or months of salary. Not Flooz employees. "You realize," Levitan says, "that you may not be proud of the end result, but you're proud of the way you conducted yourself. Years later, I had people come to me and say, 'I heard you closed the business right, you treated everyone correctly.'" At the age of forty, he took time off to travel around the world, and for almost three years he did consulting work for other companies. "I wondered what I was going to do next."

Today, Levitan is CEO of Pando Networks, an Internet start-up in lower Manhattan that has developed a fast file-transfer program that allows entertainment companies and individual computer users to distribute bulky media files. "I realized I enjoyed being an entrepreneur," he says. "I figured I must be pretty good at it, because people paid me a lot of money to help them be entrepreneurs. I didn't seek them out. People kept contacting me, and just when I'm thinking I'm ready to get back into it, some [venture capitalist] calls up and says, 'We need a CEO, and if you come on board, we'll fund it.'"

And Levitan doesn't share CNET's view that there was anything fundamentally wrong with Flooz. In many ways, he says, Flooz was superior to his previous Internet start-up blockbuster, iVillage. "We grew the revenue faster, and I think we ran a better company and we had a better business model at Flooz than we did at iVillage," he says. "Yet iVillage went public for $1.3 billion." The lesson he takes from the experience is this: "You realize it's not just the results you get. You can't be satisfied if you get bad results. But what's also important is the level of karma, for lack of a better word, that develops around you. It becomes your personal safety net. All those people who you have done business with, whether they have been successful or not with you, they still could be part of that business safety net if you've treated them correctly, if they think you've been honest."

Among the most important differences between Middle-Class Millionaires and the middle class is how they deal with setbacks and failure. Our survey results illustrate the old saying that few things are more important in the pursuit of success than perseverance. For instance, in both of our sample groups, 9 out of 10 reported having made "a major career or business decision that had a very bad outcome." However, the Middle-Class Millionaires had, on average, 3.1 such incidents, while the middle-class respondents reported only 1.6. Middle-Class Millionaires are also about twice as likely to credit "learning from bad business or career decisions" as being very important to achieving financial success (73 percent vs. 36 percent).

The greatest measurable difference in the two sample groups' behaviors, however, involved the actions they took in response to failure. The Middle-Class Millionaires were far less likely than the middle class to take failure as a signal they should try something different. They were about five times more likely than those in our middle-class sample to try again in the same field following a bad business outcome (77 percent vs. 14 percent). On the other hand, just 2 percent of Middle-Class Millionaires said their most common course of action following a bad outcome was that they "gave up and focused on other projects." Among the middle-class sample, more than half (51.5 percent) said that giving up was their most common response.

Dan Sullivan, now a highly successful executive coach based in Toronto, likes to tell how his first two attempts at starting consulting businesses failed. After the second failure, while he was working out his debts with his banker, the man suggested to him that maybe he should take a hint and look for regular work. He even offered to put in a good word for Sullivan at the bank. Sullivan recalls laughing in response and telling the banker, "I just haven't gotten this right yet, that's all." Today Sullivan's firm, The Strategic Coach, runs 500 workshops for entrepreneurs every year all over North America and Great Britain.

Perseverance is a uniformly attractive middle-class value to all our survey respondents, even if some are better at persevering than others. Our survey found very little difference in stated attitudes toward perseverance between the Middle-Class Millionaires and those in the middle class. The Middle-Class Millionaires were only slightly more likely than those in our middle-class sample to say that "perseverance" and "not giving up" are very important or extremely important in achieving financial success (83 percent vs. 73 percent). The difference seems to be that Middle-Class Millionaires tend to act on their belief more often when failure and adversity stare them in the face.

In 1981, a little Seattle-area office-remodeling firm called Pacific Crest hit one of those disasters that put most small businesses in the ground at an early age. The company's young owner, Steve Bell, had created a niche market in redoing dentists' offices in western Washington State when the general contractors who generated most of his work were suddenly arrested on federal cocaine-trafficking charges. All the money they owed Bell was seized by the federal government. Bell in turn owed more than $100,000 to his own subcontractors and suppliers with no way to pay off the debt.

At the time, Bell was married with two children and a third on the way. He sat down with his lawyer, who tried to break the news to him gently. Bell, the lawyer said, had no choice but to declare bankruptcy; otherwise, within a month a dozen creditors would sue him and his life would become a living hell. "I looked at him and said, 'Sir, life is already a living hell,'" Bell recalls. "'You may be right, but before I do it your way, I'm going to do it my way. I'm going to pay all these people back.'"

He wrote letters and made phone calls to all the people he owed money to and asked them to trust him. "I said, 'If you'll allow me to pay you back on my terms, not yours, then I will pay you every dime with interest. All I'm asking for is time.'"

Bell took a job with a local cabinetmaker, but it wasn't long before he realized that working for someone else would never yield enough income to feed his family and settle his debts. So he started over in the kitchen-and-bath remodeling business. Within six years he had paid off his creditors and opened a showroom and small cabinet shop. His reputation for financial integrity came to his aid. "I lived three years with no credit," he says. "I was able to purchase the showroom with no credit because the guy believed in me, because I was a man of my word."

It took six years, but Pacific Crest started growing again, thanks in large part to retail sales of cabinets through Washington's Eagle Hardware chain. Then Eagle was swallowed by the retailing giant Lowe's. Again, Bell's business faced disaster. Forty percent of the Pacific Crest business volume was about to be lost in one big gulp. With only a lot of smaller clients and no big customer to depend on, it was likely that the company would slowly bleed to death. Instead, Bell made the hard decision to lay off one-third of his workers and reinvent Pacific Crest as a maker of upscale product lines. It was a financial gamble, but today Pacific Crest has 162 employees. Revenues reached $27 million last year, and one of Bell's old suppliers from his 1981 business meltdown, a company he struggled to pay $5,000, now gives Pacific Crest an unsecured line of credit worth $2 million.

A common misperception about entrepreneurs who try and fail and try again is that they somehow aren't as deeply bothered by feelings of regret and despair as other people. Before Greg Hund sold his MBE franchise, he bought into a start-up bakery franchise in Manhattan. Within months, even before the shop had opened, Hund knew he was facing a disaster. His renovation costs had gotten so high that he knew he'd never make any money, no matter how many pastries he sold. He grew despondent and emotionally numb. He reckons he's the only person ever to lose five pounds while running a bakery. One evening he found himself huddled on the living room floor, despairing of how he'd ever get out from under his debts. When he finally found a buyer for the shop, the subsequent sale left him down $175,000.

In his darkest hours, when the burden of his errors in judgment about the bakery weighed most heavily on him, Hund knew that if he could just relieve himself of this mistake, he'd be able to go out and look for another business to run. The one escape he says he's never permitted himself to consider is the option of taking a job and going back to work for someone else. Today he lives in Austin, Texas, where he is in the process of opening the first of four shops in the Floyd's 99 Barber Shop chain.

Failure can be just as difficult emotionally for Middle-Class Millionaires as it is for anyone else. The Middle-Class Millionaire is simply less likely to take those feelings as a sign he or she should be doing something else. Perhaps it's telling that more Middle-Class Millionaires consider "luck" very important to achieving success (31 percent) than "having a higher IQ" (22 percent).

4. Go Where the Money Is

In early 1991, a computer science Ph.D. candidate named Ping Fu joined the staff of the National Center for Supercomputing Applications (NCSA) at the University of Illinois. Talented computer science students from all over the country came to the NCSA, and some of them worked directly for Fu. When one particularly tall, young college sophomore on her staff expressed an interest in the Internet, Ping suggested the young man work on computer code for an interface that would make other Internet applications easier to use. The young man's name was Mark Andreesen, one of the first developers of the Web browser. By 1993, Andreesen had left NCSA and moved to Silicon Valley, where he founded Netscape and became a billionaire.

Ping Fu had gone through enormous hardships to achieve her position at NCSA. The daughter of an engineer father and an accountant mother, she had been forcibly removed from her home at age seven and subjected to horrible traumas in an orphanage during China's Cultural Revolution, when it was government policy to mistreat the offspring of educated urban professionals. During her twenties, she undertook a study of infanticide in rural China that was widely lauded for its excellence until it provoked a worldwide human rights uproar. The embarrassed government imprisoned Fu and deported her to the United States with $80 in her pocket. She persevered through terrible difficulties here as well but managed to pursue a career in computer science, after which she set her sights on NCSA. By 1991, she had landed her dream job at one of the world's most important computer research institutes. She had even found love at NCSA and married a fellow computer scientist. For just about anyone—and especially for someone with such a troubled background—it all added up to a successful and satisfying life.

But what Fu took from her experience of having mentored a future dot-com billionaire was this: Andreesen had created something of tremendous value and made it his own. He hadn't possessed anywhere near her talent as a computer scientist. He was only an average programmer, and he hadn't wasted much time getting better at it. Taking the browser and the name "Mosaic" with him to California was an audacious move (NCSA sued him for appropriating its intellectual property), but he didn't let the risks stop him. Instead, Andreesen was driven to create something great, and he kept his focus on how it might stand to reward him financially were it ever to reach its potential. Fu resolved to follow Andreesen's example someday. She would develop a product that might rival the Web browser in potential.

It took a few years, but by 1996, Fu was ready to make the leap. She left the NCSA and started a company called Geomagic. Her product was a software program, developed with her husband, that uses laser scanners to create computer models of three-dimensional objects. The potential applications seemed to be endless, and with a $500,000 loan from her sister and $8 million from venture capital, she has built up Geomagic into a global leader in DSSP, "digital shape sampling and processing." Among Geomagic's thousands of clients are NASCAR teams, which use the Geomagic process to streamline the inspection and production of cylinder heads, and NASA, which uses Geomagic software to analyze the condition of the Space Shuttle's protective tiles and initiate repairs while in orbit. In 2003, a research team from Texas Tech University spent four days laser-scanning the Statue of Liberty so that if it is ever destroyed by a natural disaster or a terror attack, the 16 million data points saved with Geomagic software can be used to build an exact replica. In 2005, *Inc.* magazine named Ping Fu its Entrepreneur of the Year.

The insight that turned Fu from research institute employee to Middle-Class Millionaire is reflected in our survey results: By an overwhelming margin, the Middle-Class Millionaires we surveyed express a greater need than that of the middle-class survey respondents to benefit financially from their work. The vast majority of Middle-Class Millionaires—more than 80 percent of them—either own their own businesses or are part of professional partnerships. Almost two out of three Middle-Class Millionaires (65 percent) consider "obtaining an ownership stake in your work" very important to financial success. Among our middle-class sample, just 28 percent consider ownership important to their success. In a variety of ways, Middle-Class Millionaires are more focused and proficient at maintaining their financial interests in what they do. They are far more inclined to put themselves consciously in what might be called "the flow of money."

For a good number of Middle-Class Millionaires, this is the last hurdle that sets them apart from the middle-class herd. As with so many successful middle-class people, Ping Fu had already demonstrated a degree of proficiency in three of the four areas of Millionaire Intelligence. She was an industrious and conscientious worker. She naturally developed a supportive network of people she trusted in her work, including her own husband and sister. Her perseverance had been tested to an almost indescribable degree. And yet, by working for a nonprofit computer center, Fu was out of the flow of money. Had she not taken a deliberate step to do otherwise, she might have stayed in southern Illinois and remained a successful and much-admired teacher. But she never would have become a Middle-Class Millionaire.

The business of Middle-Class Millionaires is business. On average, Middle-Class Millionaires have about the same levels of formal education as those in our middle-class sample, which is extraordinary given the difference in their relative net worths. Many middle-class occupations offer pay raises for the accumulation of educational credentials, but among Middle-Class Millionaires, continuing education happens on the job. Many are proud to have graduated from what used to be called the school of hard knocks. In our interviews with Middle-Class Millionaires, they often refer to their first business failure or some early trial-by-fire business experience as "how I got my MBA." People with professional degrees often become Middle-Class Millionaires, but usually because they have leveraged their academic training in order to run their business, not by humbly plying their trade for wages. In this sense, Ben Franklin's lifelong habit of signing his name "Benjamin Franklin, Printer" was really something of a cunning pose. Printing was Franklin's trade, but it was not his primary occupation. Franklin made a lot of his money in printing-related businesses—as print-shop owner, as publisher, as investor in other print shops. Yes, he was a printer. But as soon as he was able, Franklin put his financial interests ahead of the time he spent tending to his trade. He placed himself in the flow of money.

By and large, salaried professionals are not Middle-Class Millionaires, while professionals with an ownership stake in their practice or firm might be. Physicians who own their practices are far richer than physicians who don't. The same goes for lawyers, engineers, and architects. In the corporate world, Middle-Class Millionaires are found mostly among company employees with incentivized or pay-for-performance compensation. There are salespeople who take home more money each year than vice presidents several levels above them. Bonuses and stock options in the executive suites also account for the creation of many Middle-Class Millionaires.

Those who put themselves in the flow of money do so consciously. Our survey indicates that Middle-Class Millionaires are almost three times as likely to say that choosing a career on the basis of its prospective financial rewards is important to financial success (73 percent vs. 28 percent). By contrast, the middle-class respondents were about twenty-seven times more prone to believe that the maxim "do what you love and the money will follow" is very or extremely important to financial success (54 percent vs. 2 percent of Middle-Class Millionaires). Middle-Class Millionaires are also more apt to embrace some of the harsher realities of achieving success than those in our middle-class sample. Middle-Class Millionaires are more than twice as likely to say that the keys to financial success include "believing you have to be Machiavellian to succeed" (48 percent vs. 21 percent) and "taking advantage of weakness in others" (52 percent vs. 22 percent). Middle-Class Millionaires are nearly twice as likely to characterize their approach in negotiating as "doing whatever you need to do to win" (65.5 percent vs. 34 percent), while members of our middle-class group are more than eight times more likely to describe their negotiating approach as "losing is acceptable if you doubted your chances to win in the first place" (25 percent vs. just 3 percent among Middle-Class Millionaires). If the Middle-Class Millionaires are to be believed, keeping yourself in the flow of money often means defending your position by taking a hard line with others in the business world.

As the head of the Glastonbury, Connecticut, investment company Symmetry, Patrick Sweeney frequently has to defend his bottom line from the not-so-subtle demands for "revenue sharing" from the large brokerage firms. "When the advisors we work with moved to a larger firm, the new firm tried to bully us," Sweeney says. "They wanted us to share revenue with them, which is pretty normal, but you and I would call it a good old-fashioned kickback. I just tell them no."

Revenue sharing is supposed to compensate brokerage houses for maintaining their distribution channel of financial advisors, and most companies like Symmetry would rather pay than dare run the risk of being cut off from the advisors. As Sweeney sees it, however, his company's products are very popular among financial advisors, so his firm doesn't need to pay revenue sharing, even though some of his competitors do. "We've had three or four of these negotiations in the past year. One company went so far as to ask us for a quarter of a million dollars to keep doing business with them. We said no, and they kept hammering us for several weeks about paying them this fee. They thought we had to pay because all their vendors pay, but I told them we're not going to budge."

One particular negotiation went right to the brink. "This senior-level executive said to me in my own conference room, 'We don't need you, I just want to make that clear,'" Sweeney recalls. "I said, 'We don't need *you*!' I mean, we want to be friendly with brokerage firms. We want to partner with them. But they feel like we need access to their salespeople, so they can hold us up. But I tell them, 'You don't want us, fine, you go tell your reps you don't want Symmetry any more for this program.' We essentially play a game of chicken, because in our little niche, passive investment strategies, the advisors like us. The brokerage firms can't cut us out because we happen to be popular among their best and most successful advisors. We definitely exploit that."

Being in the flow of money also helps account for the Middle-Class Millionaire propensity for hard work. Simply put, work is more enjoyable when you are pursuing your own financial self-interest every day. It represents opportunity, not obligation. This is why a lot of Middle-Class Millionaires say they feel differently about Sunday evening than most other members of the middle class do. Salaried workers are likely to mourn the start of the new business week, while Middle-Class Millionaires more commonly welcome it. They often say they have an itch that starts as early as Sunday morning, a mild anxiety to get the week started.

"There's no question that on Sunday night my brain is wound up," says Robert Levitan. "I'm thinking about everything we've got to do on Monday. And I like that. It's a good thing." It was one of the things he missed about running his own company during his three-year sabbatical in consulting. "I missed caring," he says. "I missed pushing the envelope and being around people smarter than me. Today I'm the stupidest guy in the office, and it's really terrific. It's so liberating. At my last start-up I was one of the smartest, and there's just too much pressure when you're the smartest. You don't need that."

The Middle-Class Millionaire Effect

Achieving financial independence at the age of forty-two gave Benjamin Franklin a huge assortment of options in life, and he exercised them through a hierarchy of personal values that would feel familiar to any member of the American middle class today. He secured a home and an income for his wife and family. He used this influence to help his son win a royal appointment as governor of New Jersey. He continued to write and work on his own self-development, indulging his curiosity in the invention of everything from bifocals to musical instruments to the Franklin stove. In Philadelphia he is considered the founder of its first library, first fire department, first hospital, and first university. And when the existence of the newborn United States itself was in danger, he left for France as an official envoy from the Continental Congress to petition King Louis XVI for assistance against the British—assistance that most historians agree turned the tide of the Revolution and made

American victory a reality. From these milestones in Franklin's life we see how his concerns moved outward in concentric rings, from home and hearth to self-fulfillment and then to his community, his nation, and the world.

In the next chapter, we examine our survey results that show how Middle-Class Millionaires' attitudes toward work, money, and investment are driven by a hierarchy of values that is identical to that of the middle class but very different from the values of the truly rich. Our findings help explain why so few Middle-Class Millionaires consider themselves wealthy and prefer to regard themselves as "middle-class" or at most "upper-middle-class." We'll explore what keeps the Middle-Class Millionaire hard at work, and how they are using their high incomes and superior social connections to seek fulfillment of their middle-class values in new ways that are transforming nearly every important American industry and institution they come in contact with.

When viewed as a Middle-Class Millionaire, Benjamin Franklin was unique for his time, when wealth was something one was born to, land was its primary source, and those few who managed to climb the social ladder distanced themselves from their origins. The essential formula for financial success may not have changed much since then, but its forms and expressions have evolved considerably. For one thing, self-made wealth has become dramatically more common in just the past several decades.

Today America is home to more than 8 million households in which the main breadwinner's temperament and financial success approach those of Franklin. In fact, Middle-Class Millionaires are the fastest-growing population segment within the American middle class. The next decade could see 20 million Middle-Class Millionaire households.

Imagine an America with 20 million Benjamin Franklins.

CHAPTER THREE

MIDDLE CLASS BUT MILLIONAIRES

David and Sharon Martin liked their block in Arlington Heights, Illinois, so much that they wanted to build their dream house there. In the spring of 2005, after four years of living in a modest forty-year-old split-level at 112 North Forrest Avenue, the Martins decided to demolish it and put up something more to their liking. They hired an architect to design a two-story four-bedroom house with all the latest conveniences, a three-car garage, and 3,918 square feet of floor space—twice as much room as they and their three daughters had before.

"We wanted a full basement, and my wife wanted a bigger kitchen," says Martin, a thirty-seven-year-old contractor and homebuilder who calls himself "a blue-collar entrepreneur." The old house was poorly insulated and had a cracked foundation, but they wanted to stay in the neighborhood with its tree-lined streets and nearby parks. His daughters also didn't want to change schools. "They all have their little networks of friends," Martin explains.

Unfortunately for the Martins, just a few months before they conceived their plan the village of Arlington Heights had instituted one of the strictest regulations on residential demolitions in the Chicago area. During the previous five years or so, opposition to "teardown" projects of this kind had been growing in Arlington Heights and other places in and around Chicago. Neighborhood groups railed against what they derided as "monster houses" and "McMansions," claiming that the new larger houses are a visual blight that ruin the character and charm of their surroundings. Even though the Martins' new house would conform with existing zoning regulations (they had a right to build up to 3,929 square feet), the new teardown law in Arlington Heights also required them to present their plans at a public hearing and obtain a vote of approval from the village's design commission.

By all accounts, Arlington Heights is a very nice place to live. With a population of 76,000, the village's weekly crime reports typically show nothing more serious than a half-dozen burglaries and auto break-ins. North Forrest Avenue is a quiet street of modest single-story ranch houses and split-levels. There is a ballfield at one end of the block, and the Windsor Elementary School is within walking distance. The block is also close to Arlington Heights' bustling downtown and its commuter rail station.

Although Arlington Heights had seen 162 teardowns in 2004 alone, the Martins' project was a first for North Forrest Avenue. Some of the neighbors feared that this first teardown would prove contagious and set off a wrecking-ball craze on the block. Others seemed to resent the Martins' plan on principle. "There's no reason to tear down a $400,000 house," Paul Schmidt complained in the local *Daily Herald*. "What they are saying is that they don't care about this neighborhood. Well, we care." The *Herald* reported that thirty of Schmidt's neighbors came to his house on a rainy Sunday afternoon to discuss the issue, but they had to gather for pizza and salad while huddled under patio umbrellas in the backyard. Schmidt's family room was just too small.

On September 13, 2005, the Martins debuted the plans for their new house at a public meeting before the design commission. Almost everyone on North Forrest Avenue showed up in opposition. "My jaw dropped," Sharon Martin told the *Daily Herald*. "They all had little signs saying they were against it. But it does fit in more now. It looks like a one-story house with an addition." From the Martins' perspective, their building plan proved they cared a lot about the neighborhood. They were making a huge investment in their property, and they had modified their plans repeatedly to conform to the zoning code. Besides, the Martins had previously invited neighbors to their house to look over and discuss the designs, but only a few had taken them up on the offer.

In the ensuing months, the design commission sent the Martins and their architect back to the drawing board six times, telling them to take the design and "soften it up a bit." The delays cost thousands of dollars in architectural and legal fees, but Sharon Martin said that by then she and her husband had decided to stick it out. "We thought about moving because of the hassle, but I don't want to let the neighbors run me out of my house," she said at the time. "I like the schools. I like the area." After the second public meeting, David Martin stood up and announced to his neighbors, "I'll tell the whole audience here that I am not stepping down. We are going to build this house sooner or later."

In recent years, during the latest run-up in nationwide housing values, the teardown phenomenon has roiled many of the country's most desirable suburbs. Real estate prices in many communities have soared to the point where houses have proved to be far less valuable than the land they are sitting on. The National Trust for Historic Preservation has decried the teardown trend as "an epidemic that is wiping out historic neighborhoods one house at a time." The trust now keeps a running tally of teardown hot spots, counting 300 communities in thirty-three states.

Each teardown community generally conforms to one of two patterns. A minority of them are resort towns, where development pressures are replacing seaside bungalows with modern construction. Most of the places on the National Trust's list, however, are inner-ring suburbs near major cities, built around commuter rail stops or prewar trolley lines. These tend to be prosperous bedroom communities, noted for the quality of their public schools. Some have famous names long associated with affluence, such as Brookline, Massachusetts; Bryn Mawr, Pennsylvania; Bethesda, Maryland; Wheaton, Illinois; and Santa Monica, California. Many more, though, rank among the fairly undistinguished suburbs that shaped the public image of mass middle-class prosperity in the 1950s and 1960s, places such as Pasadena, California; Teaneck, New Jersey; and Arlington Heights, Illinois.

On its Web site, the National Trust has produced a color-coded map of the fifty states, classifying each for the intensity of its teardown activity. California, Florida, Illinois, Michigan, New Jersey, and Massachusetts are all depicted in bright red. Certain metropolitan areas are singled out for exceptionally high concentrations of teardowns. Besides the New York, Chicago, and Los Angeles areas, the trust singles out Dallas, Denver, and Atlanta.

This map is called "Teardowns by State and Community," but it could just as well go by another name: "Middle-Class Millionaire America." Building big new homes in older suburbs—suburbs most likely to remind them of where they grew up—is just one way Middle-Class Millionaires are transforming America. The National Trust's top 300 teardown communities are all places where Middle-Class Millionaires are coming home to roost.

As with the Martin family project in Arlington Heights, new houses in these older towns are seldom greeted warmly by their neighbors. Disparaging nicknames for the new houses vary by region and include "bash-and-builds," "bigfoots," and "plywood palaces." One such house in Chevy Chase, Maryland, was egged, which prompted the mayor to make a public plea for civility in the little town. A new house in the Atlanta suburb of Decatur was vandalized twice in two days. "Save Our City" was spray-painted on the garage doors.

The common complaint aired by aggrieved neighbors is that the developers and owners of these big new houses are invaders who don't share the community's values. But as the Martins' story makes clear, the exact opposite is usually true. The Martins' values are identical to those of their neighbors. They want to build a home on North Forrest Avenue for the exact same reasons all the other residents moved there in the first place: The schools are good. The streets feel safe. It's a convenient and attractive place that is perfect for raising a family. David Martin bristles at the idea that he's a rich businessman imposing his big mansion on his neighbors. "I wake up at five, five-thirty every morning, and I don't get home until seven every day," he says. "I'm sacrificing myself for the benefit of my children. I do everything for my children, you know?"

The Martins share their neighbors' values, but perhaps not in a way that the neighbors immediately recognize. Most North Forrest Avenue residents have lived there for at least twenty years. Many paid under $100,000 for older homes that not all of them can afford to maintain today. The Martins, on the other hand, paid $295,000 five years ago for a house they want to demolish and replace with something that will be worth $1 million or more. The Martins are middle-class homeowners who are behaving like millionaires. Their focus, their persistence, and certainly their financial calculations are all redolent of Millionaire Intelligence. Despite their neighbor's objection that tearing down a house worth $400,000 doesn't make any sense, the Martins know that newer, larger houses are holding their resale value more surely than smaller ones. When construction is completed, the Martins' house will probably represent the soundest investment on the block. The neighbors might not like the idea, but the Martins and other families like them see themselves as the future of North Forrest Avenue. They are reinventing the traditional suburb in a way that reflects both their middle-class values *and* their superior access to wealth.

Despite the objections of preservationists, some urban planners see an upside to teardowns. Suburban sprawl, they reason, might be contained if teardowns are allowed to revitalize old-style communities where homeowners are aging and dying off. Property values are climbing in these communities because the surging demand to live in them far outstrips the supply of available homes. There is a finite quantity of traditional commuter suburbs with good schools, but the nation's population keeps growing, and the population of Middle-Class Millionaires keeps growing even faster. Home prices are essentially being bid skyward in these towns, but few people capable of carrying a $500,000 or $1 million mortgage want to live in an old 2,000-square-foot Cape Cod.

What is really happening in teardown communities is not so different from what has taken place in run-down inner-city neighborhoods for decades. The proud homeowners in these towns may not want to hear it, but they are undergoing suburban-style gentrification. It can be painful to see the home next door, one just like your own, reduced to a pile of rubbish in a single day. Once these new, supersized homes are completed, their owners literally look down on the older houses around them. And yet the influx of newly constructed Middle-Class Millionaire homes in a given community serves as a profound testament that the town has preserved its middle-class character and remains a good place to live—even if longtime residents rarely see it that way.

More than a year after they attended their first design committee meeting, the Martins were finally granted a permit to have their old house torn down and carted away. The new house will at last be ready for the Martins and their three daughters in early 2008. At the time of the final design committee approval, at least one neighbor, Lucille Szybisty, was willing to accept the Martins' project as a natural sign of progress and to suggest that the Martins are really no different from anyone else. "Most people here, if they had the money, they would build a second story on their home," she told the *Daily Herald*. "If I had the money, I would."

There is no single source or sociological field manual that provides an authoritative list of middle-class values. In the first chapter we named just a few—family, security, education, health, self betterment, and community—as abiding values of the middle class, but the actual inventory remains a subject of debate.

E. D. Hirsch, the author and education reformer, has long pondered the effect of what he calls middle-class values on children's classroom behavior and academic achievement. In his *Encyclopedia of Cultural Literacy*, Hirsch defines "middle class" in part by stating, "Values commonly associated with the middle class include a desire for social respectability and material wealth and an emphasis on the family and education." Other texts and studies on the subject similarly stress the central importance assigned by the middle class to securing upward mobility for the next generation, sometimes at considerable sacrifice. George Bernard Shaw said, "I have to live for others and not for myself; that's middle-class morality."

Does this mean that people who live above and below the middle-class social stratum don't value family or education as much? Of course not. But values have, as sociologists might say, emotional and symbolic components. People of all classes make choices from among competing values, and in doing so they express the importance of those values in relation to one another. For example, most middle-class families place a high value on rearing small children themselves and would not want to send them away to boarding school, which is more of an upper-class tradition. On the other hand, when a seventeen-year-old goes off to college, the event likely represents a proud moment of upward mobility in the lives of most middle-class families. In a blue-collar household, the same event is just as likely to represent abandonment and betrayal of the family unit. Studies have shown that while middle-class families and working-class families may both claim to place a high value on education and their children's well-being, middle-class families are far more likely to sacrifice significant time and financial resources helping prepare their children for adult life.

If values are difficult to define, so is the simple notion of what constitutes the middle class in America. The term "middle class" has at times been stretched to include everyone who is not obviously lower class or upper class. This was especially true in the postwar Levittown era, when it appeared that almost every family with one steady breadwinner could afford a new house and a lawn—symbols of middle-class respectability. More commonly, though, the middle class is defined as an occupational stratum encompassing salaried professionals, executives, and small-business owners. By this definition, you're not middle class if you work for hourly wages and punch a time clock. A $30,000-per-year schoolteacher is middle class, but a $50,000-per-year bus driver is not.

Contradictions such as this one and others lead some sociologists to refer to the "middle classes," since there are meaningful differences within portions of what is most broadly called the middle class. There are upper-middle-class executives, middle-middle-class professionals, and lower-middle-class clerks. But as we found in our own survey, confusion encroaches here as well. For instance, many survey respondents in our "upper" group think of themselves as "middle," and almost as many of our "middle" survey respondents regard themselves as "upper."

Most of the Middle-Class Millionaires in our survey said they consider themselves "upper-middle-class" (67 percent), while the rest said they were "middle-class" (33 percent). Among our non-millionaire households (with incomes of $50,000 to $80,000), 79 percent referred to themselves as "middle-class," and almost 21 percent said they considered themselves "upper-middle-class."

This large overlap between upper and middle—in which one of five in the lower income category consider themselves upper middle class, while one-third of the upper income group considers itself just plain middle class—is partly why we had to define our survey around income and wealth qualifications. Had we surveyed, for instance, self-identified members of the "upper middle class" and self-identified members of the "middle class," we would have gotten a very poor picture of the

Influence of Affluence. One out of three of our more affluent survey subjects would have volunteered to lump themselves in with the rest of the middle class, even though their earnings put them in the top 2 or 3 percent of national household income.

While their class self-perceptions may seem somewhat muddled, our two groups have almost identical pictures of their financial well-being and financial security—despite the enormous financial advantage one group has over the other. Among our Middle-Class Millionaires, only about 9 percent consider themselves "financially wealthy" today, while about 4 percent of the middle-class sample considers itself wealthy. Both groups, by an overwhelming margin, consider themselves "very or extremely concerned about their ability to maintain their current financial position." Slightly more Middle-Class Millionaires actually feel that way (78 percent) than the middle-class non-millionaires (76 percent).

So what constitutes wealth? In this regard, there is such a sharp division of opinion that it's easy to see why Middle-Class Millionaires share the same financial worries as the rest of the middle class, even if their tax returns place them miles apart. On average, our Middle-Class Millionaires said they would need a net worth of about $24 million in order to feel wealthy. The median answer to this question was $13.4 million, meaning that half the group estimated they would need *at least* that much to consider themselves wealthy. Among the middle-class sample, our survey respondents estimated on average that they would need a net worth of $2.3 million in order to feel wealthy, and the median response was just $1.1 million. Essentially, our entire middle class would feel wealthy if they had what most Middle-Class Millionaires have today. But 90 percent of Middle-Class Millionaires don't think their net worth has made them wealthy at all.

To us, these results help explain how Middle-Class Millionaires might feel very much at home in communities where they run the risk of being regarded by their neighbors as "rich people in McMansions." As we discovered, there is a fairly predictable hierarchy in middle-class values. Some things are more important than others to most members of the middle class, and in the case of choosing a place to live, we can see how, for instance, good schools, safe streets, and a high quality of family life are all more important than what other people happen to think.

In 1999, a Chicago-area securities trader named Brian Hickey was ready to move his family to a larger home in Hinsdale, Illinois, an affluent town not very far from Arlington Heights. The home he was selling was old and fairly small, and as the real estate market picked up, he came to realize that its value as a home paled in comparison to the value of the lot it was sitting on. Eventually, Hickey agreed to sell his house for $725,000 to a homeowner who promptly demolished it and built a $2.5 million replacement.

To Hickey's securities-trader sensibilities, the entire transaction seemed grossly inefficient. He had gone through the trouble of fixing up his house and showing it to prospective buyers, but in the end every piece of it was carted off by dump trucks. It bothered him, too, that he had to pay a full commission to his real estate agent for showing a house that ended up having no value. "I scratched my head and said, 'Why wasn't there a company to handle this kind of thing?' I would have used it, so I figured others would need it as well."

Hickey knew from securities trading that there's always money to be made when you figure out a way to bring buyer and seller together more efficiently. So he founded Teardowns.com, a service that allows homeowners to market their prospective teardown properties directly to builders at a flat 2 percent commission, far lower than the 6 percent traditional real estate agents charge.

By Hickey's reckoning, a neighborhood is ripe for teardowns if new houses are selling for about three times the price of old houses nearby. One of Hickey's partners ran the numbers on 274 Chicago-area teardown properties in 2002 and 2003. He found that builders typically were able to sell new houses built on teardown lots for more than three times what they paid. A $1.2 million house would typically rise where a $400,000 bungalow had come down.

The effect of teardowns on Hinsdale has been staggering. Three out of ten houses in the 120-year-old town have been torn down and replaced in the past fifteen to twenty years. Preservationists consider the town a national teardown "poster child" for how redevelopment can erase a community's historic character. The town nonetheless remains a very desirable place to live. It has a small, vital downtown and a rail stop for commuter trains that whisk riders to Chicago's Loop in twenty-two minutes. More important, the schools are among the best in Illinois. Test scores at all three of the town's elementary schools, for instance, rank among the top twenty-five in the state.

Just as the map of teardown towns resembles a map of Middle-Class Millionaire America, it also resembles a map of America's best public school districts. Public schools, after all, play a large part in determining local real estate values, and teardowns take place only where real estate values are very high. Teardowns.com now operates in eight states, and its Web site advertises dozens of communities that the company is interested in. "The communities are usually wrapped around good schools," Hickey says. "If you really narrow it down, school systems are important because a lot of these communities are very family-oriented." In affluent Hinsdale, where many households could afford private school, Hickey says that with rare exceptions, "public schools are it."

Until ten or fifteen years ago, most new people who moved to Hinsdale sank their money into rehabilitating and enlarging the village's older housing stock. But housing tastes have changed in recent years, Hickey says. Affluent buyers are more likely than ever to look at houses the way they look at cars—if they can afford the latest new model with all the bells and whistles, then that's what they want. The main problem with new houses, however, is that they are often built in the wrong place. Affordable land for new houses is most abundant at the fringe of suburban development, but these are places where school districts that were rural not so long ago have undistinguished educational records. To meet the demand for new houses *and* good schools, some builders started looking for the last scraps of vacant land in established communities. Once all the vacant land was gone, smaller homes in these communities became the next prime targets for redevelopment.

"That's what fueled the teardown activity," Hickey says. "Homebuyers find schools that meet their expectations for quality. And what they couldn't get in older homes—theaters in the basement, whirlpool baths—could now be found in these great older communities. It's kind of the best of both worlds. You can now buy a new home in the community that you want, and get the features that people seem to want."

Today Hickey lives in a 1950s-era brick Colonial in Hinsdale, but his memories of the hundred-year-old Victorian he grew up in include his father having to snake the creaking plumbing system, and a musty cellar where most homeowners would want a finished basement. "People may feel, 'I love this old house, yet I'd like it to be safe for my kids, I'd like to have the room and space that's livable from basement to attic,'" he says. "It was difficult to rehab them without taking them down to the studs." To Hickey, it's only natural that affluent families want for the children what they had for themselves, which is why Hinsdale has been regenerated so rapidly from the ground up. "A lot of the people in Hinsdale are from this same geographical area, and they are trying to have the same experience they had when they were growing up," he continues. "However, the housing stock isn't supplying that same experience. So they're looking to upgrade their living experience and their housing experience—because they can afford to."

One of the most interesting sets of results we obtained in our survey was how closely the middle-class sample and Middle-Class Millionaires mirror each other in terms of their stated hierarchy of values—how, in fact, Middle-Class Millionaires can sometimes in practice remain closer to the middle-class ideal than the rest of our "middle-middle" sample. It would be natural to assume that affluence would generally lead Middle-Class Millionaires away from the rest of the middle class. Instead, our results suggest that they use their affluence in some important ways to behave *more consistently* like middle-class people than the rest of the middle class does.

For instance, to test for a middle-class hierarchy of values, we asked both sample groups to go down a list of value statements and assess the personal importance they ascribe to each. The consistency between the two groups in this portion of the survey was extraordinary. "Being ethical" was rated "very or extremely important" by 96 to 97 percent of both groups. About 90 to 92 percent of both groups rated "your responsibility to loved ones," "being a good parent," and "protecting your family from crime" as values that are very or extremely important. Roughly 85 percent of both groups put the same high value on "providing your children with the best possible education." The value of "honesty" also ranked in the 85 percent range for both. The value of "being a good spouse" was highly ranked by about 79 percent of both groups. "Caring for others" and "authenticity" were highly ranked in the 67 to 68 percent range by both groups.

With both groups, "your own interests and hobbies" are clearly subordinated to spousal and familial concerns. They were ranked important by only 50 percent of Middle-Class Millionaires and by 65 percent of middle-class respondents. "Protecting the environment" also comes after family, at 55 percent for Middle-Class Millionaires and 65 percent of the middle class. "Keeping the community safe" and "being well-regarded" were ranked highly by just 55 to 57 percent of both groups. "Helping your community to grow" was highly ranked by just 38 or 39 percent of both groups. There was some difference between the groups who considered "your responsibility as a member of the world community" important. Only 23 percent of Middle-Class Millionaires ranked it very highly, while 34 percent of the middle-class sample ranked it highly. In general, however, the two groups tracked each other fairly consistently in terms of shared values.

The consistency of these results raises one obvious question: Isn't this simply a hierarchy of fundamental human values? Surprisingly, that isn't so, according to our research. Consider the answers to the same set of questions provided by individuals whose net worth exceeds $25 million. "Being ethical," which was regarded with universal primary importance within both middle-class groups, was considered very or extremely important by just 51 percent of these high-net-worth respondents. "Providing your children with the best possible education," which was held as very or extremely important by 85 percent of both middle-class sample groups, was considered just as important by only 60 percent of the high-net-worth group. "Being a good spouse"—highly regarded also by 80 percent of both middle-class groups—was ranked very or extremely important by just 41 percent of those with high net worth. And "your responsibility to the world community" ranked high in the esteem of only 10 percent of those with high net worth, versus 23 percent of the Middle-Class Millionaires and 34 percent of the middle-class sample.

Here is where George Bernard Shaw's assessment—that sacrifice is the hallmark of middle-class morality—comes to life. We've already shown that only about one-half to two-thirds of the middle class ranked "my own interests and hobbies" as very important, far below all other responsibilities to loved ones. Among high-net-worth survey respondents, however, "my own interests and hobbies" was ranked very or extremely important by 80 percent, trailing only "protecting my family from crime" (97 percent), "protecting my family from accidents, fires, car crashes, etc." (95 percent), "career" (92 percent), and "being financially independent" (97 percent).

It shouldn't be surprising, however, that Middle-Class Millionaire values pull away from middle-class values and more clearly resemble the high-net-worth group's values in areas involving money and careers. Like the high-net-worth individuals, Middle-Class Millionaires almost unanimously (97 percent) place a high value on "being financially independent" (only 67 percent of the middle-class sample places the same high importance on that value). Middle-Class Millionaires also put a higher value on their careers than do those in the middle class (82 percent vs. 43 percent).

In some cases, values seem to shift in consistent steps with wealth. The importance of "friendship" and "responsibility to the community and neighbors" declines with the accumulation of wealth. Friendship is important to 84 percent of the middle-class group, 64 percent of the Middle-Class Millionaires, and just 42 percent of high-net-worth individuals. When it comes to the community and neighbors, 60 percent of the middle-class survey respondents regard them as very important, 46 percent of the Middle-Class Millionaires see them that way, and just 26 percent of those with a high net worth believe they are very or extremely important.

It may seem surprising that people with a net worth of $25 million or more are far from unanimous in the value they place on being good parents and securing the best possible education for their children and that many more of them consider their own interests and hobbies of greater value. This doesn't mean that high-net-worth individuals don't care about their children. More than 60 percent of them ranked these child-related values as very or extremely important. We are seeking to measure those values held most frequently in common, to the point where they can be said to be a defining characteristic of a given class. It would be hard to say, based on our evidence, that education is an essential, commonly held value among those with high net worth when survey respondents were more likely to count their hobbies and personal interests as very important.

From our survey data, then, the Middle-Class Millionaire emerges as a unique breed. On one hand, Middle-Class Millionaires are deeply rooted emotionally in the middle-class values they assumed during childhood, but on the other hand, they are equipped with attitudes toward career and personal success that far more closely resemble those of high-net-worth individuals. As we showed in Chapter 2, the urges to maximize and optimize, to focus and win, set Middle-Class Millionaires apart from other members of their social class. Their values, however, compel Middle-Class Millionaires to remain in close proximity with the rest of the middle class. Our survey data help explain how, in matters related to money or success (as with the Martin family's new home on North Forrest Avenue), Middle-Class Millionaires are likely to express their middle-class values in ways that members of the middle class may not appreciate.

In a very specific way, our survey data actually detect the very seeds of the teardown phenomenon. Both Middle-Class Millionaires and middle-class survey respondents (about 85 percent each) put a high value on "securing the best possible education for their children." Consistent with that stated value, 77 percent of the Middle-Class Millionaires cite "the school system" as very or extremely important in choosing a community to live in. Among the middle class, however, only 57 percent cited the school system as important in choosing a home. Almost as many middle-class members placed a high value on "convenience to work" (52 percent) and "convenience to shopping" (43 percent), two considerations that were rarely cited by Middle-Class Millionaires as important (8 percent and 18 percent, respectively).

What are we to make of this? A good number of middle-class respondents who claim it is important to get their children "the best education possible" did not find the school district an important factor in deciding where to live. Digging deeper into the survey, we find that while education is ranked highly important with equal frequency among middle class and Middle-Class Millionaire alike, it seems that the Middle-Class Millionaire has more at stake in the matter. Both groups care, but for starkly different reasons.

We asked the survey respondents if this statement was very or extremely accurate: "A child's academic achievements reflect one's success as a parent." Just 16 percent of the middle-class sample agreed, but more than 46 percent of the Middle-Class Millionaires agreed. In a similar vein, in response to the statement "You will feel you have failed as a parent if your children are not as successful as you," just over 15 percent of the middle-class group agreed, while 40 percent of the Middle-Class Millionaires agreed. The same share of Middle-Class Millionaires, 40 percent, feel it is very or extremely important for their children to attend a prestigious college or university. Only 7 percent of the middle-class group feels that way.

While their stated values about education may be nearly identical, many Middle-Class Millionaires have a completely different outlook on education than the one possessed by most of the middle-class survey respondents. These results suggest that many Middle-Class Millionaires are singularly devoted to their children's academic success and are more apt to blame themselves if their children fail to achieve it. In terms of personal sacrifice, personal responsibility, and a commitment to upward mobility, Middle-Class Millionaires are more likely to embody and act upon their middle-class values more completely than the rest of the middle-class group.

Given the choice between a big new home on a cul-de-sac in a mediocre exurban school district and an old house in an excellent school district, Middle-Class Millionaires have rejected both and blazed a trail of teardowns through some of the nation's most prosperous suburbs. As we see it, this is partly because of their wealth, partly because of their Millionaire Intelligence, but entirely due to their middle-class values, arranged in a hierarchy that puts their family's safety above schools,

schools above family comfort, comfort above personal convenience, and convenience above whatever the neighbors might think. Considered in this light, teardowns are an utterly predictable phenomenon in any excellent school district with no land left for development. As often happened in the writing of this book, it makes us wonder what other values-driven trends are poised to catch fire due to the influence of Middle-Class Millionaire affluence.

Although the deflation of the housing bubble had caused a slowdown in real estate activity at the end of 2006, Hinsdale, Illinois, managed to set a new record in 2007 with its most expensive teardown, a $5.6 million home on an acre of land. Brian Hickey doesn't expect to feel too much pain from a slowing of sales. "We never got into this business because it was a fad," he says. "We got into it because we saw that these more affluent communities are full of inferior housing stock. Something's got to give if people with the means continue to want to live in these desirable areas." Our survey suggests that they always will.

During the spring budgeting season in 1985, the school board in Westport, Connecticut, was faced with some difficult decisions about the future of the town's only high school. Staples High had long been a source of civic pride for Westport. Its students often won state and national scholarship competitions, and more than 10 percent of each graduating class went off to the Ivy League and other elite colleges. But enrollment at Staples was projected to drop dangerously low in the next several years, from 1,700 to about 1,000. With such a small student body, Staples would no longer be able to offer the same range of advanced science and language electives that had helped make it one of the most academically distinguished public schools in the state. For the first time in decades, the board was under pressure—particularly from homeowners without children—to cut courses and lay off teachers.

Westport is a historic river town of 26,000 with a commuter rail station that connects it to Grand Central Station in Manhattan, forty-four miles to the southwest. Over the years, the town has been a suburban middle-class bellwether of sorts, one that occupies a unique niche in the popular culture of baby boomer America. Westport was the home of *The Man in the Grey Flannel Suit,* the bestselling novel and movie with Gregory Peck that examined how pursuit of the American dream can cast a shadow on family life. When Lucy and Ricky of *I Love Lucy* finally quit their Upper East Side apartment to start a family, Westport was where they chose to raise Little Ricky. And when TV producers dreamed up a farcical sitcom about an attractive suburban housewife who happens to be a witch, they decided that their *Bewitched* Samantha Stephens should secretly wreak havoc on the neighbors in sedate, secure Westport.

There never was a movie or a TV show about the schools crisis that hit Westport and its neighboring communities in Fairfield County in the 1980s. That was when the baby boom, which had brought so much prosperity and notoriety to Westport, went bust. Greenwich, Darien, and other affluent towns in southwestern Connecticut laid off teachers and shut down elementary schools in those years, but Westport was hit hardest of all. Five out of its seven elementary schools were closed, and the Department of Education predicted in 1984 that Staples High School would lose 60 percent of students in its three upper grades, the largest such drop for any school district in the state.

The *New York Times* reported in 1985 that Westport's school board was being squeezed by what appeared to be several trends beyond its control. Westport was graying, the article stated, and soon nearly one-quarter of the town would be populated by childless retirees who "form an increasingly potent voting bloc, with little interest in taxing themselves to educate the children of others." High real estate values meant that the town remained attractive to the corporate executive set, but the *Times* speculated that "few young families can afford the $250,000 that is considered the minimum price for many of the houses in Westport."

It was hard to see the future of the town as anything more than a stuffy geriatric enclave that tolerated children and families but would no longer indulge them financially.

That year, the school board decided to close a $250,000 funding gap by dropping an ecology course, paring back some music offerings, and merging several elective history courses. By 1990, however, the situation had worsened, and Westport's finance board ordered an $890,000 cut in the school board's $33.2 million budget. The school district's teachers, who ranked among the state's highest-paid, were an inviting target. A beloved elementary school art teacher with twenty-two years of seniority had her position eliminated. So did a math teacher, an industrial arts teacher, and the head of Staples's English department. Two hundred Staples students protested the layoffs at a demonstration in front of town hall. School supporters demanded that the district look at other ways to economize, but the town's elected board of finance made clear that firing teachers should be the first priority.

Not long afterward, however, Westport's schools and Westport itself began to undergo a surprising reversal of fortunes. Part of the revival was owed to simple demographics. A new generation of echo boomers—children of baby boomers—began refilling classroom seats all across the United States. The other factor in Westport's turnaround emerged from another, wholly unexpected and unpredicted source. The town's high housing costs, long assumed to be a formidable obstacle to attracting young families with children, were not an impediment for more affluent couples starting families later in life. By the mid-1990s, Westport was in the throes of a Middle-Class Millionaire influx, part of a larger migration of well-paid baby boomer professionals, with their little echo boomers in tow, who were willing to pay top dollar to live in suburban towns with quality schools. Westport again became an iconic town of sorts. In 1993, Martha Stewart chose an 1805 farmhouse in Westport to show us how to live well from her home-cum-broadcast studio, Turkey Hill.

There are only about 9,000 single-family homes in Westport, most of which were built in the 1960s or earlier and sit on large zoning-restricted lots that can't be subdivided for new development. They are spread out over twenty square miles, a land area just slightly smaller than all of Manhattan island. This mix of good schools and older houses on big parcels all but ensured that Westport would reign as the teardown capital of Connecticut. More than a hundred Westport homes have been carted off and replaced every year since the mid-1990s. The Web site WestportNow.com has a handy interactive feature called Teardown of the Day, which allows users to see properties slated for demolition by simply rolling a cursor over pinpoints on a town map.

Contrary to the 1985 predictions, the growth of childless retirees in Westport slowed down during the 1990s and never reached one-quarter of the town's population. Many older residents sold their modest 1950s- and 1960s-era houses to homebuilders eager to throw up mini-mansions in their place. With each teardown, Westport grew less geriatric, more family-oriented, and more Middle-Class Millionaire. By the 2000 census, two-thirds of Westport's single-family homes were worth more than $500,000, and one in six was worth more than $1 million. The overall population grew by 1,200 between 1990 and 2000, while the number of children under age eighteen had grown even faster, by 2,200. The demographic disaster forecast for Westport's schools had been averted. School district enrollment, which had cratered at about 3,400 in 1994, grew to 5,400 by 2006. It is now expected to top out around 8,000 by 2010. Children, not retirees, are now one-quarter of Westport's population.

Accommodating that many new schoolchildren isn't cheap, but by 1997 there were signs that a new consensus in town was ready to tax itself in the name of public education. That year, the traditionally Republican town elected a Democrat named Diane Farrell as first selectwoman—the mayor's job—with 61 percent of the vote. At age forty-two, Farrell had ties to three generations of Westport public education. Farrell herself had been an elementary school teacher before going into advertising. She had attended a Westport elementary school, while her mother was a teacher at another Westport school. When Farrell's own daughters attended one of Westport's elementary schools, she headed the PTA there. Both girls had since gone on to Staples High School.

By 2000, the school district and the board of finance had approved a $150 million building program for new and renovated elementary and middle schools. One of the long-closed elementary schools was taken out of mothballs and rehabilitated. The big project that remained was a multimillion-dollar makeover for Staples High School. The current school building was too small for an anticipated enrollment of 1,800, and its 1958-vintage classrooms were ill suited for education in the age of the Internet. Controversial early estimates of the project's cost ranged from $54 million to $65 million.

Evidence of how much Westport had changed came with Diane Farrell's 2001 bid for reelection. She was running against tradition. In the past twenty-five years, Westport voters had thrown out every incumbent first selectman after a single term. Her Republican challenger, John Izzo, ran on a tax-cutting platform that seemed geared to appeal to aging empty-nesters—that "potent voting bloc" cited in the *Times* article sixteen years earlier. Izzo claimed that no one had actually committed to a ceiling on Staples's renovations and that the price tag might reach $135 million. GOP bumper stickers showed up around town promising that a vote for Izzo would "save $100 million in taxes."

It didn't work. Farrell won reelection with 70 percent of the vote. The people of Westport had spoken, and they voted for more taxes *and* better schools. The next year, Farrell backed a $73 million bond issue—the largest in Westport's history—to rebuild half of Staples High School. The bond was overwhelmingly approved, but only after a half-hearted movement arose to stall its passage by making its approval subject to a ballot referendum. Farrell made an eloquent plea against the delay at a public meeting that was reported in the *Westport News*. "We are not just spending $73 million," she said, pointing out how good schools yield a return in the form of strong property values. "We are making an investment because we are a community that values education. It is imperative that we all commit to protecting that investment."

In April 2004, the *Wall Street Journal* studied the makeup of freshman classes at ten of the most selective colleges in the nation—the eight Ivy League universities plus the University of Chicago and Pomona College in California. The *Journal*'s reporters pored over the freshman "facebooks" at these institutions and recorded the high school alma maters of all 11,000 students. They came up with a list of just sixty-five high schools nationwide that had sent at least twenty of their 2003 graduates to these cream-of-the-crop colleges. Of the sixty-five schools, thirty-six were elite private academies such as the Harvard-Westlake School in California and Phillips Exeter in New Hampshire. A handful were famously selective urban public "magnet schools" such as Boston Latin and Bronx Science. Twenty-two were public schools in affluent suburbs, including Westport's Staples High School. Not surprisingly, out of those twenty-two suburban feeder schools to the nation's most highly selective colleges, fifteen were located in towns that also appear on the National Preservation Trust's list of "teardown" communities.

Within a mere fifteen years, Westport changed from a town at loggerheads over school spending into a town devoted to preserving its image as a proud bastion of public education. The high school that once considered dropping fourth-year French as a cost-cutting measure now offers classes in Mandarin Chinese and Latin. Westport's cost per pupil, at about $14,500, is among the highest in Connecticut. The town's taxes are high, too, but that's really only because housing values are so high. The actual tax *rate* on Westport real estate—the tax per $1,000 of assessed value—ranks among the lowest in Connecticut. And when the new Staples High School opened in 2005, although its ultimate cost came in at around $80 million, it could hardly be considered a Taj Mahal. At one point in the construction process, the school board decided to save $800,000 by switching to sealed windows that can't be opened.

What is happening in Westport and in Middle-Class Millionaire enclaves all over the country is a revitalization of what were already fairly prosperous suburbs. Looking back on Westport's recent history with the schools, it's plain to see how Middle-Class Millionaires set off a virtuous cycle. Families willing to shoulder sky-high mortgages to gain access to Westport's superior schools helped bid up housing prices to the point where the only people willing to make the financial sacrifice of buying a house in Westport were those attracted to Westport's schools. After all, if you don't have kids, there are plenty of nice places where the houses are much cheaper. In Westport today, taxes on high home values have ensured that the schools will remain well funded, and the political support for school funding is all but assured for years to come. And if the schools continue to remain desirable, today's Westport school parents will be able to recoup their investment in their homes decades later, when they've become empty-nesters and are ready to move on.

Not everyone with a child in Westport's schools is a Middle-Class Millionaire, but it was the influx of Middle-Class Millionaires—with their middle-class values and Millionaire Intelligence—that shifted the town's primary focus back to children and families. This is a kind of transformative success-breeds-success dynamic that we find often when Middle-Class Millionaires coalesce in spending decisions and lifestyle choices that influence and direct the rest of the middle class around them. The Influence of Affluence is one of the chief mechanisms by which Middle-Class Millionaires are transforming America.

CHAPTER FOUR

THE RICH WORK FOR THE POOR

Back in 1999, Manhattanites William K. Joseph and his wife, Stephanie, were facing a familiar middle-class rite of passage: getting their child into college. Max Joseph was a bright, talented high school junior with aspirations of becoming a filmmaker. He always did well on standardized tests and was an excellent student at the exclusive Dalton School in Manhattan. In years past, a student with Max Joseph's academic profile might have expected little trouble getting into one of the nation's eight elite Ivy League universities the following fall.

But the Josephs knew that the race to get into such prestigious institutions had grown far more competitive than it was during their own college days. The numbers of applications submitted to each university had surged in recent years, to the point where top schools were accepting only one out of every eight applications and even lesser-known institutions, once considered "safety schools," were rejecting 60 or 70 percent of applicants. As junior year began, the Josephs grew concerned that they weren't up to the task of making sure their son filled out all his applications properly and hit all the deadlines. The Dalton School had a professional counseling staff, but getting a teenager to complete all the steps required for each application wouldn't be the school's responsibility.

With mixed emotions, the Josephs decided to hire a private college admissions counselor, one of a small but rapidly expanding field. William Joseph says he and his wife felt self-conscious at the time about hiring a coach to help get their son into college. He was also concerned about the expense and whether it would be worth it. The family picked a then-new Manhattan firm called IvyWise, headed by Katherine Cohen, a Yale Ph.D. who once worked in the admissions office there. At about $100 per hour, Cohen provided an initial assessment of Max's qualifications, arranged for an SAT tutor, and advised him on his course selections for senior year. Once she learned of Max's interest in filmmaking, she lined him up for internships at local film production offices. When it came to submitting an essay for his application to Brown University, Cohen encouraged Max to substitute one of his fictional short stories instead, in the hopes it would help him stand out. In April 2000, after about eighteen months' worth of assistance from IvyWise, Max was rewarded with a thick packet in the mail from Brown—an invitation to join the class of 2004.

For the past ten years or so, a growing number of parents have been getting this kind of pricey admissions counseling for their college-bound children. In 1999, there were perhaps 500 private college admissions counselors in the entire United States. Today there are 4,000, and the Independent Educational Consultants Association expects the number will double again within the next five years. Of the 200,000 freshmen who entered four-year private colleges and universities in 2006, at least one out of five had received professional help during the application process.

Behind the Trend

That a field such as admissions counseling has taken off during a decade in which the population of college-age echo boomers grew steadily *and* the number of Middle-Class Millionaire families in the United States more than doubled is largely a case of demography as destiny. With so many more teenagers emerging from families possessing so many more dollars in disposable income, a kind of competitive "arms race" to gain advantage in the college admissions sweepstakes was perhaps inevitable.

But that's not the whole story. While it is true that Middle-Class Millionaire parents have more resources to devote to polishing their children's college applications, remember that we also found Middle-Class Millionaires to be much more emotionally invested in the competition for college than the rest of the middle-class pack. Again, nearly half of all Middle-Class Millionaires feel that their children's academic achievements reflect on their success as parents, an attitude shared by only one in eight middle-class parents. And how do Middle-Class Millionaires measure those academic achievements? Ultimately, with name-brand colleges. Four out of ten Middle-Class Millionaires told us that it's very important or extremely important for their children to attend "a highly selective or prestigious university." Just one in *fourteen* members of our middle-class sample felt the same way.

The picture becomes even more intriguing when we examine *why* such an education is important to Middle-Class Millionaires. An overwhelming majority of respondents—millionaire or no—who considered prestigious universities important agreed that such schools provide a quality education that enhances their children's employment opportunities. But 73 percent of Middle-Class Millionaires also cited the superior "peer group connections" formed at such schools to be very important as well. Just 31 percent of this middle-class subgroup—a small sample to begin with—made the same assessment.

Seen in this light, the tremendous competitive pressure Middle-Class Millionaires feel toward their children's education may have less to do with building their educational foundation than with creating a lifelong social and professional network. After all, a bright student could arguably learn just as much at a less-competitive institution. But to a Middle-Class Millionaire, access to the rarefied "Ivy League network" is an unparalleled prize.

Selling into a market of parents who are both monied *and* highly motivated, IvyWise and other top-of-the-line admissions counselors have rolled out college-preparation programs that begin as early as eighth grade and top out at a cost of $30,000 or more. Oregon-based counselor Michele Hernandez, a veteran of Dartmouth's admissions department, runs three-day college application "boot camps" priced at $10,000. IvyWise now bills at $300 per hour, and its junior-and-senior-year "platinum program" costs $32,500, which has earned Katherine Cohen a certain degree of scorn and derision. Some college admissions directors have called these fees "rapacious" and denounced the entire admissions counseling field for exploiting parental fears and insecurities. Amherst College's admissions head told *New York* magazine in 2001, "To get a private counselor is a joke; it's preposterous. In the profession we laugh at these things."

Yet every year the admissions offices at the fifty or so most selective colleges and universities in the United States are inundated with applications, virtually all of which have been filled out by students fully capable of succeeding at those schools. So Cohen, who points out that her most popular service, a three-hour application review, costs $1,000, tries to impress upon her student-clients that the first step in filling out "killer" college applications (or *Rock Hard Apps,* the title of one of her books) is to use every chance you get during your high school years to make an impact and stand out as someone special.

Cohen's advice to high school students might be summed up like this: Don't scatter your energies among a half-dozen extracurricular activities. Choose one or two things you love to do and work hard to distinguish yourself at them. Compete for awards. Try to learn from your mistakes. Study every B-minus paper carefully, and ask the teacher's advice on how it could have been improved. Make sure you get to know your teachers, and make sure your teachers know you, since you'll be counting on them to write glowing letters of recommendation.

Many of Cohen's students are the offspring of Middle-Class Millionaires, and what she urges them to do, basically, is develop in high school the same essential set of qualities that we have termed Millionaire Intelligence: hard work, networking, self-interest, self-efficacy. The four points of Millionaire Intelligence all figure prominently in the IvyWise program, and the firm's success rate suggests that these character traits really are valued by the admissions offices at the nation's top colleges. In 2006, IvyWise claimed that 90 percent of its clients were admitted to one of their top two choices and that every client was accepted by at least one of his or her top three choices. It's as if the American meritocracy were restocking its ranks in the image of the Middle-Class Millionaire.

"The Rich Work for the Poor"

Cohen's next move reveals a pattern of product development that is familiar to anyone who has purchased an inexpensive DVD player in the last few years: She scaled her concept downward to appeal to a broader audience. In 2006, she secured the financial backing to develop ApplyWise, an interactive Web site that helps coach college applicants and their parents step by step through the entire application process maze. Cohen herself, rebranded on the site as "Dr. Kat," appears in six multimedia tutorials that cover everything from how to compile a "brag sheet" of accomplishments to writing an activity essay. The cost of a two-year subscription to ApplyWise is $300, and for students who want a little more personal attention, the site offers telephone counseling and essay reviews at à la carte rates ranging from $75 to $125.

Cohen took a page from the success stories of many innovative companies in all kinds of fields that were incubated in their early stages by catering only to the extreme high end of the marketplace. That's where profit margins are greatest, commensurate with the risk of trying to do anything for the very first time. If a company has any chance of taking its range of offerings and scaling them down toward the mass market, the basic concept will need to hit it big first among consumers at the top end of the middle class—the Middle-Class Millionaires. Those are the people most likely to pass initial judgment on any product's adequacy and appeal, a judgment that carries a lot of weight. If Katherine Cohen hadn't managed to produce a high rate of success and client satisfaction at premium rates with IvyWise, it's doubtful that ApplyWise ever could have attracted enough investor interest to get off the ground.

When it comes to making spending choices that are driven by their middle-class values—values such as family, education, and the environment—Middle-Class Millionaires often function in our economy as highly discriminating testers of new products and services. They can either hold the door open to further innovation, as they have with ApplyWise, or slam it shut. The late free-market economist Milton Friedman noted how carmakers usually introduce new safety features such as antilock brakes as novel high-end options in their most expensive models. These early initial sales help carmakers gauge future demand and finance the development of less costly versions that eventually become standard equipment on all of their models. In this sense, Friedman said, innovation is a process by which "the rich work for the poor."

As the American Middle-Class Millionaire population prepares to double again in the next ten years, we think that this notion of "the rich work[ing] for the poor" holds important implications for our society. Middle-class aspirations—quality education, good health, career success, leisure pursuits, and even politics and community life—suggest how affluence in the United States will have an impact on the entire world economy as middle-class desires and standards of living are being reshaped for this new century, courtesy of the Middle-Class Millionaire.

Natural Networkers

While common middle-class hopes and dreams provide a road map for those areas likely to experience the influence of middle-class affluence, our survey questions about the way Middle-Class Millionaires view their position in their communities revealed a more purposeful and proactive role for them. Fifty-five percent of our Middle-Class Millionaire sample said that they "often know about new things before other people do," compared with just 10 percent of the middle-class sample. Sixty-six percent of Middle-Class Millionaires said people regularly ask them for advice on what to buy. Only 15 percent of the middle class said the same.

Middle-Class Millionaires report they are at least two to three times more likely than the middle class to be asked their advice about the following: automobiles, physicians and health care, investment opportunities, personal fitness, caring for young children, and children's activities. In most other categories, the difference in magnitude is even starker. They are almost sixty times more likely to be frequently asked their advice about home security systems and fifty times more likely to be asked their advice about hotels. Middle-Class Millionaires are thirty-five times more likely to be asked about networking groups, fifteen times more likely to be asked about vacations, ten times more likely to be asked about supplemental programs for children, and nine times more likely to be asked about attorneys and legal advice. They are five times more likely to be asked about personal development programs for themselves and five times more likely to be asked about caring for elderly parents.

There is only one area of rough parity reported by our two survey groups when it comes to how frequently others sought their counsel, and it happens to involve that common middle-class obsession: education. About 40 percent of both groups say they are asked very often or extremely often for advice on "teachers and schools."

Middle-Class Millionaires don't just dispense advice. They seek it as well. By an overwhelming margin, Middle-Class Millionaires count on the direct advice of others as their number one guide to spending money. Almost 79 percent of Middle-Class Millionaires say that "the prior experiences of people you know" is very or extremely important in their buying decisions. The same is true for only about one-third of the middle class. In fact, members of the middle class are more likely to put their faith in rating services such as *Consumer Reports* (43 percent) and just as likely to trust their own research on the Internet (33 percent). For Middle-Class Millionaires, on the other hand, neither *Consumer Reports* (22 percent) nor the Internet (6 percent) ranks nearly as high as a word-of-mouth endorsement from someone they know.

This penchant for leaning on other people's experiences with consumer goods reveals a much larger and more important bias in the minds of Middle-Class Millionaires: They are more likely to count on other people for everything, including their professional well-being. More than 62 percent of them told us that "knowing many, many people" is very important or extremely important to their financial success. A healthy minority, about 43 percent, of the middle class said the same. Almost 72 percent of Middle-Class Millionaires say that "knowing people who know many people" is similarly important to their financial success, as opposed to 57 percent of the middle class. It's a shared value among many members of both groups, to be sure, but it's much more clearly a defining value among Middle-Class Millionaires. No wonder Middle-Class Millionaires place such great importance on colleges that can offer a high-quality, ready-built network for their children.

In almost every way imaginable, Middle-Class Millionaires are far more likely to assign a high degree of importance to having many people in their lives. For example, while more than two-thirds of both Middle-Class Millionaires and the middle class claim to "have an active social life," 65 percent of Middle-Class Millionaires feel they are "well connected" in their communities, while just 28 percent of the middle class feel the same.

It's pretty clear to us that Middle-Class Millionaires consciously work at making this connection happen. More than 43 percent of them say they belong to a formal or informal networking group, compared with just 16 percent of the middle-class segments. But even between the subgroups of avowed networkers drawn from both groups, there is an important divide in the roles they play. Middle-Class Millionaires are far more likely to have recruited many new people into the group. On average, Middle-Class Millionaires told us they brought in 4.7 members to their networking groups over the past three years. For the middle-class networker, the average was just 0.5. Among the bottom half of middle-class networkers, four out of five brought no new members to the network in the past three years.

One of the chief benefits of networking is that it seldom costs anything—and bringing new people into the group doesn't cost anything at all. And yet not only are Middle-Class Millionaires more likely to join these formal or informal networking groups, but they are also more likely to add value to the groups in the form of new members. Exerting influence on others is a way to wealth for them, but our survey results suggest that it is also something integrated into their way of life. It affects their community work and charitable endeavors as well. While Middle-Class Millionaires are only somewhat more likely than the middle class to be involved in community or charity organizations, Middle-Class Millionaires still bring in roughly twice as many new people into those organizations as the middle class do.

The concept of a network is unique in some important ways. Most resources are spoiled by overuse. Just about everyone can name a beach or a highway that they now avoid because it's too uncomfortably congested. As Yogi Berra once said of a Manhattan restaurant, "Nobody goes there anymore because it's too crowded." The network, on the other hand, defies this rule. As more people join any kind of network, the value of that network for each individual member continues to grow. This was true in the evolution of telephone networks, and it has been true in the development of the Internet. It is true also for personal networks, and Middle-Class Millionaires, either instinctively or because they see their self-interest in the matter, work at increasing the size of the networks they belong to.

During his visit to the United States in 1830, the French-born Alexis de Tocqueville, a prescient observer of American life, saw how "Americans of all ages, all conditions and all dispositions constantly form associations." In essence, networking has been central to the American way of life from the nation's beginnings. Tocqueville reasoned that in a pure democracy, without a king or an aristocracy to provide patronage to ambitious men, individuals prosper only when they seek people with common interests and work together. "Among democratic nations," he wrote, "all the citizens are independent and feeble. . . . They all, therefore, become powerless if they do not learn voluntarily to help one another." As we've seen from our survey, Middle-Class Millionaires seem to grasp this essential fact of American life far more fully than other members of the middle class.

On a societal scale, such personal networks can powerfully affect the rate at which new ideas or products take hold—which represents yet another vital dimension of Middle-Class Millionaire influence. The role that interconnected relationships can play in the spread of innovations has been well documented, particularly in a field of social research called "diffusion theory." The most influential study of this kind is more than sixty-five years old and took place in the cornfields of Iowa.

And yet the key group it identified as prompting the spread of a new improved corn variety quite nearly fits our own definition of Middle-Class Millionaires.

Corn Chatter

In 1941, two Iowa State University researchers named Bryce Ryan and Neal C. Gross set out to investigate how usage of a more productive variety of hybrid corn had diffused through two small farming communities fifty miles west of the Iowa State campus in Ames. After collecting data from 259 farmers, they figured out that it had taken thirteen years, from 1928 to 1941, before all but two of the farmers had adopted the new hybrid corn.

The hybrid corn was more drought-resistant than the traditional seed corn, and it produced 20 percent greater crop yields. It was heavily promoted by Iowa's Department of Agriculture and by salesmen sent out by the seed companies. Yet initial adoption was slow. Ryan and Gross, the two researchers, found that in 1933, after five years, just 10 percent of the farmers had switched. Then the rate of adoption seemed to take off. By 1936, 40 percent of the farmers were planting hybrid corn, and the switchover was all but complete by 1941.

When Ryan and Gross studied their surveys more closely, they discovered that while nearly all the farmers learned about the hybrid corn from seed salesmen and agricultural agents, most had been persuaded to make the switch only after consulting with other farmers. A relatively small number, which Ryan and Gross dubbed the Innovators, seized upon the new corn immediately as an exciting opportunity. A second wave of Early Adopters learned from the Innovators and followed suit shortly thereafter. It was this group, the Early Adopters, that had the greatest influence on the next group, which was deemed the Early Majority. That was when hybrid seed corn took off, around 1936, when the Early Majority, after consulting with Early Adopters, decided to make the leap.

In his bestselling book *The Tipping Point*, Malcolm Gladwell cites this study as an example of how ideas are spread in an epidemic-like fashion by a hierarchy of temperamentally distinct groups of people. He describes the Innovators as wild and adventurous people, eager to try new things. Their results were studied by the Early Adopters, who tended to be more thoughtful individuals who were well respected and considered opinion leaders in the community. The more skeptical Early Majority wanted to see what the Early Adopters made of this new corn before they made the leap. The last, most cautious group were the Laggards, who were temperamentally the last ones to try anything new.

Gladwell invoked the Iowa study to support his notion of how the spread of new ideas is affected by groups of people with differing temperaments. But it seems to us that Gladwell overlooked two important points about the Iowa study, which remains, after all these years, one of the most important diffusion studies ever done. He states in *The Tipping Point* that the new hybrid corn was "superior in every respect to the seed that had been used by farmers for decades before." This is not entirely true. Iowa farmers were long accustomed to taking their own seeds from their best-looking plants each year. You couldn't do that with hybrid corn. It lost its effectiveness after one generation, and new seeds needed to be purchased every spring from the seed company. Switching to hybrid corn was risky. It meant you would be dependent on the seed company forever.

So who were the Innovators with hybrid corn in the Iowa study? Gladwell makes them out to be wild risk takers, but the study found them also to be among the county's largest and richest farmers. They were the ones who were most able to handle the financial commitment and the downside risk if for some reason the hybrid corn failed. They were also more or less socially isolated from most of the other farmers in the county, like the ultra-high-net-worth individuals of today. So when they switched to hybrid corn, they had relatively few face-to-face conversations about it with other farmers.

They did, however, discuss the corn with farmers who were more nearly their social equals, farmers who were successful, were widely respected, and seemed to know everyone in the county. These are the people who turned out to be the Early Adopters. These Early Adopters were most like the Middle-Class Millionaires of today. They weren't as well-off as the Innovators, but they could afford to take a chance on the new corn. And since each of them knew so many other farmers, once they switched to hybrid corn, they influenced everyone else's decision. In Greene County, Iowa, in 1935, these were the farmers with Millionaire Intelligence. Eventually, the livelihoods of every farmer in Greene County turned on their good words about hybrid corn.

The path that hybrid corn took through Iowa farming communities in the 1930s illustrates the very same process new ideas go through today as they make their way through middle-class communities. A good current example is the growing diffusion of backup electrical generators in Middle-Class Millionaire homes, seen most often in Florida and other Gulf Coast states.

Before 2004, expensive natural-gas-powered standby generators were usually found only at business locations where companies have special needs for electricity during power outages. These heavy-duty commercial-grade generators, which could cost $25,000 or more to purchase and install, were occasionally found at the homes of the very rich as well. Brief power outages from storms and high winds are fairly common in the South, and most homeowners who are not content to live by candlelight have portable gasoline-powered generators, costing about $1,000, which they have to haul out, fill with fuel, and plug in to give their homes minimal emergency power.

Between September 2004 and October 2005, Florida was hit with three hurricanes, each of which left millions in the dark for days, if not weeks. Hurricane Frances knocked out power to 5 million Floridians in 2004. It was one of the most widespread storm-induced outages in history. Some people had to wait eight weeks to have their electricity restored, and even those who owned portable generators couldn't find fuel to run them. A year later, millions of Gulf Coast residents who were lucky enough not to have their homes destroyed by Hurricane Katrina faced weeks more without power. By the fall of 2005, the few Florida companies that installed residential standby generators were inundated with orders and forced to compile months-long wait lists.

"What happened was, the affluent people felt what it was like to be without electricity," says H. J. Frank, of Personalized Power Systems in Boca Raton. "Before, my generator had been a toy for boys. It was more of a status symbol, to show you could afford $25,000 or $30,000 on something rare that you don't really need. But after the storms, it's turned into a necessity. They realized that without electricity for seven or eight days, it's an affordable item for a home worth half a million dollars or more."

With two thousand installations completed in south Florida, Personalized Power is the largest company of its kind in the nation, and until recently it wasn't even necessary for the company to advertise. Home generators tend to sell themselves. Referrals from neighbors flow naturally once the lights go out, and everyone in the neighborhood notices who still has power.

Andre Biewand and his family suffered through five-day power outages each time one of the three 2004–2005 Florida hurricanes struck near their suburban Orlando town. Biewand, a real estate developer, and his wife had twin toddlers to contend with at the time. To preserve the food in his refrigerator, he begged local storeowners to share some dry ice with him. The next year, with their third child on the way, Biewand used his contracting and construction savvy to get together with four other neighbors and wangle deals on $15,000 generators for their homes that would have cost much more if they'd paid retail. He regards it as an insurance policy on a four-bedroom house in a neighborhood of million-dollar homes. "I know that if another hurricane comes, it's life as usual," he told the *Christian Science Monitor*. Seven of his sixteen neighbors have their own generators now. During the last power outage, he says happily, the family barely noticed that the house was humming along on generator power.

In a very brief period of time, the home standby generator has graduated from an ostentatious status bauble to a wise investment that expresses fundamental middle-class values of home, security, and family. After all, when the lights go out, not only does the food spoil, but the collection of chilled wine may go bad, humidity threatens the home's furnishings, and the high-tech security system goes out, too. Affluent homes are more dependent on electricity than ever before, says Frank, which is why he believes his company's market is now driven by security-conscious women. In the diffusion model, gadget-crazy rich guys had been the Innovators that put Frank in business. Now affluent mothers who want to protect their homes and families are the Early Adopters, helping push the industry toward the mass market. By one estimate, homebuilders in Houston say that one in five new luxury homes are now built with standby generators, and other new homes are advertised as "generator-ready." Big air conditioner companies such as Rheem and Carrier just recently started making standby generators. Kohler, the maker of luxury bath fixtures, has a new "residential power" division. Kohler's brochures promise "life without interruption" and show a glowing image of a young mother cooing over her infant.

Frank now considers it his job to make standby generators increasingly more affordable—"to work down the pyramid," as he puts it. His company is the first in the nation to try popularizing the systems by offering sixty-month financing for homeowners, with payments starting at $299. Frank also speaks hopefully of recent breakthroughs in "smart switch" technology that automatically shifts the power load around the house while on standby power. Smart switches mean that soon a $20,000 generator will provide the same level of power produced today by a much larger $30,000 unit. That's good news for the majority of people who have postponed buying generators for their homes. For the Early Adopters, however, it means they are likely to find themselves saddled with obsolete systems long before the units' useful lives are over.

That's typical of the risks that Early Adopters of all innovations invite upon themselves. It's also the kind of risk we see Middle-Class Millionaires more willing and able to endure, just for the chance to try new ideas that might make their lives run more smoothly. Along with their natural predisposition toward networking, recruiting, and sharing what they know with others, taking that initial leap toward immature and formerly unproven products and technologies is an essential step in the diffusion of such values-based innovations throughout society.

Throughout this book, we've dubbed this process of discovery and dissemination, rooted in Millionaire Intelligence, the Influence of Affluence, because it depends on both the affluence and the influence of the Middle-Class Millionaire—affluence because this attribute makes their opinion more credible on certain matters than the opinions of middle-class peers, and influence because they actively disseminate their opinions to their friends, family, workers, and colleagues.

Middle-Class Millionaires and the Electric Car

Take a ride through a typical middle-class suburb in the evening when most people are home, and you're likely to see two kinds of vehicles in the driveways. There's the SUV or the minivan, which serves the purpose of hauling the whole family everywhere, including long trips out of town. And then there's the second car, or maybe a third car, which is relegated to the very limited duty of taking one of the wage earners in the family back and forth to work each day.

For forty years or more, entrepreneurs, activists, and legislators have decried the rush-hour smog produced by all these second household cars shuttling their lone occupants between home and the workplace. Untold legions of gearheads—from eccentric home garage tinkerers to an entire division of General Motors—have tried to develop an emission-free electric commuter car with an attractive combination of power, range, comfort, and curb appeal at a price the public is willing to pay. For forty years they have failed. In a nation of 300 million automobiles, there are today only a few thousand electric cars that are legal for highway use.

Popular explanations for the electric car's failure have varied. Some have said that the cars haven't been marketed properly. Some blame a lack of government subsidies. Some say the technology is not yet mature. Still others complain that it's the public's fault for rejecting the lifestyle compromises that electric cars demand. An award-winning documentary called *Who Killed the Electric Car?* claims that a conspiracy of oil and auto industry executives put an end to General Motors' billion-dollar electric-car experiment in the 1990s.

None of these explanations seem as satisfying as our own simple conclusion: Makers of electric cars have never developed a vehicle that accommodates what we have defined as the middle-class hierarchy of values. The earth's environment, as we found, is considered a very important value by almost two-thirds of both our middle-class and Middle-Class Millionaire survey samples. There is no shortage of middle-class families who would like to have a non-polluting car. But for most of these families, ranging in income from middle class to Middle-Class Millionaires, the high cost and poor performance of electric cars would force them to make unacceptable compromises with other middle-class values that they regard even more highly than the environment. That's why the electric car has never found a home in the driveways of suburbia.

Take another look at those driveways, and you'll see two distinct kinds of commuter cars. A middle-class family of fairly modest means will likely have an inexpensive compact as a commuter car, or perhaps even a used "beater" vehicle. In a Middle-Class Millionaire household, however, the commuter car is more apt to be an indulgence item, such as a luxury sedan or a sports car.

For the first family in this scenario, the purpose served by a commuter car is affordable utility, which leaves more money in the household budget for items higher on their middle-class values hierarchy—the home, education, and security in retirement. For the second family, which presumably has satisfied the financial demands of these most highly ranked values, the second car is the one they most enjoy driving and being seen in. Consider also that most Middle-Class Millionaires are skilled professionals, small-business owners, or corporate executives. The car that's parked each day in the company lot is often an important accessory to the Middle-Class Millionaire's professional image. And remember that in the hierarchy of values for Middle-Class Millionaires, careers rank almost as highly as the education of their children.

In this light, it's fairly easy to see no electric car has ever provided an appealing alternative for either of these two distinct classes of commuter car. Electric cars have always been relatively small, expensive, and strange-looking. The cheapest electric car today is a tiny sedan that costs about $10,000 and has three wheels. It can't go faster than 40 mph, and it needs to be parked and recharged every 40 miles. More conventional-looking electric vehicles can cost $50,000 or more. A Toyota Scion xB can be bought in a customized electric version for $69,610, well above the price of luxury SUVs such as the Porsche Cayenne or the Cadillac Escalade. The sticker price on a gas-powered Scion xB is just $14,600.

This has been the pattern for the past four decades. Every fledgling electric car that promised to break through to the mainstream has turned out to be both overpriced and underpowered. Each model was either too costly and too limited for the striving middle class or too weak and too homely to appeal to the Middle-Class Millionaire. Despite the high value assigned to the environment by both segments of the middle class, no one has ever come up with an emission-free electric car that could deliver a level of owner satisfaction sufficient to satisfy those more highly ranked middle-class values.

Until now. The year 2008 marks the debut of the world's first high-performance electric-powered production car. The Tesla Roadster is a two-seater convertible similar in size and appearance to a Porsche Boxster. It has a range of about 200 miles between charges and a top speed of 130 mph, and it can zip from 0 to 60 mph in about four seconds—faster than the Porsche. With a lightweight aluminum chassis and carbon-fiber body designed and built by the British sports car maker Lotus, the Roadster is the first electric car that can compete with gas-powered cars in its class on both price *and* performance.

For this reason, the rollout of the Tesla has been unlike that of any electric car before it. *Time* magazine hailed it as one of the 25 Best Inventions of 2006. A prototype was mobbed by members of Congress during a 2007 visit to Washington. Secretary of State Condoleezza Rice took a spin in it. A *Vanity Fair* profile of the Tesla's founders hailed the car as a "dream come true" and foretold the end of the internal combustion engine. A fashion magazine actually declared the Roadster this year's Car to Be Seen In. When a *Popular Mechanics* writer took a ride in the Roadster test vehicle, his response was "Who knew saving the planet could be this much fun?"

Tesla Motors priced its first "Signature One Hundred" limited-edition Roadsters at $98,000, and all hundred cars sold out before they were even available to test-drive. Buyers include the super-rich, such as George Clooney and the founders of Google, Larry Page and Sergey Brin. Among these famous members of the Innovator class are a good number of ordinary Middle-Class Millionaires, too. The Roadster is a dream come true for Bob Bressler, a car enthusiast and Napa Valley vineyard owner patiently awaiting its early-2008 delivery. At the time he decided to buy a Roadster, Bressler already owned a three-wheeled electric single-seater called a Corbin Sparrow and a high-performance turbocharged Callaway Corvette that guzzled a gallon of high-octane gas for every eighteen miles of driving.

"It was always a dilemma for me," he says. "I wondered, why can't I get a high-performance car that would also be cheaper to operate and would directly address all the problems—political and environmental—that come from petroleum-based fuel?" Bressler spent years working in Silicon Valley before retiring to open Bressler Vineyards, and he can't think of a better place for Tesla Motors to start out. "If you want a place for Early Adopters, there it is," he says. "There are a lot of people in Silicon Valley who can spend a hundred thousand dollars on a car."

Tesla's founder, Martin Eberhard, grew up on a farm in Nebraska and has been a car enthusiast ever since he learned to drive at age thirteen. With a master's degree in electrical engineering, Eberhard made his millions as CEO of an electronic book company during the 1990s Internet boom. In 2003, he decided to start a company that builds electric sports cars, he says, prompted by a mix of environmental concern and love of fast cars. "I guess the real thing is I wanted one for myself," he told ABC News in 2007. "It's time for us to do something about our dependence on foreign oil. It's time for us to do something about global warming. But I wasn't ready to go driving around in some goofy little car." As an engineer, he was impressed by the efficiency of electric motors. For about sixty cents' worth of electricity, an electric car can go as far as a $3 gallon of gas would take a similarly sized car. As a driver, though, Eberhard was taken by the electric motor's torque—its raw power. The Tesla Roadster has only two gears, and it can go up to seventy mph before shifting into second.

Eberhard dreamed up the Tesla Roadster in much the same way that John Hutchins and Bruce Spector conceived PinnacleCare and Brian Hickey came up with Teardowns.com. These are all bold new ideas in multibillion-dollar industries—health, real estate, transportation—at high-end consumer niches that the big players in those industries have been all but blind to. These enterprises are cases of the entrepreneur class in America innovating for the satisfaction of themselves and their entrepreneur peers. Tesla Motors has gotten this far only because so many other middle-class-bred Silicon Valley moguls share Eberhard's dream. PayPal founder Elon Musk was looking for a way to convert his Porsche to electric power when he was introduced to Eberhard in 2003. Today he is chairman of Tesla Motors. He heads a partnership that has sunk $27 million into the company and raised another $80 million from other Silicon Valley venture groups. Google's founders are among the investors.

The company now plans to build a thousand Roadsters per year, with prices starting at $92,000. Showrooms are opening in California, Illinois, New York, and Florida. Musk plans for Tesla Motors to become a multibillion-dollar company with a full line of electric cars. "My goal," Eberhard has said, "is ultimately to get people to stop burning gasoline in their cars."

The road from here to there is pure Milton Friedman. The next Tesla model, code-named "White Star," will be a luxury sedan in the $55,000-to-$68,000 price range. A $30,000 "Blue Star" model will follow after that. "Our strategy is to enter at the high end of the market, where customers are prepared to pay a premium," Eberhard explained to a Senate Finance Committee panel in 2007, "and then move down-market as quickly as possible to higher production levels and lower prices with each successive model." The Roadster is destined to become Tesla's high-end niche car, like the Chevy Corvette, atop a line of more affordable models. Bressler, the proud early Tesla owner, sees the strategy in more concise terms: "The purpose of selling five hundred Roadsters is not to sell five hundred Roadsters," he says. "It's to sell a hundred thousand White Stars. If you want to influence everyone else in the world who will never buy a Roadster but might buy a White Star, you want them to say, 'Oh, look, electric cars are real! Maybe I can buy a White Star instead of a BMW.'"

To Eberhard, this is the same route to widespread adoption traveled by every technology from cell phones to flat-screen TVs. Making the Roadster has given the company the chance to perfect its lithium-ion battery technology, build up a network of suppliers, and develop some manufacturing expertise. Leveraging the technology and the publicity will allow Tesla to go from importing 1,000 Roadsters annually to building between 15,000 and 25,000 White Stars per year at its new factory in New Mexico.

Even more important to Eberhard, the Roadster also promises to change the public's perception of electric vehicles. Forty years of failed attempts at making clunky everyman electric vehicles has given the industry a terrible black eye. "People thought about them as dork-mobiles," he told one interviewer. "Just ugly little golf-carty things." Tesla's promotional materials promise that its cars will be "gorgeous and thrilling to drive," claims usually reserved for gas-guzzling Maseratis and other high-performance cars. The Tesla Roadster is filled with ingenious features that any luxury car owner would want, such as a PIN-coded ignition pad that makes the Roadster impossible to hotwire, and an electronically set "valet mode" that limits the speed and range of the car so parking lot attendants aren't tempted to go joyriding.

Perception of the product is, of course, what lies at the heart of diffusion theory. No matter how great the so-called relative advantage of an innovation might be, the rate at which people actually take it up is controlled by what they think of it. And what they think of the innovation is largely controlled by what influential people say about it. Dozens of hapless electric-car inventors have been getting it wrong for forty years, as any of the researchers on the Iowa hybrid corn study could have told them. One after another, electric-car makers have brought out a series of "dork-mobiles" that few people with any influence would want to drive, and their cars never had a chance of catching on.

Tesla Motors, by contrast, seems to be riding the diffusion model in exactly the right direction. If the Roadster is aimed primarily at the wealthy Innovators, the White Star luxury sedan, with a $55,000 starting price, seems to be aimed at the influential Early Adopters—the Middle-Class Millionaire market. By the time the Tesla Motors factory starts rolling out the White Star in 2009, there will be thousands of Tesla Roadsters driving around, and most prospective White Star buyers will have had the chance to get a look at them. Being Middle-Class Millionaires, they'll go out of their way to research the matter with existing Roadster owners. Assuming the White Star lives up to its billing, you can bet that soon thousands of Middle-Class Millionaires will be plugging them in and talking them up as embodied by the Influence of Affluence. In the process, they'll help create demand for the "Blue Star," Tesla's next down-market model.

There are signs other electric-car makers are catching on to what Tesla Motors has accomplished. At least one builder of "dork-mobiles" is now promoting the imminent launch of its own Lotus-designed luxury sedan, which claims a far greater range between rechargings than the Roadster's. Competition doesn't seem to bother Eberhard and Musk. Tesla Motors has even licensed its proprietary battery technology to another electric-car maker in Norway. As veterans of Silicon Valley's network culture, Tesla's owners know that competing with the internal combustion engine will require the creation of an electric-car infrastructure that is beyond the reach of any one company, however successful it becomes. In 2007, Tesla Motors won a grant from the state of California to develop a 16-kilowatt charging station—what some electric-car fans are calling the gas station of the future. Eberhard says he expects the first public charging stations will appear in the garages of luxury hotels eager to attract affluent Tesla drivers.

An electric car still can't be considered emission-free, of course, if the power plant that charges the car's batteries runs on coal or oil. Musk has got this problem covered. He is a lead investor in an alternative-energy company called Solar City, which installs and maintains rooftop solar panels. For $6,500, Solar City will come to a Tesla owner's home and install a small solar energy system that permits the Roadster to recharge directly from sunlight. The car's entire "energy pathway" would be free of emissions *and* operating costs. "It closes the loop," Musk told *Outside* magazine. "It makes the car fully eco-friendly."

With California already subsidizing the construction of 1 million residential solar roofs in the next twenty years, the idea of emission-free cars run for free from the sun doesn't seem like such a far-off dream. Battery and energy technologies keep improving year by year, and as the economies of scale climb, the unit costs will continue to fall. Over the years, if electric cars can displace enough gasoline-powered cars on the road, the demand for foreign oil would likely weaken, bringing down gasoline prices for everyone—including those millions who may never be able to afford a Tesla. It's a case of the rich working for the poor on a scale perhaps not even Milton Friedman could have imagined.

CHAPTER FIVE

THE DOCTOR WILL SEE YOU WHENEVER YOU'D LIKE

Bradley Tavel already had a problem with hypertension, which is why he was in a Washington, D.C.-area internist's waiting room for his 10:00 A.M. appointment. Sometime after 11:00, a nurse practitioner took his blood pressure and sent him back to the waiting room. Tavel didn't see his doctor until after noon, when his blood pressure was taken again. He remembers the internist telling him, "You're still very high." Tavel adds, "I found out that my blood pressure was elevated because I had been jerked around all morning!"

As sole proprietor of a small Maryland real estate development firm, Tavel says he cannot comprehend how badly the business of medicine is transacted today. To draw an extreme comparison, he asks, "How would you feel if you sent your child to school and the teacher didn't show up until ten or eleven?" The forty-nine-year-old Tavel once spent four hours in a physician's waiting room, from 8:30 A.M. to 12:30 P.M. "I told the doctor, 'You owe *me* for this visit,'" he recalls. "'It's not my problem that you can't run your practice.'"

The Tavel family has had more than its share of chronic medical problems. Bradley's wife was diagnosed with lupus years ago, although the condition is currently in remission. His daughter was more recently diagnosed with epilepsy. It adds up to a lot of time spent in waiting rooms, which does little to help Tavel's hypertension. He finally decided to seek out a different way of managing his health, he says, because "The only mechanism I have to voice my opposition is to buy something better."

What Tavel bought is something called "concierge medicine." Tavel now pays $1,650 per year for a spot in a Bethesda, Maryland, concierge physicians' practice—one that accepts only a limited number of patients, all of whom enjoy direct cell phone access to their doctors, same-day or next-day appointments, extended office visits, and a personalized preventive health care program to follow. As Tavel sees it, the $1,650 he spends for this level of care "has got to be less, when you break it down, than the lost earnings opportunity from hours of waiting around in doctors' offices." The unhurried office visits and thoughtful discussions he has with his doctor remind him of the professional treatment he expects, for instance, from his lawyers. "You go to an attorney and you become an integral part of your legal representation," he points out. "Now I feel that way about my health care, that I'm a part of it. It's all about the manner in which the care is delivered. I'm not a piece of cattle." His only disappointment, he says, is that there is no similar style of pediatric care to help him and his wife with their daughter's epilepsy.

Without facing the risk of a long layover in the waiting room, Tavel feels free to stop by his doctor's office more frequently these days. His blood pressure readings have been going down, and he suspects it's because he's been able to follow his doctor's advice more faithfully. The more closely Tavel and his doctor can collaborate on lowering his blood pressure, the less likely he will someday end up hospitalized with a stroke or a heart attack. Bradley Tavel has Millionaire Intelligence in spades. He refused to do business with a health care system that failed to meet his own personal standards for efficacy, and the decision may well save his life.

There have always been expensive fee-for-service physicians—so-called Park Avenue doctors—who operate outside the medical insurance system and attract a well-heeled clientele. But until about a dozen years ago, no one had ever thought to ask affluent working people for a flat annual retainer-like fee to guarantee privileged, on-demand access to their favorite primary care doctor. Today more than 100,000 Americans pay for concierge medicine, a generic name that doesn't sit well with many doctors but effectively evokes its accommodating, customer-oriented approach.

It is hardly a coincidence that services with the concierge label have been attached to everything from medicine to premium credit cards during a decade in which the number of millionaire households in the United States has more than doubled. As general customer satisfaction continues to drop in most industries, affluent consumers have been avidly buying themselves better service experiences whenever they can. "Concierge" has become a code word that evokes Continental traditions of quality and hospitality while signaling to consumers that responsive, customer-focused attention can be theirs if they care to pay a little extra.

The term *concierge* has seeped into common parlance in America only in the last several decades. A 1993 article in the *Cornell Hotel and Restaurant Administration Quarterly* noted that "the rise of the concierge" in U.S. hotels had barely begun in 1983, but within the following decade no quality hotel could do without one. A Chicago concierge recently remarked, "Ten years ago, every third or fourth guest wanted to know what a concierge was. Today guests come in looking for the concierge." The American chapter of Les Clefs d'Or, the international organization for professional concierges, now counts about 450 members working at more than 250 four-star and five-star hotel desks.

Les Clefs d'Or (The Golden Keys) unabashedly refers to its members as "part Merlin, part Houdini"—proud specialists who "make the impossible possible." Luxury hotel concierges are much more than glorified gofers. They take a personal interest in each guest's needs and cultivate the relationship in order to generate goodwill and repeat business for the hotel. The motto of Les Clefs d'Or is "In Service Through Friendship."

A few years ago, the management of Hampton Inns hired Holly Stiel to study their operations and advise them on upgrading their standards of service. Stiel is perhaps the best-known concierge on this side of the Atlantic. She wrote *Ultimate Service*, the authoritative tome on the subject, and she holds training seminars for service personnel all over the country. Thirty years ago, she started up the San Francisco Hyatt's concierge program and claims the distinction of being the first American woman ever admitted to Les Clefs d'Or, having been inducted in a 1977 ceremony in Vienna.

At the time, the midpriced Hampton Inn chain (a part of the Hilton hotel empire) was undergoing a vast branding overhaul that entailed rethinking every identifiable "touchpoint" in a typical guest's experience. Company officials had no plans to add concierges to the 1,300 Hampton Inn locations, but they wanted Stiel's expert opinion on how the existing staff might learn to think and behave in a more concierge-like manner.

The Hampton Inn assignment gave Stiel the chance to ponder what might constitute the essence of hotel concierge service in the absence of a genuine hotel concierge. Concierges, she concluded, are "people who say yes, and then they figure out how to make it happen. They're creative. They're resourceful." The process of solving a guest's problem should also make that guest feel special. That's what lends the concierge's work its sense of exclusivity, she says. "The essence of it is really about 'Yes, I'll help you. This is what I'm here for.'"

At five-star hotels, a cheerful, can-do attitude is only the starting point for staff concierges. The best of them also possess a discerning eye for what is most important to hotel guests and superior knowledge of what's available. It's not enough to know the best places to eat. A concierge should know firsthand what the best dishes are and which restaurants are most appropriate for a given social occasion. Top-notch concierges also have connections. They have pull with the box office at the sold-out show or the maître d' at the restaurant that may be booked solid. They twist arms if they must, and theater managers and restaurateurs who benefit from concierge referrals try to stay in their good graces. Concierges like to say that as long as it's legal and ethical, they will do their best to come through for a guest or client.

During nearly thirty years in the concierge field, Stiel says, she has seen a steady rise in the value placed on service in most businesses as the newly affluent shift their interests from having things to having experiences. "All of the symbols of affluence keep changing," she says. "It becomes more and more incumbent upon concierges to provide exclusive experiences." Concierges trade war stories of how they booked last-minute helicopter charters or managed to reopen Tiffany's for after-hours shopping. It is that feeling of being catered to and cared for that breeds guest loyalty to a hotel and justifies the hotel's investment in a concierge staff. Stiel speaks of the "lifetime value" of the loyal business traveler who returns to a hotel several times a year largely because of his or her familiarity with the concierge staff.

In recent years, the concierge concept has even been used to create "lifetime value" in the selling of ordinary consumer products. When Sir Howard Stringer was named the head of global entertainment giant Sony's U.S. division in 1997, he discovered the new job carried one responsibility that no one had told him about: Everyone he knew, from fellow corporate chieftains to Sony's roster of international film stars, was calling his office asking to be first in line for the latest gadgets from Japan. They also wanted his advice on custom-installing Sony's home theater equipment. Stringer decided he needed a VIP program to handle all the requests.

With a jump start from Stringer's own continent-spanning Rolodex, he launched the invitation-only Sony Cierge. For a $1,500 annual fee, Sony Cierge members get a personal shopper who keeps up on all their electronics preferences and is on call to help out with everything from selecting a pocket camera for a gift to designing a home theater installation. Amy Berman, Sony Cierge's director, confesses it's hard to list all the services she can offer, because "everything depends on the client's request, which is great for the consumer, but a challenge for us."

Berman's team of personal shoppers is hired not for technology expertise but for customer-service acumen. "We say there are no nos," Berman adds. "Even if they need something tomorrow and I can't get it to them, I'll ask, if they're traveling, if I can have it shipped to the hotel the next day. Just thinking about those little things is what people want." Sony Cierge members also have exclusive access to a members' lounge in Sony's midtown Manhattan store and a private showroom on the Sony movie studio lot in Culver City, near Los Angeles.

Based on the success of the Cierge program, Sony sought to grow beyond its own list of best customers and Stringer's personal circle of high-powered acquaintances and struck a partnership with American Express to reach one of the world's most selective lists: American Express's Centurion cardholders. Begun in 1999, the Centurion, or "Black Card" as it's known by its members, is offered by invitation only to qualified American Express customers who generally spend $150,000 or more annually on their American Express card. For an annual membership fee of $2,500, Centurion cardholders receive benefits including elite status on most major airlines and easy upgrades in many hotels—services that are highly desired by the globe-trotting businesspeople who typically qualify for the card. Cardholders are also introduced to a personal concierge team who helps them plan travel, secure tickets to events and the theater, and make dinner reservations, along with other personal shopping services, including Sony Cierge. It's rumored that many popular upscale restaurants hold back a few tables every evening for VIPs and Centurion cardholders.

Behind the scenes, the company providing this team of round-the-clock concierge services for the famously demanding Centurion clientele is Circles, perhaps the most successful of several national concierge firms. Circles was started in 1997 by Janet Kraus and Kathy Sherbrooke, two classmates from Stanford's MBA program. The two partners started the business on their credit cards as a call center and Internet-based service and then raised more money from friends and family. Once they secured millions of dollars from venture capital firms, they were able to invest in phone technology, database development, and staffing. Circles extends its services to about 250,000 people, a number that includes American Express cardholders. Other companies such as Merrill Lynch, Aramark, and Ernst & Young provide their employees with access to Circles as part of their benefit plans.

Eighty percent of Circles' work involves the mundane—tickets, flowers, reservations, gifts, and petsitting—but the founders like to talk about fulfilling unusual requests, such as the engagement planned at the top of the Eiffel Tower or the hiker who needed to be taken down from Mount Everest. When an employee of a Circles client company needed to catch an escaped house cat that was mewling in darkness outside, the firm delivered him a pair of night-vision goggles.

The size of Circles' clientele means the firm has leverage with vendors that a hotel concierge could only dream of. For instance, because it is thought to be the third-largest purchaser of flowers in the United States, Circles gets preferred pricing on floral orders.

For a concierge company to have attracted such scale and quality of clients in just ten years is a testament to the ability of its management, but its growth also occurred at a time when demand for concierge services was beginning to come from nontraditional places and for unexpected reasons. The Pepsico headquarters in Purchase, New York, for example, had earned some notoriety in 1992 for hiring what was thought to be the first corporate concierge in America. Andy King, then thirty-one, was depicted in a *Wall Street Journal* story as a harried juggler of twenty requests per day, doing "what housewives traditionally did before they got jobs outside the home. He does what secretaries did when there were still secretaries." With the advent of the corporate concierge, busy professionals could spend long hours at work while their concierges arranged for theater or concert tickets and reserved vacation flights and hotel accommodations.

As the concierge economy has been steadily expanding and moving down-market, a cottage industry of boutique operations with one or two employees and names such as Gofer Girls has sprouted up. Even Circles has announced a direct-to-consumer Web site. Soon anyone willing to pay a small annual retainer might be able to avail himself or herself of Circles' services.

This decline in exclusivity has led to some chafing over the use of the word *concierge*, with hospital greeters and apartment-building doormen adopting the title. Some companies use it to describe their call center staffers, or, in the case of a rental car company, a driver who delivers the car. One national firm that operates a network of concierges in various cities explicitly states on its Web site that "we are not home-based errand-runners who call ourselves concierges." Some of the highest-end personal concierge services are starting to walk away from the "concierge" label entirely. The newer rubric for high-end personal concierge firms is "lifestyle management."

If the concierge name is being abused at the fringes, it doesn't bother Holly Stiel very much. Service, she says, is so poor in this country that if using the word *concierge* makes people try to live up to the quality implied in the name, then she's all for it.

Stiel has a theory about the fact that after thirty years or more of experts extolling the virtues of quality service, it continues to decline. "In North America, we're not that interested in service," she says, pointing out how other cultures, especially in the Far East, have an ethic of service that American culture lacks. Customer service would improve, she says, if management treated service employees with more respect. "That is the essence of why service is terrible in America, I believe. We have a service economy that does not honor the service provider."

Holly Stiel wasn't talking about the medical profession. But she could have been.

In the spring of 1996, two Seattle internists sent a letter to each of their approximately 8,000 patients announcing they would be retiring soon from their medical practice. Among those thousands of envelopes, however, a select few hundred contained something extra. It was an invitational brochure that ultimately led to the birth of concierge health care.

Before Howard Maron and his partner, I. Scott Hall, prepared their mailing, the two doctors set aside the names of several hundred patients whom they either knew or suspected were very wealthy. They were the ones who received brochures inviting them to join Maron and Hall as clients in their new business venture—a unique medical practice with a select patient roster limited to only one hundred families.

The partners promised that with just fifty households each to look after, they could practice medicine the old-fashioned way. Office visits would be unrushed. Appointments would start on time. Maron and Hall would perform thorough annual physicals, make house calls, and even have prescription medicines hand-delivered. The new practice offered some modern conveniences, too. Each patient would get the doctors' personal cell phone numbers and e-mail addresses. Maron and Hall would make themselves available around the clock—and around the world, if necessary. They promised to accompany their patients to appointments with specialists and see to their care in the event of hospitalization, even if that meant going to medical centers out of town or overseas. Tellingly, they began referring to their patients as "clients."

The new company was called MD²—pronounced "MD squared"—a name suggesting an exponential leap in the quality of service and care.

The price of that leap was steep: In its first year, MD^2 charged an annual membership fee of $12,000 for individuals with an additional $6,000 for spouses and $1,800 for children. At those prices, Maron and Hall could afford to keep their patient roster extremely small. Membership fees from just one hundred families generated more annual income for MD^2 than all the insurance reimbursements and co-payments they had previously earned from 8,000 patients. With such a rich flow of fee income, the two doctors discovered they didn't even need to charge for visits or file for insurance reimbursements anymore, which in turn allowed them to cut way back on billing-related overhead.

MD^2 promised to practice "medicine in the ideal," something Howard Maron felt he already had plenty of experience with. Maron had previously served for twelve years as team physician for the Seattle SuperSonics NBA franchise. When he traveled with the players each spring during the playoffs, he recalls, "I had a very defined assignment: Take care of these twelve guys. Spare no expense. Do whatever is necessary, but keep them healthy and put out fires." He learned two things from the experience that would influence the founding of MD^2. First, he discovered he enjoyed being able to devote all his time and attention to a medical problem when the situation required it, without being rushed. Second, he was amazed at how eagerly medical specialists and hospital officials would toss away their appointment books to accommodate the schedules of famous athletes. "What I realized also," he adds, "was that if the owner of the team or another VIP had a medical problem, it would have been more difficult to get that same response."

Now, with just fifty families to care for, Maron could provide the same level of attention he had lavished on his dozen SuperSonics. "There is nothing we won't do," he says of his practice. "If I send a patient to a consultant, I might go to that appointment, especially if the subject was complex. If my patient is having a cardiac catheterization, I may be in the cath lab. House calls are common. Nothing is prohibited." Maron recently responded to a request for a last-minute checkup from a patient who was about to go overseas. He did the exam on the patients' private jet as it awaited takeoff on the airport tarmac.

Within months after launching their new practice, Maron and Hall had filled the hundred slots and had to start a waiting list. News of MD²'s success spread fast, first among doctors in Seattle and then throughout the nation's medical community. Physician practices began to experiment with lower-priced, scaled-down versions of the MD² model. Just over a decade later, there are at least 100,000 people all over the United States paying monthly or quarterly fees to approximately 300 physicians for what is generically known as concierge health care—and the vast majority of these patients are paying a fraction of the fees charged by MD².

A 2005 study by the federal Government Accountability Office (GAO) found that 90 percent of 111 concierge practices it surveyed charged less than $4,000 per year per patient and that half of all concierge practices charged between $1,500 and $2,000. Although these lower-priced practices offer fewer perks and privileges than MD² does, they retain many of the fundamental service advantages that set MD² apart. According to the GAO report, almost all concierge practices offer direct twenty-four-hour access to a physician by phone and e-mail, same-day or next-day appointments for non-urgent care, and extended time with a physician during office visits.

Concierge medical practices remain a rarity in most communities. Even in the Boston and Seattle areas, where concierge medicine is most popular, many practices are filled and no longer accepting new patients. Nonetheless, about 18 percent of our national Middle-Class Millionaire sample already employs some form of "concierge or customized health care," and 43 percent of the rest say they expect to sign up with a concierge physician within the next three years. Ninety-two percent cite their unhappiness with the current state of traditional health care as an important reason for joining a concierge practice. An almost identical share—90 percent—regards the desire for "the best health care available" as a primary motivation for seeking concierge care.

Our survey shows near-unanimous agreement that "good health is more important than money." Approximately 92 percent of both middle-class samples—millionaires and non-millionaires alike—said this statement was either very accurate or extremely accurate. Good health is such a fundamental middle-class value that when doctors began to offer concierge medicine as a market-driven method for delivering it, Middle-Class Millionaires were among the first to grasp the new idea's appeal and open their wallets. Among the middle-class sample, however, very few have made the financial sacrifice that concierge medicine likely represents for a family earning between $50,000 and $80,000 per year. Less than one-tenth of 1 percent—one in a thousand—of the middle-class sample has concierge medical care, and just over 2 percent say they expect to join a concierge medical practice within the next three years.

Middle-Class Millionaires, it appears, have both the inclination and the means to act on the growing consensus that mainstream health care in the United States is on the decline in terms of quality and service. Particularly at the level of the primary care physician—on whom insurance companies and HMOs rely as gatekeepers for referrals to specialists—satisfaction levels among doctors and patients alike have hit all-time lows. A 2003 study published in the *New England Journal of Medicine* revealed that U.S. physicians were so overscheduled that they ignored the recommended best practices for diagnosis and treatment of disease in about half of their appointments. Other research has shown that although a thorough physical exam following all the prescribed diagnostic steps should last about ninety minutes, primary care physicians on average spend only eight minutes with each patient. As recounted in another medical journal, one disgruntled patient memorably complained to his doctor that each office visit reminded him of Disney World: a three-hour wait for a twenty-second ride.

Practitioners of concierge medicine have discovered what every five-star-hotel concierge knows very well: Affluent people are willing to pay for what they value, and in addition to good health, what they value highly is *time*. Nearly 56 percent of the respondents in our survey claimed that not having to wait for treatments and testing was an important reason for patronizing concierge health care. More than most people, Middle-Class Millionaires see the relationship between time and money in an almost reflexive way. Their careers depend on the effective management of their time, partly because they have so little of it to waste. As we showed in Chapter 1, Middle-Class Millionaires work on average seventy hours per week. For someone with such a punishing workload, cutting back on time-consuming hassles is not a matter of mere convenience but something much more serious.

When offered the option, Middle-Class Millionaires would rather pay to jump the line with any service provider—a hotel, a bank, a doctor—that respects their tight schedules, expresses familiarity with their needs, and treats them as valued clients. This rich potential clientele has been growing yearly, both in numbers and in appetite, and the concierge model of service has exploded as a result. Inevitably, the trend at the top has generated a renewed interest in customer service on a pay-as-you-go basis throughout the economy, opening up new forms and possibilities in customer service that wouldn't have existed without the primary patronage of the Middle-Class Millionaire. In the case of concierge health care, there are those who believe that what MD² began in 1996 represents nothing less than the leading edge of a revolution in preventive medicine.

A small start-up company in Boca Raton, Florida, called MDVIP is the nation's single largest developer of new concierge medical practices. With 150 affiliated physicians in seventeen states and Washington, D.C., MDVIP recruits and supports experienced primary care physicians in the practice of "personalized health care," the term the company prefers to use in place of concierge medicine. MDVIP was started in 2000 by

Edward Goldman, a retired family physician and medical entrepreneur who for more than thirty years has been pursuing the practical, cost-saving possibilities of preventive health care. Though the name MDVIP was certainly conceived to appeal to consumer notions of exclusivity, the company's brochures claim that "VIP" really stands for "Value in Prevention."

Back in the 1970s, Goldman was among a lonely few doctors who welcomed the advent of the HMOs—health maintenance organizations. He was attracted to their stated business approach: that they wanted to *maintain* their members' health by emphasizing preventive care. The HMO promise was that they would profit by keeping people out of the hospital.

While still practicing medicine, Goldman and a partner developed a computer program they thought the HMOs would love. They sank thousands of dollars into software that would take a variety of measurements and patient responses from a physical exam and use the data to evaluate a patient's condition in terms of relative aging. An overweight forty-six-year-old smoker might be told, for instance, that the computer estimates his "health age" at fifty-nine. The program also identified a set of preventive measures the patient would need to take to turn back the clock.

This was before the invention of desktop computers, and developing the software was difficult and expensive. But Goldman was convinced the program could provide HMOs with a valuable tool for promoting preventive care. He hoped that the HMOs would want to underwrite putting the software in other doctors' offices. Instead, as Goldman remembers it, the HMO executives he met with were less than thrilled. Some were openly hostile to the idea, stating that it would prompt patients to enroll in smoking-cessation programs and other expensive treatments. A few told Goldman they'd prefer that he not even use the program at no charge with his own patients.

Goldman left the practice of medicine in 1992 and joined a physician practice management company as a partner. By 1996, he had moved on to a medical Internet venture, and after selling his interest in that, he had some time on his hands to figure out what he wanted to do next. He began conversations with Robert Colton, a Boca Raton internist who was fed up with the grind of seeing dozens of patients per day. Colton wanted Goldman's advice on quitting medicine. The two veteran doctors discussed how much had changed in medicine, for better and for worse, since they started out. They lamented what seemed to be a cruel paradox: In the past thirty years, medical knowledge about detecting and preventing disease has advanced greatly, but primary care physicians no longer have enough time with their patients to make use of what they know.

"Back in 1970, we were still asking questions like: Does high blood pressure really influence heart disease? Is cholesterol really involved in it?" Goldman says. "Today we know every risk factor for every major disease. The problem is, how do I individualize that to you, your genetics, your particular history?" Goldman and Colton began entertaining the question of how primary care might be redesigned around the twin goals of disease prevention and early detection. After all these years, they wondered if there was finally a cost-effective way to fulfill the HMO promise of health maintenance.

Colton and Goldman agreed they would need to develop a new diagnostic instrument—a comprehensive set of tests, procedures, and patient questionnaires—that would help them arrive at each patient's risk for developing any of the full range of known diseases. Annual follow-up exams would track the course of each patient's highest risk factors. Should a disease materialize, it would be detected in an early, pre-symptomatic stage when treatment is easier, less costly, and more frequently successful.

Colton estimated such an annual exam would take approximately ninety minutes. A doctor with a typical 2,500-patient roster would have to work sixteen hours a day for a year and do nothing else in order to spend that much time with each patient. The two sat down with Colton's medical charts and calculated his existing rate of office visits scheduled annually by various categories of patients. They determined that if his patient roster could be cut down to 600, he could devote approximately half his office hours to scheduled ninety-minute preventive health physicals and reserve the rest of the day for his patients' other needs. By paring back his patient roster from 2,500 to 600, however, Colton's practice would face a revenue gap of about $1,500 per year per patient.

Goldman and Colton made the rounds of local insurance companies in the hope of finding that $1,500. As Goldman remembers it, "I asked them, 'If I could truly keep people healthy, would you be willing to pay for it?' The resounding answer was no. We didn't even get to the phase of skepticism." Their inquiries with Medicare fell on deaf ears as well. If there was any value at all in the prevention and early detection of disease, the two major funders of health care in this country didn't seem interested.

"We were in a quandary," Goldman says. "We wondered if the patients themselves would pay for this." That's when an article in the *Journal of Medical Economics* caught Goldman's attention. It was about MD². Goldman and Colton experienced what might be called an Influence of Affluence epiphany.

"The article said that patients were paying as much as *twenty thousand dollars* per family," Goldman says with a laugh. "We said, 'My God, let's get together with groups of patients and ask if they would pay fifteen hundred!'" After holding half a dozen focus groups in and around Boca Raton, Colton was encouraged enough about the response to try to convert his practice over to the new model. He held a big party for his patients at the Boca Raton Hilton to distribute literature about his plans and took questions. Not everyone was happy about the idea, but within a week, Colton had signed up the 600 patients he needed.

Creating a business that could help other doctors replicate Robert Colton's success took some time and effort. Goldman wanted to make sure that what Colton was doing didn't run afoul of any insurance rules or state and federal medical regulations. Medicare, for instance, doesn't allow doctors to charge some patients more than others for the same service. MDVIP patients nominally pay $1,500 per year for the company's prevention package—the special annual physical, a customized Web page with their medical records on it, and a library of online preventive care educational videos. MDVIP patients don't really pay for the privilege of longer consultations, same-day appointments, and phone and e-mail access to their doctors. Those features are side benefits that arise from having a physician who can afford to carry a small patient load. MDVIP physicians generally agree, however, that longer office visits and the ease of making appointments are an important part of giving good preventive care.

To develop and roll out MDVIP's business strategy, Goldman brought in a friend named Steve Geller as CEO. Geller had retired from the toy manufacturing business and moved to Florida years earlier. He was a patient of Colton's and had his own personal reasons for promoting concierge medicine.

"I'm old, I'm fat, I smoke, and I'm rich," Geller told *Fortune Small Business* magazine in 2004. "I got fed up with the lousy service I was getting from doctors. You wanna know the last straw? I was standing at the Plexiglas window in some guy's office trying to get the nurse's attention. And there's a sign taped to the window: DO NOT TAP ON THE WINDOW. I'm sick. She's ignoring me. And I'm afraid to tap on the window! What kind of business can survive with that kind of service? To hell with that!"

MDVIP's design is that of a membership organization. The 55,000 patients under MDVIP's care enroll directly with the company and pay their quarterly fees to the Florida headquarters. For their one-third of the membership fees, MDVIP handles billing, medical software, electronic medical records management, and all the development and distribution costs of its preventive care program. MDVIP then sends $1,000 per patient back to the doctors, who are under contract with MDVIP to provide the preventive care program.

For every hundred doctors who apply to join MDVIP, only twelve end up in the network. Some are rejected because MDVIP decides they're not experienced or distinguished enough. In other cases, MDVIP's analysis of a given patient population shows a lack of interest or ability to pay the quarterly fee. "This is the early stage of a new model, so we've set the bar very high," Goldman explains, so for now they're turning down good doctors who aren't excellent, and passing on practices with weak demographics.

MDVIP runs patient zip codes against the Claritas company's breakdown of the U.S. population into sixty-six discrete demographic clusters. Goldman acknowledges that for a practice to switch to MDVIP, the doctors need to have a good number of what we would call Middle-Class Millionaires already in their patient population. Based on the zip code analysis and a spot survey of the physician's patients—some doctors are not as highly regarded as they think—Goldman says that he can reliably predict what percentage of a doctor's existing patient base is likely to sign up with MDVIP within the first twelve weeks following the changeover.

Goldman notes that MDVIP's retention rate is over 95 percent. "We have a saying around here: People either pass away or move away, but they will never go back to a standard practice once they've tasted this."

The mezzanine dining room at Le Bec-Fin is a narrow, windowless space in the rear of Philadelphia's most highly rated French restaurant. On a summer evening in 2006, nearly two dozen middle-aged primary care physicians from greater Philadelphia had been invited to the mezzanine to enjoy Le Bec-Fin's tiny portions of fois gras and lamb and to learn how MDVIP might rescue them from the daily grind of life at the bottom of the U.S. health care system's pecking order.

The evening was hosted by Andrew S. Ripps, one of MDVIP's founders and its vice president in charge of recruiting new physicians. Ripps started his talk by flattering everyone in the room with the results of MDVIP's study of the Philadelphia region's medical community. They all had been hand-picked for the evening's invitation, he said, because their reputations and backgrounds had been checked out, and they are among the best and most experienced primary care physicians in the local market. MDVIP, he explained, is building a nationwide network of distinguished practitioners of concierge medicine, and the doctors present had made the first cut.

Ripps proceeded to describe the crisis that his guests are facing, with the aid of a PowerPoint presentation that flashed on a movie screen crowded into one corner. Primary care physicians are now entirely dependent on insurers and HMOs to steer patients in their direction, and as a result, these same third-party payers have squeezed physician incomes, forcing them to schedule more and more patients each day just to keep up. A show of hands in the room indicated that most had examined at least thirty patients earlier that day. Good doctors suffer the most, Ripps acknowledged, because they are most apt to disregard the rigid reimbursement rules and simply give the best care they know how. "If you're doing that," he said, "then you're giving philanthropic care."

With physicians' incomes flat and their workloads growing, primary care medicine is headed toward a crisis. Approximately 21 percent of the primary care internists who were board certified in the early 1990s have since left the field, and there are fewer young doctors stepping up to replace them. Between 1997 and 2005, the annual number of medical school graduates who chose to specialize in primary care each year dropped by more than half. Ripps flashed an image of a smiling nurse practitioner in a Wal-Mart store. "This is your new competition,"

Ripps announced. The retailer is one of several, including the CVS drugstore chain, that now have walk-in clinics charging flat fees of $60 or so to treat minor ailments.

As Ripps went on to describe the MDVIP program, the star of the evening was Alan Sheff, a soft-spoken, unassuming internist who happens to be the physician for Bradley Tavel—the hypertensive real estate developer at the opening of this chapter.

Sheff told the gathering that he was earning the same income with 450 patients as he did previously with 3,000, and no, not all of those 450 patients are rich. His patients include schoolteachers and bus drivers, he said, and he can afford to waive his fee entirely in the form of "scholarships" for a small percentage of his patients. The difference now is that he takes enough time with each patient to practice medicine the way he was taught. His days are more manageable. During his first week in concierge practice, he had time to eat breakfast with his wife for the first time in ten years.

By the end of Sheff's talk, the doctors were in a mild state of shocked silence. There was a palpable look of envy on a few of their faces, and some of their questions for Sheff had an angry edge to them. Several couldn't understand how, with all the panicky hypochondriacs out there, it was practical for Sheff to give out his e-mail address and his home and cell phone numbers, as required by MDVIP. Sheff admitted that during the first few weeks "my hypochondriacs called me a lot. But I think they just wanted to make sure I was really there. They wanted to test me." Then the calls stopped, he says. Prima donna patients are inevitable, he added, but he finds them much more tolerable now that he has time to deal with them.

Some doctors had a hard time grasping Sheff's claim that he now regards insurance reimbursements as mere "tip money." Primary care physicians rely on reimbursements as the lifeblood of their practices, and the doctors peppered him with questions about how he bills insurers for his patients' care. Sheff had to repeat himself, saying that since his membership payments from MDVIP account for 85 percent of his income, he doesn't worry much about reimbursements, and he doesn't even bother to haggle with insurers when they reject a claim. As the evening ended, the invited doctors seemed more irritated than interested. It appeared from the looks on their faces that MDVIP hadn't won a single convert. But within weeks, eight of the fourteen doctors had begun the MDVIP application process.

Sheff says he's seldom seen such a careworn, beaten-up bunch of doctors as he did that evening at Le Bec-Fin. He admits, though, that he'd once displayed the same symptoms from years of doing what he calls "traffic-cop medicine." Four or five years ago, Sheff's patients started asking if *he* was feeling all right. "I was threadbare," he says. "I was visibly worn, and maybe my communication skills had suffered." He figured something was seriously wrong if his patients were worrying about their doctor's health.

That's when Sheff decided he should think about quitting the practice and reluctantly began exploring his career alternatives. The opportunity to join MDVIP came along soon after. In February 2003, he and Lee Pennington, another doctor in the fourteen-member Potomac Physician Associates, jumped to MDVIP while continuing to share quarters with their colleagues. Potomac is now technically two separate practices, with separate doors and waiting rooms on the ground floor of a suburban office tower. On one side, Sheff, Pennington, and two other MDVIP physicians share a small waiting room that offers coffee, fruit, and pastries and is almost always empty. On the other side, six Potomac physicians tend to a traditional bustling waiting room with thirty chairs, and an impressive aquarium as a diversion.

One experience all concierge doctors share is a sense of surprise that some of their richest patients reject concierge care when it's offered to them. "Some people have deep pockets and short arms," Sheff says with a shrug. He was certain, for instance, that one patient who always arrived for office visits with a butler in tow would sign up for an

MDVIP membership. Instead, Sheff recalls that the man was outraged at the idea of spending more than a $20 co-pay to see his doctor. "He said to me, 'If Medicare says that's all you're worth, don't come crying to me.'" Sheff reasons that the switch to concierge care has left him with more patients who really value seeing him. At the time of the change, he received his share of angry notes from disappointed patients who felt he was abandoning them. Since then, he's gotten many more notes from patients thanking him for his time and attention. When an elderly patient recently passed away after years of battling a variety of ailments, the old man's son wrote Sheff with a touching boxing analogy: "Thanks for being my dad's cornerman."

Sheff and Pennington do not pose as Park Avenue doctors. There is nothing about the decor in their offices that visibly sets them apart from other doctors at Potomac. The two share a single fluorescent-lit workspace, and their exam rooms down the hall look as sterile and cold as the ones on the other side of the practice. There is a difference, however, in the quality of Sheff and Pennington's office hours. On their busiest days they will each see perhaps twelve patients, as opposed to the typical day previously, when they would have seen twenty-two. They spend more time now consulting with specialists about lab data and X-ray results, something that was hardly ever practical when they were juggling as many as thirty patients per day. His daily approach to medicine is far more proactive now, Sheff says, and he is certain that his patients are healthier as a result.

"My patients' medical problems are under better control," he says. "I know this because the patients I started with who had chronic medical problems—hypertension, diabetes, weight gain—these problems are now all tuned up and tight. We're finding that now, after the third or fourth annual physical, there's less and less to talk about."

From its inception, concierge medicine has been treated with almost universal disdain by elected officials and the medical establishment. Concierge physicians were commonly accused of catering to the rich and selling out their ethical responsibilities as healers. Dr. Richard Roberts, then chairman of the American Academy of Family Physicians, complained, "If you have a substantial portion of America's doctors doing this, who's going to take care of everybody else? We've got over 40 million people in this country without health insurance, and another 20 million who are underinsured. What's wrong with this picture?" California Congressman Henry Waxman introduced a bill that would bar concierge physicians from seeing Medicare recipients and complained to the Department of Health and Human Services that concierge fees amount to double-billing the patient and the government for office visits.

Since concierge medicine originated with what remains today among the highest-end practices in the field, MD² was targeted for the most acid-tongued attacks. In a write-up about MD², *Forbes* magazine quoted Princeton's medical economist Uwe Reinhardt as saying, "It was inevitable that physicians would join the coterie of professionals (like estate planners and private tutors) looking to exploit the neuroses of the very rich." In the *New York Times Magazine,* a critic from Harvard Medical School made the sour prediction that concierge doctors would work just as hard as ever, and that the hours saved by seeing fewer patients would be consumed by the urgent need to market themselves.

Twelve years after MD²'s founding, however, little of what critics had foretold has come true. Far from draining the supply of available doctors, concierge medicine might well be keeping a small number of experienced internists and family doctors from quitting the practice of medicine altogether. Concierge practices also tend to locate in fairly wealthy metropolitan areas that are oversupplied with primary care physicians to begin with, so their loss is barely felt. The 2005 federal

GAO report on concierge medicine noted that concierge practices were most commonly found in or near Seattle, Boston, and southeast Florida and that "the ratio of physicians to overall population in each of these metropolitan areas exceeded the nationwide average for all metropolitan areas in 2001."

Marketing has also proven not to be a problem. With annual patient retention rates typically above 90 percent, many concierge physicians maintain waiting lists. Those concierge physicians who still have room for more patients find that personal referrals from their existing patients are the predominant source of new patients. It might be said they can count on the Influence of Affluence. Our survey, for instance, showed that Middle-Class Millionaires with concierge health care have on average referred about twenty people to their respective doctors in the past three years. By our measures, there is no other service that Middle-Class Millionaires recommend more enthusiastically than concierge medicine. People are also far more likely to rely on Middle-Class Millionaires for physician referrals. Our survey found Middle-Class Millionaires are more than twice as likely as the middle class to report they are very often asked for their advice about a variety of medical matters.

Former Wisconsin governor Tommy Thompson was President Bush's Secretary of Health and Human Services when the first objections to concierge medicine were raised. Thompson had long been an advocate of preventive medicine since his days in Wisconsin, and after he left the Bush administration in early 2005, he started doing consulting work for MDVIP. During a report on concierge health care that year, he told *NBC Nightly News*, "I know the criticisms are there, but it just doesn't hold any water. There are so many different kinds of practices that MDVIP is going to bolster and strengthen the health care system, not in any way detract from it."

Thompson now chairs an MDVIP panel of health care experts who are studying the company's model and discussing how it might be offered to lower-income people with no loss in quality. The company is working with medical centers in Boston, Houston, and Los Angeles to open primary care practices based on the concierge model for inner-city patients. What has the universities intrigued is this: MDVIP's affluent members are part of what might be the most extensive real-life experiment in preventive care in modern medical history. It is an experiment, Goldman will remind you, that neither the federal government nor insurance companies were interested in underwriting.

"We're doing all this front-end work to keep patients healthy," Edward Goldman says. "But is it working? If it's working, I should be putting fewer people in the hospital, and I should have fewer people coming to emergency rooms. Well, in the state of Florida, which has the highest Medicare admissions rate in the United States, we have had sixty percent fewer admissions. We have had fifty percent fewer admissions than the best HMOs in the state."

In other states where MDVIP is active, the company's patients are hospitalized 60 to 75 percent less frequently than other patients with commercial insurance, despite the fact that MDVIP patients tend to be older and are more likely to have chronic conditions to begin with. To Goldman, these statistics lead to a clear diagnosis: It is the health care system that is diseased. He points out that 70 percent of all doctors in the United States are specialists who treat people when they are ill, and only 30 percent of doctors are primary care physicians who try to keep their patients well. The ratio, Goldman says, should be the other way around. Goldman's goal with MDVIP is nothing short of turning the U.S. health care system upside down.

As medicine improves its ability to identify health risk factors, concierge medicine only stands to grow in importance. Leland Kaiser, a Colorado health care consultant, sees the technology of genetic testing pushing medicine toward an inevitable emphasis on prevention, with concierge medicine at the head of the trend. For instance, Kaiser thinks that there are many common medications available today that physicians should avoid prescribing without knowing their patients' genetic profiles. "The literature is pretty clear," he says. "You give a medication to a person that's genetically not fit for it, you can kill him." But genetic testing is costly, he acknowledges, "and it's not going to be covered by insurance initially." Concierge medicine is likely to give the technology its earliest test.

Several years ago, Kaiser predicted in a medical journal that concierge medicine might account for 30 to 40 percent of all primary care appointments within the next decade. He no longer thinks its growth will be quite so fast, but he still maintains that the growth of concierge care is inevitable as baby boomers age, and that the Influence of Affluence will become increasingly evident.

"Here's the brutal truth," he says. "The more money you have, the longer you're going to live and the better you're going to live. We're not going to escape that. The one thing that helps is that as the technology gets used and demonstrates its value, the cost comes down, because you're dealing with more units. Finally, people will demand that their insurance cover it. So there's a trickle-down effect, which is wonderful." The alternative, he says, "is to take the sort of democratic ideal and push it to the point of absurdity. You'd say, 'Nope, we're not going to have one of anything until everybody can have one.' Well, you get nothing if you take that view. That stops everything."

Even without assistance from insurers, one doctor has extended the influence of concierge care all the way down to people who currently carry no insurance at all. In July 2007, a Seattle concierge physician named Garrison Bliss opened a monthly fee practice in downtown Seattle that charges just $34 to $74 per month. Underwritten by venture capital funding, Qliance Medical Group offers primary medical care with the goal of providing all the benefits of concierge care to the working poor and the uninsured.

Qliance doctors are each assigned a maximum of 700 patients. They offer half-hour doctor visits (instead of the fifteen minutes normally budgeted in practices with insurer co-pays) and hour-long medical exams with X-ray facilities and lab services on-site.

"Among our first fifty members, we have families of venture capitalists and cabdrivers," Bliss says. "We have blue-collar, middle class, and upper-class, and everybody I've talked to says that they've never seen medical care like this. That's what I wanted." Bliss interviewed the first fifty patients in his new venture. Overwhelmingly, he says, the most common reaction has been, "I can't believe someone spent this much time with me."

Bliss happened to be present at the birth of concierge care back in 1996. When Howard Maron and Scott Hall decided to leave Seattle Medical Associates to start MD², Bliss was one of their partners. "What Howard did was create a marketplace in medical care that hadn't existed before," says Bliss. "This is a consumer issue, not a physician's issue. If you create a real marketplace where patients are buying and doctors are providing, then consumers can have some power."

At the time that Maron and Hall jumped ship, Bliss and another partner—admitting to feelings of envy—began to ponder their own alternatives. Bliss was the first doctor to take MD²'s practice model and run a series of spreadsheets to determine how far down he could scale it (Bliss and his partner decided to keep 800 patients each, and eventually they charged $95 per month).

By 2006, Bliss was the president of the national Society for Innovative Medical Practice Design, all of whose members are engaged in some form of concierge or fee-based medicine, including a few who had scaled down the concierge model to as little as $50 or even $25 per month to cover what seems to be the absolute bottom line in all concierge medicine: unhurried visits with the physician, next-day or same-day scheduling, and twenty-four-hour telephone access.

Bliss began to wonder, "What if you could buy all your primary care for $50 or $60 per month? It meant that if you were sick you could be seen today. If you thought you broke a finger you could go to someone who might splint it, X-ray it, or send you to someone who could give you a cash price for doing it. What if you didn't have to go to emergency rooms for anything other than serious emergencies?"

He started Qliance, he says, out of his own need to answer these questions. "Someone had to do it, and no one was stepping up," he recalls. "I was enjoying my practice, but at the same time I was realizing that this movement will kind of wither and die if it doesn't extend itself to take care of a much larger portion of America. I also didn't feel very good that there is an inexpensive and effective form of primary care that could be designed to take care of a huge proportion of people in the United States and could outperform every insurance company—and nobody's doing it."

Bliss believes Qliance's type of low-cost concierge care could end up changing the health care system on a grand scale. As he sees it, if Qliance's monthly fee-based care were coupled with high-deductible catastrophic insurance coverage, 80 percent of the nation's 47 million uninsured could get improved, affordable care for 80 percent of their illnesses at just half or two-thirds the price of regular insurance. "You have financial protection in case you really get trounced with something bad," he says. "In between, it's your money to spend, which means you may be more intelligent about spending it. Then you begin to have some price pressure for the rest of medical care. Do I really need to see the GI specialist? Maybe I'll wait a week. Maybe I don't need a CAT scan for my headache. It reduces costs over time. It gives a lot more power to the patients. It gives physicians a reasonable role in medical care. The doctors will do better financially and the patients will get their money's worth. That sounds good to me."

Ultimately, Bliss puts faith in the marketplace. "There's an extraordinary market out there of people who are uninsured," he says. "It's a group that no one seems to want to take care of. It's a group that no insurance company seems to be able to get their fingers on. These are the people who won't buy unless it's a reasonable deal, because their employers aren't paying."

Prior to 2005, the Society for Innovative Medical Practice Design had a simpler, more memorable name: the American Society of Concierge Physicians. The word *concierge* never sat right with the doctors, though, and even at the association's founding, the president explained apologetically, "We use the name 'concierge' because it was the most easily recognizable way to get the word out about the society. But we don't think it really describes what it is we're doing."

The truth is that doctors in concierge practices appeal to their patients for the same basic reason the word *concierge* has gained so much cachet in recent years—because there are so few places remaining that can commit to quality service. Edward Goldman says that concierge health care changes the physician-patient relationship in a way that is more gratifying to both parties. That sounds like nothing so much as the motto of Les Clefs d'Or: "In Service Through Friendship."

Fundamentally, it was the dissatisfaction of patients such as Bradley Tavel that led to the development of concierge medicine. It is a testament to the Influence of Affluence that some think concierge medicine might revolutionize preventive care and others believe it could also provide an answer to the health insurance crisis.

Through their fees, however large or small, patients who purchase concierge medicine are willing to pay extra to express the value they place on their health. The nature of concierge care, of preventive care, moves the patient-doctor relationship to another step beyond the concierge model of service. A patient in preventive care is more likely to see a doctor as an advocate and a "cornerman," as Alan Sheff learned. Some elevate the doctor to the role of a trusted coach—someone you hire to better yourself and gain a better understanding of yourself—which is the subject of the next chapter.

CHAPTER SIX

THE BEST ADVICE MONEY CAN BUY

In the fall of 2004, Mark Little had a scheduling problem that was nagging at him. As head of a wealth management firm in San Antonio, Texas, Little was required to take a continuing education course before the end of the year in order to maintain his registration as a financial advisor. His appointment book, however, was jammed through January. As the deadline for enrolling in the classes kept creeping closer, Little kept pushing back the course dates.

Procrastinating to avoid an inconvenient obligation may seem like a minor failing for a busy professional, but there was one person in Mark Little's life who wasn't about to let it slide. Anne Bachrach, Little's personal "accountability coach," finally grew tired of watching him procrastinate, week after week. Normally, Bachrach would address a chronically incomplete to-do item by confronting him over whether it should be dropped from his schedule altogether. That wasn't an option in this case, since Little needed the course to keep his professional registration.

So Bachrach tried a different tack. She "created a consequence" for him. She told him to write out a personal check for $2,000 and send it to her. If the continuing education classes weren't scheduled and paid for by their next coaching session in two weeks, Bachrach said, she would forward the cash to one of her favorite charities, a political cause she knew that Little didn't care for.

That was enough to get Little's attention. He mailed off the $2,000 check and scheduled the classes on the same day. As Little says now, money and politics were never the real issues at stake in the matter. The check was just a coaching tool. It gave him the nudge he needed during a hectic time in his career to focus on a bothersome task. It's also an indication of how thoroughly integrated coaching has become in running his life.

Eight years ago, Mark Little was working nights and weekends to keep up with 1,242 financial planning accounts. He weighed 313 pounds and suffered from diabetes. In the intervening years, he has employed at least seven professional and personal coaches who have helped him turn around both his health and his work life. He trimmed his weight down to 173 pounds, overhauled his business, and reduced his client list to fewer than one hundred choice accounts. Today he works only three days a week, his income has tripled, and he has competed in four triathlons.

By most measures, Little had already achieved a great deal of success by the age of forty-three, before he'd ever hired a coach of any kind. On the other hand, he felt miserable from eating all the wrong things and representing all the wrong clients. A dietician and a trainer helped set his health straight. It took him just nine months to lose the first 121 pounds. Under the direction of a "lead coach," a string of three other business coaches—top-of-the-line experts in helping entrepreneurs focus their talents and energies—assisted him in the difficult decision to drop all but the best seventeen of his 1,242 clients and helped keep him on track as he rebuilt the practice to a very select group of ninety-one clients—nearly all of whom were Middle-Class Millionaires like himself.

Business coaching of this kind is a phenomenon that has grown with the rise of the Middle-Class Millionaire. All but unheard of twenty-five years ago, professional coaches and "life coaches," as they are sometimes called, have been hired by almost half the Middle-Class Millionaires in our sample (45 percent) over the past three years. Another 42 percent of Middle-Class Millionaires say they expect to hire a coach within the next three years. Of our middle-class sample, just 13 percent said they've hired a coach, although 26 percent say they expect to hire one soon.

"The most successful clients of mine had coaches," Little says. "I think it's a pattern. I think a lot of entrepreneurs kind of naturally gravitate toward the notion that a coach is going to point things out and make insights that maybe your closest friends and employees are not willing to make about you. It's all with the idea of making progress faster, accelerating results, and pointing out things that are a little bit tough."

Top athletes and performing artists have always employed their own personal coaches to help them hone their skills. Personal trainers have been around for a long time, too. But until fairly recently, ordinary individuals who wanted to improve their efficacy at work had to rely on the advice of friends, peer networks, mentors, or psychotherapists. Coaching—which prompts an individual to identify personally meaningful goals and stretch to fulfill them—simply wasn't available.

Dan Sullivan, the Toronto-based founder and head of The Strategic Coach, says he gave the business consultancy that name in 1986 simply because that's what his clients had begun calling him. "As near as I can figure, it was around '83 or '84," he says. "I noticed that when they would introduce me or talk about me, they would use the word *coach*. Since they were thinking in those terms, I simply adopted the word."

It wasn't until 1995 that coaches had a credentialing association, the International Coaching Federation (ICF), whose membership has tripled since 2001 to 11,500 today. That membership, more than half of which is located in North America, includes a wide variety of personal business coaches and life coaches. A recent ICF study estimates that the average coach makes about $50,000 per year and has eleven active clients at any one time. Sixty-nine percent of coaches and 56 percent of coaching clients are women.

As a marketing concept, coaching has caught fire in recent years, spreading outward to the fields of education and medicine in particular, as we've already seen. Besides SAT coaches, there are parenting coaches, too. There are coaches for people suffering from diabetes, attention deficit disorder, and compulsive smoking. The ICF has organized specialty groups on wellness coaching, adolescent coaching, addiction recovery coaching, and "political leadership" coaching. Within the business professions themselves, coaching specialists abound in almost every discipline. The *Wall Street Journal* reported there is a coach for engineers who calls himself "the geek whisperer."

Among all the survey respondents who report having hired coaches, we found a distinct and significant divide in the purposes those coaches serve. The middle class were much more likely to consider coaching an important factor in improving their personal lives (65 percent), while only 16 percent of the Middle-Class Millionaires saw coaching that way. Among Middle-Class Millionaires, the most commonly cited important or very important reason for hiring a coach was that it "provides you with a way to improve your career skills" (90 percent). In our middle-class sample, by contrast, just 44 percent pointed to career skills as an important reason for having a coach.

These results imply that Middle-Class Millionaires are much more likely to hire a coach as an investment in their self-efficacy and financial autonomy—two important distinguishing features of Millionaire Intelligence. For instance, 83 percent of our Middle-Class Millionaires regard their careers as "extremely or very important." Just 43 percent of the middle-class sample assigned the same level of importance to their careers. Middle-Class Millionaires also place, with near unanimity, a high degree of importance on "being financially independent." Nearly 97 percent said this independence was very or extremely important to them. About two-thirds of the middle-class sample—67 percent—agreed with that sentiment. These numbers suggest that while financial independence is a common middle-class aspiration, among Middle-Class Millionaires it is a defining characteristic.

There are those who find it difficult to accept that anyone as competent and successful as Mark Little would require any coaching at all. Little has even heard the question raised by one of his own coaches. One day he was huffing and puffing away on a treadmill when his personal trainer commented, "You know, Mark, you're so driven, why do you feel like you need a coach?" Little laughs now at the memory. "I said, 'What, are you crazy? A few minutes ago, when I asked you how much longer I had to go on the treadmill, that's the point: I was ready to get off. And I would have gotten off if you hadn't been standing there—if I hadn't been *paying* you to stand there!'"

To Anne Bachrach—the woman who made Little write out that $2,000 check to charity—having a coach means that there is at least one person in your life who is dedicated solely to helping you achieve what's most important to you. "You can't do it for yourself," she says. "This is my belief. There are too many distractions, too many people trying to hold you back or hold you down, whether they do it intentionally or not. The coach is the only one really in your corner. Everyone else has their own agenda."

Bachrach says that if most Middle-Class Millionaires don't emphasize the benefits of coaching in their personal lives, it's probably because when you are a boss, the professional inevitably becomes the personal. "What I do is not brain surgery," she says. "I try to help people create balance in their lives. It's not just about work. Most of my clients happen to be men, and they tell me, 'Oh, my wife loves you!' They actually have a home life, in addition to working. Coaching is not just about ramping up one thing to the detriment of something else. When their business goes up, their personal side should go up, too."

Perhaps the reason why Middle-Class Millionaires find coaching a more compelling investment of their time and money is that 80 percent of those in our sample either own their own business or are partners in professional practices and therefore stand to profit directly from increasing their personal productivity. Only 20 percent identify themselves as corporate employees, compared with 46 percent of our middle-class sample. Still, the escalating demands on management are felt universally.

One of Bachrach's clients is a fifty-something workaholic who was staying late at the office every evening while complaining that his social life was terrible. He set a new goal for himself: He would leave work at precisely 6:00 P.M. each day. But his efforts failed miserably. So Bachrach created a consequence for him. "I asked him to name something he really can't stand," she says. "He paused for a moment and said, 'Cats. I hate cats.'" So Bachrach mailed him a pledge card to Siamese Rescue of San Diego, where she lives. The client had to agree that every day he fails to leave work by 6:00 P.M., he's got to mail a $50 check to San Diego's homeless Siamese cats. He posted the Siamese Rescue pledge card above his desk and has yet to send the cats a single dollar.

When Dan Sullivan was growing up on a farm in northern Ohio, he remembers deciding at a young age that he wanted a very different life for himself, and that it would require him to strike out on his own and work for himself. He pursued a career as a business consultant and went bankrupt twice trying to establish himself in the field. During one particularly lean spell, he spent ten months living in an apartment with no furniture except for a sleeping bag and an air mattress. He says now, "It never occurred to me during that time that I wouldn't continue doing what I'm doing."

Today, at age sixty-three, Dan Sullivan has become a life coaching guru of sorts to businesspeople from all over the world. In the past twenty years, his Strategic Coach program has schooled thousands of

Middle-Class Millionaires in the art of seeking personal happiness while growing a thriving business. The program has achieved cult-like status among some of its devotees, and although a typical $6,500-per-year curriculum lasts three years, about 250 of Strategic Coach's clients have remained under the firm's continuous tutelage for ten years or longer. Sullivan has his own line of inspirational books and CDs, featuring pithy aphorisms for self-made self-starters such as "Your number-one responsibility as an entrepreneur is to protect your confidence."

Enrollees in the basic three-year program gather for daylong sessions four times a year in Atlanta, Chicago, Los Angeles, Toronto, or Manchester, England. They are sorted into groups according to their income levels, and during the day they perform a series of exercises to help them work out specific goals for themselves and their businesses in the coming quarter, the coming year, and the coming three years. The idea is to get them out of the office to think strategically about the things they consider most important in each part of their lives. In 2004, *Inc.* magazine told the story of a thirty-three-year-old Strategic Coach client who jumped from the $100,000 income group to the $1 million group in the course of three years. During that time, he cut his workweek from seven days to four, lost 50 pounds, and started hobbies including photography and scuba diving. "It's made me a more interesting person," he told *Inc.* "I could die tomorrow, and I know I love my life."

The basic principle behind the Strategic Coach method can be summed up by Sullivan's maxim "You can have everything you love in life if you give up everything you hate." The program pushes each participant to identify at least two or three of his or her "unique abilities" at work and then delegate or outsource every task or duty unrelated to those abilities. Over the three-year coaching period, the participants are encouraged to ramp up their operations and take more time away from the office, the better to keep their unique abilities sharp and focused on the long term. The loss of hands-on responsibilities can give fits to the control freaks in the program, but the Strategic Coach curriculum preaches the importance of seeing employees as investments in future profits, not as a drag on the bottom line. The belief is that increasing your capacity will force you to make things happen. As his book *The Quotable Dan Sullivan* puts it: "If you want the energy to create the show, sell the tickets first."

At the urging of his lead coach, Mark Little arrived at his first Strategic Coach session in Chicago in 1998. Within his niche in the financial services world, he was not just an overachiever. He was a star, the top producer for his affiliated broker-dealer firm. But he didn't feel like a star. He was the classic frustrated businessperson—overworked, overweight, and beating his head against the same wall each day. Dan Sullivan says that businesspeople who enroll in his program are extremely determined individuals (he lovingly calls them "killers") but that they are "also not necessarily self-focusing people." They tend to load themselves down with so many responsibilities that they can't think in strategic terms. That was Mark Little in 1998. Some of Little's 1,242 clients were earning him almost nothing but grief, and yet he had no strategy for crawling out from under his crushing workload.

Financial planning started to undergo big changes in the mid-1990s. It had grown up through the 1970s and 1980s as an exclusively commission-driven industry. Planners such as Mark Little offered their advice at no charge or for a modest fee and earned their income by selling insurance and other financial products to clients through sponsoring broker-dealers such as Merrill Lynch. As middle-class affluence grew more widespread in the 1990s, however, increasing numbers of planners set their sights on becoming "wealth managers" instead. For a flat annual fee equaling a small percentage of a household's liquid assets, usually around 1 percent, wealth managers handle all the financial planning and investments for clients without needing to sell them anything.

Little enrolled in Strategic Coach because he suspected he was better suited to the wealth management field, and the first few quarterly sessions in Toronto began to confirm those suspicions. For years he had been selling products to clients and explaining their investments to them, and although he was adept at both tasks, neither involved what he identified as his unique abilities. Wealth management required a different set of skills far more suited to Little's talent for engendering trust, developing relationships, and managing large portfolios. The big question remained how he might transition from one type of business to the other while maintaining his income for himself and his family.

In the summer of 1999, Little attended his broker-dealer's annual convention in Newport, Rhode Island, where the featured speaker was Bill Bachrach, author of a popular business title called *Values-Based Selling*. Bachrach's provocative theme that day was that financial advisors can build very lucrative wealth management businesses, but only if they dare to be choosy about whom they accept as clients. Basically, he told this roomful of successful salespeople that they should stop selling. They could make more money with less effort, he said, once they began *rejecting* all but the wealthiest and most agreeable client prospects. Using this concept, Bachrach has developed a system of what he calls values-based financial planning, which plumbs each client's deepest feelings about money. The system, he says, helps clients see the function of money in their lives more clearly. It can make planning a more fulfilling experience for planners and clients alike, and it tends to sift out difficult, high-maintenance clients.

Little was so excited by what he heard that he grabbed a seat right next to Bachrach at the luncheon following the speech and peppered him with questions throughout the meal. In the following months, he tested Bachrach's ideas, working from books and audiotapes, but eventually decided he needed hands-on help. First Little enrolled in Bachrach's three-day academy for role-playing and coaching. Next came an advanced coaching program that cost $15,000, followed by a five-month-long weekly mentoring and daily accountability program.

Little estimates he spent more than $50,000 participating in every coaching series Bachrach had to offer. A year after meeting Bachrach, Little chose him as his lead coach.

The goal of all this coaching is something Bachrach calls "Being Done," a phrase he has trademarked for the financial planning industry. A wealth manager with a strictly limited number of select, high paying clients can raise his or her income level high enough that it's no longer necessary to spend any time trolling for new prospective clients. That's Being Done. Little, who had begun the Strategic Coach program hoping he might whittle his client list down to 600, discovered now that if he could cut back all the way to just one hundred "ideal clients" with investable assets of $1 million or more, he would earn more than $1 million annually in fees—almost three times what he'd made with more than 1,200 clients in his commission-based practice. At that point he could spend his time tending to those hundred accounts, educate himself further about the business, and give up worrying about building the practice. He would Be Done.

Little developed a strict set of criteria for those ideal clients. Requiring $1 million in assets was just the start. He realized he didn't enjoy working with clients who played the stock market themselves and second-guessed him about investment decisions. To be his client, you would have to agree to put every investment dollar you have under his care. He also asked his new clients to promise him they wouldn't watch stock-hyping "financial pornography" on cable channels such as CNBC. He didn't want the kind of client who would call to ask his opinion about some hot new investment gimmick in this month's *Money* magazine, either. In his commission business, Little spent hours with clients going over the whys and wherefores of their investment portfolios. He asked his new clients to agree that they weren't interested in hearing about such details. He wanted to work only with people who were content to hand over all their financial worries to him so that they could go and enjoy their lives. If they weren't ready to trust him completely with their money, he would be glad to recommend another wealth manager.

Out of Little's 1,242 existing commission-based clients, however, all but seventeen failed to meet his minimal $1 million asset qualification. Among those seventeen, there were a few trusts and institutions, which were also outside the "ideal client" profile he had developed. They were profitable accounts, but boards of directors are unpredictable, and Little didn't find them very satisfying to work with. His promise to himself, and to his coaches, was that he would stick with the plan to have a hundred ideal clients who trusted him completely, so the trusts and institutions would have to go.

By the summer of 2000, under the watchful eye of Bachrach, Little was ready to begin three daunting tasks at once: politely disengaging from 1,225 clients, courting seventeen ideal clients under the new fee structure, and setting out to find eighty-three new ideal clients. It was a terrible time to try something like this. The Internet stock bubble had burst in March 2000, and investor portfolios had lost billions in equity. Little was cutting loose some of his most faithful clients and raising high standards for new ones at a time when investor assets had taken a beating and other financial advisors were closing up shop.

He resisted the temptation to compromise his plan or modify his new client standards, but keeping up the momentum was a problem. Bachrach and Sullivan had given Little great ideas and wonderful tools to work with. Little had even added one of Bachrach's own coaches, Michael Gerber's E-Myth Mastery Program, to his coaching lineup. "But you know," he says, "when you get back to the office and the daily grind sets in and your staff is asking for vacation time and your clients are demanding attention, you just slip back into the normal routine. Who's sitting there reminding you of your priorities, of actually working 'on' your business instead of 'in' your business? The one thing I had missing was accountability."

That's when Little hired his fourth coach, Anne Bachrach. She was a perfect fit for what he'd set out to do. She had been one of Dan Sullivan's seminar leaders at The Strategic Coach for about one year, and she knew Bill Bachrach's planning system backward and forward—in no small part because she is married to him. For $600 per month, Anne would review Mark Little's weekly e-mail reports, which tracked his progress making new prospect contacts and letting go of existing clients. In a follow-up phone call, she would press him for answers about areas where he either risked falling behind or needed to make his interim goals more aggressive.

Anne Bachrach does her coaching entirely via e-mail and phone from her home in San Diego. She almost never meets her coaching clients and says she doesn't even know what half of them look like. Bachrach's follow-up calls usually last less than half an hour and take place without any superficial chitchat. "This is my unique ability," she says. "I'm very direct. I tell the truth as I see it. I just try to help people put things together." Her motto, she says, is "Excuses don't count unless you're dead." She recalls a client who called to say he'd been sick for two days. "I said, 'I'm supposed to be nice to you now? That was two days out of two weeks. You can make it up!'"

Some people thrive on this kind of structure. To them, coaching puts a helpful and benign authority figure in their lives—sort of a boss you can fire. But Bachrach has also had clients who have cracked under the pressure and quit. She has fired other clients because their lack of progress was frustrating her. "One-on-one coaching is very difficult," she says. "It's not for everyone. I've seen people just burn out because they couldn't handle it." Two clients have told her they get nightmares prior to her calls, Bachrach says, "and these are calls about *their* goals, for crying out loud." It wasn't long before her weekly phone calls became a source of dread among Mark Little's staff, too. Whenever Anne called, the buzz in the office was "Mark's going to go in and get his whuppin' on what he didn't do. And we're going to get ours next."

By July 2001, Little was all the way down to seventeen clients. More than twelve hundred accounts had been referred out, and his overall revenue or "production" was projected to fall by half. It was a nerve-wracking time. With the market in shambles, he was terrified the plan would fail and he'd be forced to rebuild his traditional financial planning practice all over again. Both of the Bachrachs assured him that with only seventeen clients to service, he now had the gift of time to go out and find eighty-three more just like them. Little remembers putting his trust totally in his coaches during this period, if only to protect his investment in them. "If you buy in to a methodology, what really makes it work is that you're either all the way in or all the way out," he says. "Any coach will tell you that the people who are half in never realize the greatest success." He recalls the story of the Spanish explorer Hernán Cortés, who burned his ships off the Yucatán so his men were left with no choice but to help him conquer Mexico. "That's what this kind of coaching at this level is. They burn the ships, so you're not only all the way in and paying attention, but it's *got* to work. There's a lot of magic in that."

All seventeen of Little's remaining clients had decided to stay with him after he'd explained how his wealth management practice would work. He told them about his goal of Being Done and how, once he had achieved a hundred clients, he could service their accounts undistracted by the need to find new clients. This simple fact gave Little's clients an urgent incentive to help him get to a hundred. The sooner he was Done, the sooner he'd be all theirs. Once they saw their self-interest in the matter, they started sending him referrals at a rate he'd never experienced before. One client sent him sixteen prospects. "See all the other advisors you like," another client told her friends. "But see this guy last because he's the one you really want."

Little was all the way up to forty-three clients in September 2001 when the 9/11 terror attacks shut down the stock market for six days. Anxiety in the financial community mounted, since no one could say for sure what might happen when the markets reopened. For Little, those days were the first test of whether his new clients were really prepared to delegate all their money concerns to his care. Following the stock crash of September 1987, he had spent long days on the phone debating with clients how they might have to adjust their portfolios, speculating on the effects of interest rate changes, and the like. This time was different. He called all forty-three clients and told them, "You're going to hear some wacko financial advice about what could happen, and I want to say how grateful I am that you're not paying attention to it." He advised that the best thing to do in the face of such uncertainty was to stick with their existing plans. All forty-three clients happily agreed and were grateful for his call.

By 2004, Mark Little had attracted ninety-one ideal clients and had what would be considered a first-rate wealth advisory practice, with annual fees approaching $1.6 million. In fifteen years, he had built up a business on his own, and then with the help of some of the best coaches money can buy, he ramped it up into something exceptional. He told Bill Bachrach at one point that he knows that every client loves him because he's fired every client that doesn't. There was just one problem.

"I didn't like it," he says. "It was still a business I had cobbled together out of another business that was a mess at one point. After I had built it up into this world-class business, I didn't like it. I had made the best of a bad situation." Having worked for three solid years with the goal of Being Done, Little found that prospect less and less appealing the nearer it drew. He didn't want to live out his life as just another well-to-do wealth manager. At age fifty, he started looking for a way out, to find a new challenge for those unique abilities he had grown to master. Mark Little decided he wanted to coach.

Self-betterment was one of the most conspicuous traits that Ben Franklin shared with today's Middle-Class Millionaire. It was a lifelong obsession. The first self-help book in America was his best-selling *Poor Richard's Almanac*, which was filled with such immortal dictums as "No gain without pain." Franklin's self-help book about business, *The Way to Wealth,* has remained in print for 249 years. What Franklin preached in these publications he practiced in his personal life. He kept track of his daily habits by checking them against a list of thirteen virtues he considered essential, including Industry ("Be always employed in something useful") and Resolution ("Perform without fail what you resolve"). At the end of each day, Franklin would open a little book he had printed up for just this purpose and make a mark next to each virtue he'd transgressed. Every thirteen weeks—four times a year—he'd study the direction his habits were trending. Ben Franklin was his own accountability coach.

As we pointed out in Chapter 1, the estimated number of Middle-Class Millionaire households in the United States may reach 20 million within the coming decade. We wondered what a nation with 20 million Ben Franklins might look like. Based on our survey results, it will likely be a nation bursting with coaches. Three out of four Middle-Class Millionaires either have a coach or say they will employ one within the next three years. Middle-Class Millionaires not only employ coaches three times more frequently than members of the middle class do, but they also recommend their coaches to others about *five* times more frequently. This likely explains how coaching continues to grow so fast without the benefit of any mass marketing. Coaching, as an idea and an industry, has permeated the culture through the Influence of Affluence.

Among survey respondents who have hired coaches in the past three years, the Middle-Class Millionaires on average refer their coaches to 5.7 people. Middle-class people with coaches refer them to an average of 1.2 people. The survey shows Middle-Class Millionaires aren't apt to keep their self-betterment regimens a secret. They let others know about all their self-betterment tools—seminars, courses, books, and

CDs—at a far greater rate than those in the middle class. They constitute a virtual volunteer sales force for the entire industry.

When we look at our survey results in light of Millionaire Intelligence, we see that the coaching emphasis on developing one's strengths—those things Dan Sullivan would call our unique abilities—is entirely consistent with the Middle-Class Millionaire fondness for maximizing opportunities and optimizing their competitive edge. The survey found, in particular, some coaching-related results regarding children and education that strongly bear out this idea.

According to our survey, almost all members of the middle class, millionaires and non-millionaires, place a high degree of importance on getting their children the best education possible. This is a markedly different result, as we showed in Chapter 2, from the one produced by the sample of high-net-worth individuals. Sixty-one percent of them considered their children's education very important, which supports the commonly held thought that education is a very basic and defining middle-class value.

Our two groups of middle-class survey respondents part company, however, on the practical question of how and when educational resources should be deployed. This is a point we first raised in Chapter 4, but it bears repeating here in greater detail. Middle-Class Millionaire parents are more than three times more likely than middle-class parents to provide their children with "additional education services such as lessons or tutoring" (72 percent vs. 23 percent).

As we drilled down through this result, we found that among this subgroup of all middle-class parents inclined to give their children extra lessons or tutoring, the reasons for doing so split distinctly along income lines. Most middle-class members of this subgroup—76 percent—said that lessons and tutoring were important in order to help their children "keep up." Among the Middle-Class Millionaires, however, 71 percent said these services were important in helping their children "get ahead." The less affluent, in other words, are overwhelmingly interested in shoring up their children's academic deficiencies, while Middle-Class Millionaires are just as singularly interested in coaching that refines their children's academic strengths. This difference in motivation appears to reflect a distinctive aspect of Millionaire Intelligence on the part of the Middle-Class Millionaire: an innate proclivity to gain a competitive advantage, for themselves and their children, in a competitive world.

The survey shows a similar split along income lines when it comes to attitudes toward personal or professional development seminars and conferences. A majority of both groups have attended such events recently or plan to go in the next three years, but the reasons given for attending are different. Among Middle-Class Millionaires, 79 percent cited "a way to improve your career skills," which was also cited by 65 percent of the middle-class sample. A majority of the middle-class respondents, however, also pointed to other benefits of such events, including "a way to improve your personal life" (50 percent), "meeting people who can help you get ahead in your career" (60 percent), and "benefit from the support" (64 percent). None of these three reasons for attending personal or professional programs or courses were ranked important by more than 26 percent of the Middle-Class Millionaires. Overwhelmingly, they go to be coached on improving their career skills.

One of the more surprising findings in our study was that even while on vacation, Middle-Class Millionaires consider self-improvement just as important as relaxation. Among the middle class, 68 percent regard "rest and relaxation" as a very important reason for vacationing, while just 14 percent mentioned "self-improvement." With Middle-Class Millionaires, the two reasons are basically tied. About 38 percent of this group sees "rest and relaxation" as an important reason for vacations, while 42 percent cited "self-improvement." Even "education" was considered important by 29 percent of Middle-Class Millionaires during vacations, compared with just 12 percent of the middle-class sample.

Ben Franklin wrote, "Leisure is the time for doing something useful," and a lot of Middle-Class Millionaires evidently agree. Middle-Class Millionaires don't go on vacation just to feel better. They want to *be* better. Miraval, the Tucson, Arizona, luxury spa resort, regularly competes with neighboring Canyon Ranch for top destination spa accolades from major travel magazines. Miraval's point of distinction is that it balances its more traditional relaxation-oriented offerings by coaching its guests in a range of "challenge activities" that involve climbing poles and swinging from ropes.

Miraval's latest move is to open a 350-unit "inspired living residence" on Manhattan's Upper East Side, in which each resident will enjoy the services of a wellness advisor and access to a wide range of New Age-inspired programs. The company hopes to build a dozen or more such developments in major cities around the United States and expects the residences to be popular among regular visitors to the main Miraval resort. The company's marketing chief told *Forbes* magazine that Miraval guests want to take a piece of the experience home with them. "It's a little like taking piano lessons without a piano at home," he said. "If we give you a little piano to practice on, you will improve."

Dan Sullivan thinks this widespread interest in being coached, even for fun, has a lot to do with the rise of digital communications in recent years. Sullivan theorizes that the personal computer in the 1980s and the Internet in the 1990s together have spawned a generation of independent-minded businesspeople who are self-motivated and self-directed, building dynamic companies that weren't even possible in earlier decades marked by bureaucratic corporations.

"These are people who definitely didn't want to be managed," Sullivan says. "But they like having a structure that allows them to focus. They like having someone to report to. They like having an accountability structure. That is where the role of the coach began to emerge. You want someone who is going to be an observer, [but] you are the one who is setting out the agenda."

Sullivan believes that the current computer age is as pivotal a time in human history as the advent of the printing press. He paints a picture of an emerging global economy in which "the whole emphasis is on creativity, the whole emphasis is on independence of thought, the whole emphasis is on utilizing your unique ability and packaging your unique ability out in the world." The biggest winners in such an economy are these highly coached businesspeople who "independently and spontaneously create value for other people."

These are the people Sullivan says he wants to coach in the skill of building a lifetime of happiness, in large part because, in his experience, they rarely keep their prosperity to themselves. Having coached thousands of people over the years, he has observed how the concerns of Strategic Coach enrollees move upward and outward as they grow more successful. They start out obsessed with fixing their business in the first year, and by the fourth year, they've got ideas about fixing the world. As we would put it, they move their focus upward in their middle-class hierarchy of values.

"There's a clear-cut pattern," Sullivan says. "The reason they want to be more successful is that they want to take care of their families, and they also want to free up more of their time so they can be really, really good spouses and really, really great parents. Once they get beyond that, there's a tremendous move toward giving back to the community in some way." Clients become more influential in their communities, start taking part in politics, and involve themselves in charities.

That was Ben Franklin's pattern, too. First he achieved personal affluence as a printer, author, and investor. His private wealth provided him the autonomy to exercise his public influence in ways that shook the world. A nation of 20 million Benjamin Franklins, with a million coaches behind them, might shake the world beyond anything Franklin himself would ever have dreamed.

By 2005, Mark Little's wealth management practice had grown so successful that he was ready to release clients who had once met his stringent criteria but since strayed from the ideal. One of these clients had so much money under management with Little that his annual fees were $20,000—about one-twentieth of the entire annual revenue Little had been earning from 1,242 clients just a few years earlier. The problem was that this same client also liked to play the stock market on the side with a $200,000 E-Trade account. Little put him on notice. Once the practice reached a full complement of one hundred ideal clients, he would have the choice of closing the E-Trade account or finding another wealth manager. Little would drop cryptic notes in this client's copy of his quarterly statement, just to tip him off that the day of reckoning was growing near. The notes made sense only to Little and the client. One quarter, it read "23/100." Three months later, it said "43/100."

By tightening his standards and selectively sloughing off less-than-ideal clients, Little likely could have gone on like this for the rest of his working life and retired a very wealthy man. He was a role model for financial advisors everywhere. Bill Bachrach brought him on stage during seminars to discuss his experiences with hundreds of financial advisors in the audience. Little had achieved this enviable position through years of diligent work with all his coaches. It was that same coaching process, however, that also helped sow the seeds of Mark Little's discontentment with the business.

Years earlier, during one of his many self-betterment seminars, Little had been guided through a series of exercises to help him identify his true calling—what he really felt his life was all about. In a sense, he was asked to draft a personal mission statement. The result was this: "I am continually looking for ways, for myself and others, to stretch and grow." Bill Bachrach had attended the same seminar years earlier and had recommended it to Little. Only later did Little discover that Bachrach, his coach, had defined his own purpose in life in a very similar way. It had taken years of being coached to understand it, but Little began to see coaching itself as his own true calling.

"As tough as they are on the outside, the coaches I know are people who are really suited for caring," Little says. "The only word that comes to mind is *love*. It's a kind of brotherly love, but you love your clients. You care about them. You have to be happy for other people. When you talk to the best coaches, they really are happy for the people that they coach." He remembers a day when he and Bachrach were taking questions from a large audience of financial advisors, and someone asked Bachrach which of Little's professional accomplishments made him most proud. "He sat there for a minute and tears started welling up in his eyes," Little recalls. "He started crying. Bill told the guy that it's not professional. He said, 'It's his health. After all those years of coaching him, Mark took my advice to take control of his physical fitness. He lost all that weight, and now he's going to live a long life.'"

Little came to realize that even if he ran the best wealth management firm on earth, he would only rarely get a chance to live up to his life's purpose and help someone truly "stretch and grow." The values-based financial planning advice he dispensed did a lot to help clients express their personal values through their financial holdings, but that went only so far. For a good number of those clients, money mainly meant security, and they weren't particularly interested in stretching and growing with it.

So with ninety-one clients—just nine short of Being Done—and revenues of $1.6 million, Mark Little decided he really was done with his practice. He sold his interest to a larger firm and joined it as a partner, with the understanding he would be free to develop a new set of services for them. "Part of the deal is that I'm allowed to be entrepreneurial," he says. "So I can build a business on purpose, the way I wished I had."

His first project was a wealth management service fully integrated with life coaching. It's called The Freedom Experience: Life Coaching

That Specializes in Money, and it promises to help clients develop "a plan for living life on *purpose,* while making smart choices about your money." The Freedom Experience's Web site describes its ideal clients as people who are "passionate about goals," people who "focus on what's important" in life.

"For people who read that profile and say, 'That's a bunch of hogwash, it sounds like a bunch of southern California fluff,' that's fine," Little says. As a marketing approach, it's extremely pointed in a field more often characterized by bland appeals to hopes and dreams. Little says the idea is to attract people who read the ideal client profile and say, "Wow, where have you been all my life?"

Coaching, he says, is all about goals. The Freedom Experience won't take your money if all you want to do is retire quietly. "I've had clients who look me in the eye and say, 'You know what? I don't have any goals,'" Little says. "I'm not saying that's wrong, but it doesn't fit with what we do. Our whole methodology has to deal with a sense of forward movement and measuring progress toward a goal. So if somebody says, 'Look, I'm sixty-seven years old, I've got five million dollars, and the end of game for me is just playing defense with my money and never running out,' we've got nothing to talk about. They could have ten million dollars, and if they don't have any goals, we'd refer them out."

At his Freedom Experience office in the Chicago suburbs (there are eleven offices, including San Diego, Beverly Hills, and San Antonio), Little uses the coaching skills he has picked up over the years to help clients through problems that are both financial and emotional. A Motorola executive might want to know if he has enough money to leave the corporation and take a lower-paying job at a local charity. For a minimum annual fee of $12,500 per year—1.25 percent on assets of $1 million—The Freedom Experience will act as your personal chief financial officer and help you shop for cars or concierge doctors and make other big-ticket decisions. The freedom promised in The Freedom Experience is freedom not to worry about the minutiae of such things. The work is so intensive that for now each Freedom Experience advisor is limited to 100 clients, though Little is considering cutting that back to 50.

The real coaching comes when goals are in conflict or when clients need to get in touch with their goals. Little mentions the case of a married couple who had built a $6 million business together. Over the years it became increasingly difficult for them to work together, and the wife felt she'd rather be playing tennis each day at their country club instead. The couple came to him wondering if they—and the business—could afford that scenario.

Little crunched the numbers and determined it was doable for the wife to quit her job. He remembers her bursting into tears at that meeting. She had been working since she was thirteen years old, and for the first time in her life, her spouse could assure her that it was okay to stop. The husband continued to run the business by himself, and although revenues dipped for a while, the company eventually surpassed its previous numbers before the year was out.

At that point the couple returned with a new problem. The wife was tired of tennis. She was a spirited and effective businesswoman, and hitting a ball over a net seven days a week wasn't fulfilling. Little took her again through the ninety-minute coaching process, digging deep into questions about what mattered most in her life. The woman arrived at a new insight. She wanted them to donate a lot of money to start a charitable enterprise that would help women in crisis help themselves. "So now we've got a new angle," Little says. "It's not only identifying something for her to do with her life, but the question is: 'Can we afford to donate a chunk of money to get this thing going?'"

It turned out they couldn't afford what she had in mind. But Little determined that by contributing less money up front and spending more time fund-raising, the couple could proceed with the plan.

When Little started out with this couple in 2005, their charitable giving began and ended with the $3,000 a year they sent to the Society for the Prevention of Cruelty to Animals. Today the wife is a nonprofit entrepreneur. Getting to that point required moving back and forth between identifying the couple's goals through coaching and estimating the financial requirements to meet those goals. It took nothing less, Little says, to get to the bottom of what was most fulfilling to these clients. "By coming to these meetings as much a marriage counselor as a financial counselor," Little says, he helped the couple create a charity "that could really go out and make a difference in the world."

Little's innovation in the financial planning industry is spelled out in one word of his company's name: The Freedom *Experience*. Rather than approach personal finance in the typical way—protecting assets with the goal of maintaining a client's lifestyle—Little begins with the notion that goals ultimately boil down to experiences. Part of his job is to probe a client's psyche to help the client develop a vision of his or her ideal future. The rest involves making those experiences financially attainable, so that clients come away with what Little calls "a life satisfaction package."

In the next chapter, we'll look at another innovative way Middle-Class Millionaires are creating experiences for themselves. If coaching gives depth to your experience—whether it's your career or your life goals—fractional ownership gives you the breadth of multiple experiences. In fact, when it comes to anything from real estate to handbags, Middle-Class Millionaires are opting for the *experience* of ownership rather than ownership itself.

CHAPTER SEVEN

THE OWNERSHIP EXPERIENCE

Steve Case might be the closest thing imaginable to a family-oriented, self-made, middle-class *billionaire*. Like "ordinary" Middle-Class Millionaires, Case sees vacations as opportunities for his family to spend time together. Yet with all his considerable resources, he seldom had satisfactory experiences when vacationing with his wife and their five children. They owned three rarely used vacation homes around the country, which Case says left him feeling guilty when the family would vacation somewhere else for the sake of variety. On those occasions, accommodating the large family presented other problems. They'd either get adjacent hotel suites with inconvenient connecting doors or rent a vacation home sight unseen. They once rented a house in Hawaii with seven bedrooms, only to find three of the bedrooms were accessed by a flight of stairs outside the building. Rather than risk navigating the outdoor steps at night, some children wound up sleeping on couches in the living room.

Frustrated, Case began looking into vacation alternatives. During a quick online search in May 2003, he stumbled across the Web site for Exclusive Resorts, a small "destination club" that managed just four vacation homes shared by its twenty-five members. For an initial membership deposit of $120,000 and membership dues of $16,000 per year, Exclusive Resorts offered access to luxury condos at a Colorado ski resort and Trump Tower in New York and vacation homes in Baja California and Hawaii. This was everything Case was looking for: a variety of locations, predictable quality, sophisticated service, and all at a price far below that of the three vacation homes he already owned. He filled out the online form requesting more information.

When Case's name—with an AOL e-mail address—appeared on the list of inquiries at the company's Denver headquarters, co-founder Brent Handler couldn't quite believe that this was *the* Steve Case asking for a callback. He decided to make the follow-up call personally. It wasn't long into his first conversation with Case that Handler realized the billionaire wanted to join Exclusive Resorts not only as a member but as an investor, too. The two men met in San Diego three days after Case's initial inquiry, by which time Case had decided he wanted to buy the company. By November of that year, Case owned 80 percent of Exclusive Resorts, and although Handler remains president, Case installed a former AOL executive as CEO. No different from PinnacleCare's Bruce Spector in Chapter 1 or Tesla Motors' Martin Eberhard in Chapter 4, Steve Case saw something that fulfilled his own needs—and figured there were plenty of others willing to pay for the same improved experience.

As we've shown many times in this book, family is a primary middle-class value, one of paramount importance to almost all our survey respondents, regardless of income. There are differences between our two income groups, however, in how devotion to family is most commonly expressed. For instance, Middle-Class Millionaires are more than twice as likely as the middle class to say that vacations are very important as "an opportunity for the family to spend time together."

About 60 percent of Middle-Class Millionaires pointed to spending time with family as an important function of vacation time. Slightly fewer than 38 percent cited "rest and relaxation." Among the middle-class survey respondents, these two results were quite nearly reversed. For the middle class, the most commonly cited purpose for taking a vacation was "rest and relaxation," at 68 percent. Spending time with family was far less frequently chosen, at just under 28 percent.

Considering the other findings in our survey, these results make a great deal of sense. Middle-Class Millionaires work much longer each day than respondents from the middle-class group. They also take significantly fewer vacation days (twelve days on average vs. nineteen). While both groups value time with family, vacations seem to be more important to Middle-Class Millionaires—perhaps because the rest of their time is so limited by work. Here is where we see the appeal of fractionally owned vacation homes and residence clubs. Any arrangement that promises to reduce hassles and ensure a more enjoyable experience is particularly valuable to Middle-Class Millionaires, since vacations themselves are less frequent and therefore more precious.

It all helps explain why fractionally owned residence clubs and vacation clubs have emerged in just the past few years to become a $2 billion industry that is transforming the face of vacation development around the country and around the world. Destination clubs are the fastest-growing segment of the entire vacation industry. Particularly in North America, the biggest players in the field are making development decisions that have completely disrupted real estate markets in choice vacation spots such as Cabo San Lucas, Mexico. According to the market research firm Ragatz Associates, sales to destination clubs and fractionally owned real estate partnerships more than doubled to $2 billion in 2006 from $1 billion in 2004. Annual sales were under $500 million as recently as 2003.

Since Steve Case took over Exclusive Resorts, membership rolls have grown so fast that the club is having a hard time closing on enough property to accommodate all those new vacationers. Destination clubs as a rule try to maintain a ratio of six to eight members for each vacation house they own. By the time Exclusive Resorts' membership topped 2,400 in 2006, more than 200 names were stranded on a wait list because the company hadn't secured enough properties to stay within that ideal membership-to-property ratio.

Exclusive Resorts, now by far the industry leader, already boasts a real estate portfolio that exceeds $1 billion in value. Case's five-year goal of 10,000 members implies that the company will need to buy at least 1,000 more vacation homes in that brief time frame—approximately $3 billion worth of prime resort real estate. Case brags that thanks to Exclusive Resorts' buying power, developers are approaching them early on and offering first dibs on homes in some of the best remaining resort locations in the entire world.

Far from diluting the product, this growth actually benefits club members. The more members a club has, the more destinations it can offer for the same fee. It's a business philosophy based on the "network effect," in which the relative value of each membership in a network rises as more members sign up. When Case was presented with a developer's offer to sell a single high-end condominium unit in Telluride, Colorado, Case decided they might as well buy nine units instead, at a total cost of over $30 million. The company is now contracting with developers for twenty units at a time in choice seasonal locations, so as not to frustrate too many members with limited availability.

The basic concept behind fractional ownership clubs is relatively simple: Instead of an individual buyer purchasing an individual vacation home, a group of buyers acquire access to one or more properties. Ownership structures are as diverse as the clubs themselves, ranging from so-called residence clubs, which usually offer true fractional ownership of salable real estate, to destination clubs such as Exclusive Resorts, which may sell members access to real estate owned by the club in exchange for a membership fee. Even this distinction is blurring, however, as residence clubs establish reciprocal arrangements with other clubs. But while technical forms of property ownership vary, all fractional ownership clubs lay claim to the same value proposition: that you can enjoy all the benefits of a second home with none of the troubles *and* have a better experience while you're there. To make the proposition even more worry-free, most clubs promise to refund a large percentage—usually 80 percent—of the membership fee to any member who wants to leave.

Web sites and marketing materials for destination clubs are almost comically similar in their portrayals of sumptuously appointed villas, shimmering infinity pools, and vistas of incomparable natural beauty—skiing in the mountains, sunbathing on the beach, museum-hopping in the great cities of the world. The marketing for Exclusive Resorts has a slightly different look and feel, however, that reflect Case's status as a Middle-Class Billionaire who is selling to Middle-Class Millionaires. Though it has its share of postcard-pretty scenery, the Exclusive Resorts Web site puts happy and satisfied club members—mainly families with children—front and center. There is a multimedia testimonial from two grade-school-age boys who sit with their bare feet resting on a green velvet couch. Mostly, what they talk about is how they like Exclusive Resorts so much better than their old vacation homes.

In an interview with *Brandweek* magazine in 2006, Matt Garrett, the chief of market research at Exclusive Resorts, said the Web site is part of "Faces," a marketing campaign coordinated with the company's print advertising and direct-mail efforts. The "Faces" campaign was created by Resorts' ad agency in response to a survey of 1,000 prospective members. "Our members average 49 [in age] and have teenage kids," Garrett told *Brandweek*. "For them, it's not about the residence. It's about their experience and maintaining bonds with family. That's what keeps them up at night." Garrett's survey results mirror our own research into the minds and behaviors of Middle-Class Millionaires. Here are people with common middle-class values who use their wealth to express those values much more intensely—and put them into action more consistently—than any other members of the middle class.

Like coaching and concierge services (which play a large part in residence and destination club concepts), fractional ownership is a business model that has flourished in lockstep with the emergence of the Middle Class Millionaire. Members of destination clubs are overwhelmingly drawn from the ranks of today's working rich. Exclusive Resorts describes its target demographic as households with a net worth of about $2.5 million—almost identical to the median demographic of our own Middle-Class Millionaire survey sample. Most club marketing directors will note, as we have, that the number of such households is expected to grow enormously in the next ten years.

Respondents to our own survey reflect this increasing level of interest in fractional ownership clubs among the affluent. Ten percent of the Middle-Class Millionaires we surveyed already have a membership in some form of fractionally owned real estate. Another 41 percent say they expect to buy such a membership within the next three years. Members of Exclusive Resorts now pay at least $185,000 to join (along with annual fees of $9,500) in order to receive access to large, luxurious vacation homes valued at $3 million or more. These figures likely explain why none of our middle-class sample currently belongs to a fractional ownership club and why less than 1 percent—just twelve out of 3,128 we surveyed—ever anticipates doing so.

Those of us with fewer assets can appreciate the fact that fractional ownership clubs have already begun to scale down their offerings to reach a wider, less affluent market. Membership at Exclusive Resorts originally cost more than $300,000 for forty-five days of vacationing each year, but the company soon came out with a fifteen-day membership plan for $185,000. Company officials say they may develop a more affordable and separately branded club featuring smaller, less valuable homes. Today's most modestly priced destination club, Denver-based High Country Club, requires $20,000 for an affiliate membership, plus

$4,200 in annual dues. The club's 110 members have access to twenty-two homes with an average value of $850,000 in locations as varied as the Bahamas, Costa Rica, Lake Tahoe, and London. Purchasing a similarly priced vacation home would require $170,000 down and monthly mortgage payments over $4,000.

The whole notion of owning just a piece of something great has been spreading throughout the economy in recent years. In its December 2005 issue, *Entrepreneur* magazine dubbed fractional ownership one of five "burning issues business owners are thinking about," a list that included energy-efficient construction and socially responsible business practices. *Forbes* magazine's rundown of seven luxury trends that year put fractional ownership at the top of the list. Milton Pedraza, CEO of the influential Luxury Institute, has hailed what he calls "the luxury access revolution." Citing destination clubs as a prime example, Pedraza wrote in 2006 that "membership-based access programs are breaking new ground in giving access to pure experiences—selling utility without the hassles of ownership."

Name any luxury item that's much more fun to use than it is to maintain, and in Middle-Class Millionaire America you're likely to find someone making a business of replacing its conspicuous consumption with worry-free experiences. Whether it's recreational vehicles, sports cars, even designer gowns, handbags, and jewelry, it seems inevitable that when middle-class values intersect with Millionaire Intelligence, pride of ownership at some point gives way to hardheaded practical considerations of how best to spend one's time and money.

Thirteen years before Case contacted Exclusive Resorts, an advertising executive named Steve Dering dreamed up an idea that essentially launched the multibillion-dollar fractional ownership real estate industry. In the late 1980s, Dering was running a small ad agency in Park

City, Utah, where most of his clients were developers doing booming business in luxury vacation condominiums. As prices for new units started exceeding $1 million with increasing regularity, Dering began to wonder how much higher prices could go for homes that were only rarely occupied.

During a conversation with a developer, Dering remembers asking, "The person who buys a condo from you for a million-two, how often will he use it?" The answer was about five weeks per year. A typical Deer Valley condo owner might visit for three weeks during ski season and for maybe another two weeks in the summer.

While owners of less expensive units often earn a few dollars by placing their units in the development's rental pool during weeks when they're not in Deer Valley, the developer told Dering that condos costing $500,000 and up were rarely rented out. Those owners usually have too much invested in their furnishings to share them with strangers. So for the privilege of skiing Deer Valley's magnificent slopes for three, maybe four weeks a year, most high-end property buyers were bearing by themselves all the maintenance fees and amortization costs of those half-million-dollar condos. "You do the math," says Dering now, "and that's an awfully expensive day of skiing."

Dering's big idea was this: If developers sold the exact same units as furnished properties under a fractional ownership plan, with each buyer getting a one-sixth share of a unit, everyone in the deal would make out better. Buyers would pay much less—perhaps $130,000 for a one-sixth share of a condo that would normally sell for $750,000—and the developer would net more revenue. The crowning touch was that if the annual maintenance fee remained fairly high, the owners could enjoy a whole new range of hotel-style concierge services. At Deer Valley Club, Dering's first project and the first of its kind anywhere, the staff would take all your ski equipment from storage and lay it out for you in your own locker before your arrival. All your clothes and personal items would come up from storage, too. You'd be picked up at the airport and taken to your unit, which would be prepared to your specifications. If you wanted, even the refrigerator would be stocked with food. The whole premise behind Deer Valley Club was to provide an alternative to the vacation home: one that reduced the financial commitment, eliminated the worries and hassles of vacation homeownership, and added hotel-quality service. "We had people who literally could leave their office in L.A. in a suit and tie, go to the airport, ski at Deer Valley, and then go right back to the office," he recalls. No bags. No packing.

Like a lot of people with good ideas, Steve Dering was ahead of his time, which meant he had to go through years of false starts and frustrations before that idea paid off for him. He took on his first fractional ownership project with no background in real estate development and no experience in the hospitality business. But he had plenty of expertise in sales and marketing in the Park City area, and he knew the Deer Valley ski clientele very well.

A Maryland native, Dering had been lured by the skiing life to Utah's Wasatch Mountains in 1973, when Park City was little more than a worn-out mining town with a questionable future as a ski resort. Back then, if you'd predicted that Park City would host the 2002 Winter Olympics, the locals would have called you crazy. But when the Deer Valley Resort opened in 1981, Park City was on the map for good as a major ski destination. In the years before he opened his own advertising business, Steve Dering worked for the resort as its first director of marketing.

From what he knew about the skiers who pour into Deer Valley every winter, Dering was certain that a good number of those who couldn't afford a $750,000 condominium would jump at the chance to invest in a one-sixth share of one. The idea just made sense to him. "People have been doing this forever," he says now. "People would gather up three or four friends and go buy a vacation home. I used to joke that the only difference is, we're finding the friends for you."

Not long after he had that eureka moment while talking to the condominium developer, Dering and a partner started the tedious spadework of researching the ownership structures of other resort developments and drawing up legal papers to establish the new enterprise. After hours of meetings with lawyers—more hours than Dering says he cares to remember—Deer Valley Club was hatched in 1989 in partnership with a big New York developer. They located an ideal site in a convenient "ski-in, ski-out" location adjacent to Deer Valley Resort. The developer signed a large Japanese corporation to finance the construction costs. Only then did the really hard work of selling a completely unfamiliar concept begin.

If the Deer Valley Club sounds to you like little more than "time-shares on steroids" (as one early prospect put it), you've hit on the biggest marketing obstacle Dering faced. In the upscale market he was trading in, time-shares were pure poison. While a few companies, such as Disney, are known for running respectable time-share operations, the industry as a whole suffers an image problem from overaggressive marketing and the simple fact that time-shares have proven to be very poor investments. "If any of our buyers caught a whiff of time-share they'd be out the door," Dering says now. "One of my mantras was, we're not going to have anything that's color-coded or named after a precious metal. We're not going to have red season and blue season, or silver weeks and gold weeks. We're not selling 'weeks.'" Selling by the week is a time-share marketing technique, he says, and he knew that's not what his high-end buyers would want. "They're interested in a very upscale, service-intensive club where they have a deeded real estate ownership."

So Dering started framing this new idea as a variation on a more familiar institution: the country club. One of Deer Valley's key selling points was that although you were guaranteed three weeks of skiing per year, you could visit the club more often at no extra charge on a space-available basis. Any nights not reserved more than thirty days in advance could be snapped up on a first-come, first-serve basis. In the course of a year, it would mean that if some club members were rarely there, more visiting opportunities opened up for other members at no extra charge. In this sense, Deer Valley Club was like a prestigious country club for golfers. Each member owns an equal share of equity in the golf course and its facilities, but some members inevitably put in more tee time than others. "Finally, a country club for skiers" was the title for one of the Deer Valley Club marketing materials. To this day, Dering says, golfers understand fractional ownership better than anyone.

By 1990, Deer Valley Club had secured reservation deposits representing more than $10 million in sales. Start of construction was not far off when Deer Valley Club's Japanese backer pulled out. With construction financing gone, the project was dead, and all the reservation deposits had to be returned. Dering was back at square one. Though he had managed to prove that his concept had willing buyers, he no longer had a project to sell them.

Through it all, Dering was still running his ad agency, though not very well. "One of the best business decisions I ever made was sitting down with my right-hand person there and giving him fifty percent of the business," Dering says now. He basically told his top manager that he was stepping back, that the ad agency was his to run. "I said, 'Look, I've got to see this thing through. It's either going to work or it's not going to work.' I didn't want to look back and think the reason it didn't work is because I gave it a half-assed effort."

It so happened that another condominium project was planned for a site right across the road from the spot where Dering's previous project had fallen through. Dering managed to persuade the developers of this new site to work with him and sell their units through fractional ownership. Originally, the developers' business plan called for selling the entire development to individual buyers for a total of $13 million. By the time the new Deer Valley Club was sold out, fractional buyers had ponied up a total of $22 million. It was as if Steve Dering had found the development team a bag filled with $9 million lying in the snow. Dering's reward was that he saw almost none of it.

"We got squeezed and squeezed and squeezed," he says now. In the long course of construction, every time the developers faced some unforeseen setback or a rise in material costs, they would threaten to sell the development to individual buyers unless Dering gave back a portion of his interest in the project or agreed to eat more of the sales office expenses. "They kept threatening to go back the other way," Dering says. "They weren't purposely testing the courage of my convictions, but that's how it turned out." The only thing that kept him afloat financially was the health of the real estate market at the time. As his own personal home rose in value, he refinanced his mortgage at least three times, using each occasion to pull out more cash to live on.

The success of the Deer Valley Club nonetheless gave wings to Dering's new concept of the fractionally owned "residence club" as a country club for skiers. Other Rocky Mountain ski resort developers brought him in as a consultant. He went on to help build residence clubs at the Franz Klammer Lodge in Telluride, Colorado, and the Christie Club in Steamboat Springs, Colorado. He and his team kept tweaking and refining their service offerings. They started offering to stock refrigerators after one skier complained that she didn't like waiting in ski lift lines, and she certainly didn't come to Deer Valley to wait in grocery store checkout lines. One of his favorite comments from a fractional owner is one that he's used repeatedly in residence club marketing materials: "The only thing I have to worry about is when I'm coming back."

The ski resort market is a fairly limited one, however, and Dering was sure that residence clubs would work well in any vacation destination where rising real estate prices were making second homes prohibitively expensive. In 1999, he helped a developer put together a residence club in Manhattan as part of a hotel development not far from Lincoln Center. By selling one-eighth shares in eighty-two apartments, Phillips Club, the first urban residence club in the nation, opened in 2000 with sales exceeding $100 million. Its success inspired a spate of imitators, including Miami's Setai Club, whose founding members included Boris

Becker, Janet Jackson, and Heidi Klum. The club is located within the forty-story Setai Hotel, and owner/member privileges include chauffeured transportation and access to the club's "high-end cruising boats."

Today Dering's company, DCP International, is involved in thirty residence club projects, all in various stages of development, including a fifteenth-century building in Florence with 300-year-old frescoes.

Dering says he remains surprised that residence clubs didn't take off much sooner. "It made so much sense to me, I didn't understand why everyone didn't get it right away," he says. "But people are busy. It's hard to get their attention, and it's hard to get them to think in a new way."

Of course, what also contributed to Dering's problems back in 1990 was that the market for what he was selling wasn't nearly as large as it is today. There just weren't that many Middle-Class Millionaires when he started out. Hockey legend Wayne Gretzky used to say that "a good hockey player plays where the puck is. A great hockey player plays where the puck is going to be." In 1990, Dering was playing where the market was going to be, not where it was at the time. There might have been as few as 700,000 families with a net worth of $5 million or more in 1990. By 2005 that number had more than doubled. Steve Dering had a good idea, but before the market could catch up with him, the market may have needed the better part of ten years to fill up with Middle-Class Millionaires.

As a result, the same Park City real estate brokers who once laughed at Steve Dering are selling residence club memberships side by side with condominiums and private homes. Ski resort towns encourage developers to build residence clubs instead of single-owner properties, since, as community leaders figured out, fractional units bring six times as many affluent visitors through the local economy. On the original site where Dering had first planned the Deer Valley Club, another developer eventually came in to build a fractional ownership club called the Residences at the Chateaux. Dering consulted on the project. One-sixth shares of a four-bedroom penthouse there cost $695,000.

The rapid growth of fractional ownership clubs is the most visible expression of a much more widespread phenomenon in our affluent society: At some point our things—with their demands on our time and attention—start owning us. Richard Keith, the president of a club called Private Escapes, told the *Hartford Courant* in 2005 that his membership ranks are filled with fed-up former owners of vacation homes. "What they found is after the honeymoon period of owning that second single home, the real-life requirements start to creep in," Keith said. "So you're spending your vacation time not on vacation, but at Ace hardware." Even those who aren't do-it-yourselfers may prefer destination clubs to second homes because, as a 2006 *Harvard Business Review* article pointed out, they "dread spending weeks at a time staring at the walls of the same $2 million estate." The article, co-authored by Milton Pedraza, was entitled "What Is Luxury Without Variety?"

That question is now being asked every day in a wide range of luxury businesses. It's by no means a mass movement, but all around the country we see Middle-Class Millionaires starting up enterprises based on a fractional ownership or membership club model. This is partly because they see a business opportunity, but it's also because they feel the way Steve Dering originally felt about the residence club when it was no more than an idea in his head: *It just makes so much sense.* More often than not, these Middle-Class Millionaires started out as dissatisfied customers who grew determined to find—or invent—a better way.

In 2003, Jim Palmer was looking forward to the travel opportunities that early retirement would afford him and his wife, and the one place he relished exploring was America. The couple had been to any number of international vacation destinations over the years, including Mexico, Hawaii, and British Columbia, and Palmer had seen much of the world through several decades of business travel in the electronics industry. (It was a twenty-nine-hour trek home to San Diego from

Malaysia that convinced him it was time to quit.) But there were many places in the continental United States that they still had not seen, and they decided the best way to get to them would be in a motor home.

When Palmer started pricing high-end motor homes, however, the numbers gave him a shock. By his estimation, a good-sized luxury motor home would cost him and his wife more in monthly payments and maintenance than if they spent every vacation flying first class, staying at the best hotels, and eating in the best restaurants in the world. "Why would I want to do this?" he wondered. "If I gave my wife the choice of two weeks in the Four Seasons Hotel and two weeks in a motor home, you know which way she's going. And by the way, we'd save money at the Four Seasons."

Though Palmer, then fifty-six, was confident of his math, he wondered if one of his cost assumptions might be off. He walked into a couple of local RV dealerships and showed them his analysis. "They said, 'Yes, your assumptions are correct. That's what it costs,'" Palmer recalls. "I told them, 'Thanks for your honesty, but I'm no longer a potential customer. I'm not willing to spend this much money for this experience.'"

The fractional market for jets, yachts, and vacation homes had always fascinated Jim Palmer. He considered fractional ownership as something particularly well suited for Americans, because he knew that in general Americans, unlike Europeans, rarely take lengthy vacations. Many affluent Americans, those with the resources to travel, find it hard to get away. So even if you can afford a whole boat or a whole house, why buy one if you hardly ever use it? And why buy a whole motor home?

So Jim Palmer sat down with little more than a good idea and a legal pad and invented an industry. He estimated that his new company, CoachShare, could sell a $250,000 forty-foot Monaco Diplomat luxury motor coach in eight fractions that would give each partial owner five weeks of usage per year (leaving twelve weeks of the year free allows each partial owner more flexible scheduling). If the Diplomat were sold off after three years, the net cost of ownership for each one-eighth owner might add up to just $11,000 per year, versus $46,000 per year under sole ownership. The annualized financial picture gets a little brighter for the sole owner who hangs on to the motor home for five or six years, but Palmer says that after about five years, "you no longer want that motor home. You want to move up. It's just like a boat. You want more power, more space, more features."

By the start of his third year in business, Palmer had twenty-four clients sharing three Monaco Diplomats, each with a sleeping capacity for six, satellite television, satellite radio, and a washer and dryer. When a CoachShare member's reservation date comes up, the member's own personal set of monogrammed bed linens, towels, and robes is retrieved from a sealed and labeled container in the company's storage facility. Dishes, glasses, flatware, tissues, paper towels, and kitchen appliances—all the things a family would typically need to stock in a motor coach rental—are in their place and ready for use. The refrigerator is stocked on request, and a database records whether the family prefers Coke or Pepsi. When the Diplomat is ready for use, it is driven to the member's door. Palmer says he tries to make the experience conform as much as possible to that of a five-star hotel, and he even uses the same linen and bath supplier as the Four Seasons.

While it continues to maintain this degree of service for all its members, CoachShare is branching into new membership levels. The company now maintains a wait list for prospective members who want to share a $500,000 forty-three-foot Monaco Dynasty and has just started a one-sixteenth membership plan for the smaller, more maneuverable thirty-foot Monaco Monarch at a purchase price of less than $10,000 per member. With sixteen shares of ownership, the thirty-foot model allows for only two weeks per year of usage, but just as we found in our survey, that's about all the time Palmer's Middle-Class Millionaire clients have for vacationing.

Nearly all of CoachShare's customers are successful businesspeople—classic Middle-Class Millionaires—and it's Palmer's general observation that the more successful they have been, the faster they embrace his idea. Not one member, he says, has bought a fraction of a motor coach just because he couldn't afford the entire vehicle. "Some of them," he says with a laugh, "could write a check and buy three or four of these! But for them to feel good about what they've just done, they have to feel that it was smart. They're attracted to smart financial decisions."

In fact, much like Steve Dering's early experiences with Deer Valley Club, the chief obstacle to getting CoachShare up and running wasn't a lack of willing customers. It was a lack of willing partners who would take a chance on a new idea. Motor home dealers and manufacturers balked at cooperating with Palmer out of fear that fractionals, rather than expanding the pool of buyers, would actually cannibalize their sales. Another problem was insurance. Palmer estimates he contacted thirty insurers, including those that already insured fractionally owned jets and boats, before he found one willing to write up a policy for a motor coach with eight owners and almost twice as many eligible drivers.

CoachShare's start-up hurdles were almost identical to the ones endured by Exotic Car Share, the nation's first membership sports car driving club. Its founders, George and Kathy Kiebala, had started in the auto business running D &V's Auto Nook, a suburban Chicago outfit that rented climate-controlled garage space for collector automobiles. The Kiebalas couldn't help noticing that most of the Mercedeses, Ferraris, and Porsches in their care very rarely saw the light of day—some just a few weeks out of the year. In the late 1990s, they decided to expand their business by buying and maintaining a small fleet of specialty cars that paying club members "could sign out, like books from a library." They called it Exotic Car Share, and though it was a nice idea, it took forever to get off the ground. George Kiebala spent at least eighteen months negotiating with insurance companies before he could get one to cooperate. Local car dealers were loath to work with the Kiebalas. Dealers were unenthusiastic about making their exclusive vehicles more popular and visible on the street, fearing Exotic Car Share would dilute their brands' value while reducing the pool of available customers.

In 2001, the Kiebalas spun off Curvy Road, a fractional ownership organization that operates almost exactly like CoachShare and has locations in Beverly Hills, suburban Chicago, and New York. For a one-tenth share in a Bentley Continental GT, members pay $10,000 for four weeks of drive time. The car is delivered to your home or office, freshly cleaned and detailed. Exotic Car Share continues to operate only in the Chicago area and operates more as a membership rental club, which keeps costs relatively low by pre-screening its members. The luxury Web site Helium Report recently pointed out that renting a Lamborghini Gallardo from Exotic Car Share costs $330 per day for a weekend, a bargain compared to the rates at non-membership rental outfits in Las Vegas and Miami, where the same car rents for at least $1,499 per day.

Today there are more than a dozen car clubs around the country that offer either membership access or outright fractional ownership in a bewildering variety of points systems, membership plans, and partial ownership arrangements. There seems to be no end to the variety of ways that the responsibility of ownership can be transferred, shifted, diffused, or submerged, just so that the thing itself can be enjoyed. As John Caron, the president of the Otto Club in Boston, told the *New York Times*, "Ownership is not the privilege. Access is the privilege. Ownership is the burden."

This is a belief that has been stated in as many different ways as entrepreneurs have found to lift that burden of ownership. If, in the words of one fractional ownership entrepreneur, we live in a "post-consumer, post-asset-based society," one place where this concept is being readied for introduction to a much larger audience is in a small ten-person office in Seattle, where a tight cadre of former Nordstrom employees is trying to turn $12 million worth of venture capital into a billion-dollar bonanza.

The name of the company is Bag Borrow or Steal. It was founded in 2004 when a pair of Florida entrepreneurs marveled at how their wives' closets filled up with expensive and discarded handbags and vowed to do something about it. Netflix at the time was making headlines because it was beating back Johnny-come-lately imitators with deep pockets, including Wal-Mart and Blockbuster. What if, they wondered, designer bags could be rented out and rotated like Netflix's DVDs?

By 2005, they had found a venture capital backer in the form of Impact Venture Group, which is headed by Adam Dell, brother of computer billionaire Michael Dell. Adam Dell managed to persuade Mike Smith, the former president of Nordstrom.com and Lands' End, to bring Bag Borrow or Steal into the big time. Smith moved the company to Seattle and brought two key associates from Nordstrom to help him build the business, which, Smith proclaimed, would someday be worth $1 billion. That prediction was good enough, evidently, for Madrona Venture Group, the Seattle firm that gave early backing to Amazon.com and HomeGrocer.com. In March 2006, Madrona gave Bag Borrow or Steal $8.26 million in second-round financing, and by June 2007 the company had raised another $15 million from other venture groups.

Bag Borrow or Steal works like this: Each member pays a monthly fee ranging from $20 to $275 and then picks out a handbag or jewelry item to receive by mail. She can keep it as long as she likes, or send it back in exchange for something else. It doesn't matter as long as she keeps paying her monthly fee. "Imagine having a virtual closet with a wider selection than any one individual could ever buy," Dell told *BusinessWeek Online* when the Madrona financing round was announced. He pointed out that Bag Borrow or Steal is not about affordable luxury—it's for people who can afford to buy expensive bags but prefer more variety.

Even with 250,000 members, the Seattle company has more than its share of doubters, but it has a healthy number of imitators, too. It could be ten years ahead of its time, as residence clubs once were, and as CoachShare may prove to be. Clearly Mike Smith has more than bags and jewelry in mind when he predicts $1 billion in sales. Perhaps, with Madrona's money in hand, he has an eye toward becoming the post-ownership Amazon.com, the place to go for everything that's more fun to use than it is to own.

If there is one intriguing, elusive element that all these forms of commerce have in common, it is the level of trust and mutuality embedded in the notion of "sharing" ownership or joining a club. They tend to bring people together in the name of a few common values, such as the notion that it is better and smarter to share something good for a brief period of time than to hoard it for yourself. While these business models relieve their users of the burden of ownership, they must trust them instead with the responsibility of sharing, of not messing things up for the next person. "Club members," as they are called, do not congregate as they might at a country club, but as with the country club, they expect one another to take care of the property they hold in common, however briefly, whether it's the multimillion-dollar homes in Exclusive Resorts' portfolio or the $3,000 handbag from Bag Borrow or Steal. Brenda Kaufman, a fashion consultant for Bag Borrow or Steal, told MSNBC in 2007 that most members take care of a bag "as if they were borrowing it from their best friend." The influence that shared affluence has over these "club" members actually makes managing these companies in some important respects much simpler than if their assets were open to the general public, as are hotel rooms or rental cars.

With all the benefits of exclusivity and shared values that they imply, it's not too hard to imagine these notions of fractional ownership and club membership extending to an entire community. To some extent, these forms already exist in condominiums, in planned suburbs with homeowner associations, and in "active adult" communities. In the next chapter, we'll visit a southern California community that embodies these new ideals of shared values, exclusive membership, and fractional ownership of public space so fully that it's an open question whether Ladera Ranch even needs a government.

CHAPTER EIGHT

"ROOTS AND WINGS"

In 1999, twenty-five-year-old Darren Murtha was sharing a one-bedroom apartment in Huntington Beach, California, with his fiancée, Susan, while the couple began scouting for a home in pricey Orange County. Just across the ravine south of his parents' place in Mission Viejo, some fifty miles southeast of downtown Los Angeles, Murtha noticed that the first phase of a sprawling new planned community had begun construction. He and Susan drove over to give it a look.

Murtha was working for a national homebuilder at the time, and he had his real estate broker's license, so he knew a little bit about the way large residential developments work. Builders are often eager to create a buzz about a new community, so they keep their prices low during the first phase in order to attract faster sales. There is also slightly less demand at first, because, as Murtha puts it, "a lot of people won't buy without seeing what they're going to get. They don't want to take that leap." Buyers who get in early at lower prices sometimes enjoy a big boost in their property values when subsequent phases attract more buyers and drive prices upward. The catch is that early buyers face the risk that the development might not live up to expectations or that the real estate market will go soft. They also have to put up with the hassles of living in a neighborhood that is still under construction.

As the couple walked the building site and chatted with workers in the plasterboard shells of the first few sample houses, they learned they were standing in the future Oak Knoll, the first of six "villages" within Ladera Ranch, a 4,000-acre community then projected to include 8,100 homes built in stages over the next dozen years. Oak Knoll looked a little different from most southern California subdivisions, even in its construction phase. The houses themselves were slightly smaller and bunched more closely together than similarly priced properties in Orange County, but they were also exceptionally attractive and varied in their architecture. Planners had compensated for what the houses lacked in private spaciousness by paying more attention to the surrounding public spaces. With its tree-lined sidewalks and garages set back from the street, Oak Knoll was designed to feel like a family-friendly place that would encourage walking, outdoor exercise, and children's play. A small "pocket park" was set aside at the end of each street, and a series of walking paths ran through the backyards, connecting the parks to a mountain-bike trail that would encircle the west side of the village.

Murtha liked what he saw, and not just because Oak Knoll felt so new and different. Some aspects of the neighborhood felt familiar in a comforting way. "My parents had bought in Mission Viejo when it was just starting," he explains. "I grew up there from the age of three, when it was just our street and then dirt from there on out. Eventually they built the elementary school that I walked to, and then they built the high school that I walked to." Oak Knoll, he began to think, might offer his and Susan's future children a new and improved version of what he had growing up.

Darren and Susan Murtha fell in love with at least two of the nine framed-out houses they walked through that day. A few months later, they earned the distinction of being the first homeowners to close on a mortgage in what would become the phenomenally successful community of Ladera Ranch. They paid just $270,000 for a three-bedroom house done in French country style. It may prove to be the smartest investment they ever made. Three years later, the value of their little French country house had risen so high that they were able to trade up to a larger house on a hillside in Avendale, then the newest Ladera Ranch village. The 3,000-square-foot house on Smoke Tree Drive, bought in 2003 for $650,000, is within walking distance of Oso Grande Elementary School, where their three-year-old son will start attending classes in a few years.

To Susan, Ladera's special design had given the people on her block a shared commitment to community-building. "Everyone seems more apt to meet their neighbors because they know that is what they are trying to create here," Susan told the *Orange County Register* in 2003. That article, which commemorated Ladera Ranch's fourth anniversary, quoted her neighbors' glowing accounts of Friday evening happy hours with canopies pitched out on the lawns and children running and playing underfoot. One testified to Ladera's success this way: "I really believe that they marketed Ladera as a community with families and block parties, and it attracted people with family-oriented values and principles." For the Murthas, this enviable lifestyle has also managed to vastly increase their personal wealth. It is nearly impossible to find a 3,000-square-foot house in Ladera Ranch today that is priced below $1 million.

In Chapter 3 we showed how Middle-Class Millionaires are remaking older suburban communities all over the country by replacing small houses with big ones in towns that have distinguished public schools and rising real estate values. Ladera Ranch is the next logical extension of this phenomenon—a Middle-Class Millionaire boomtown built completely from scratch. It is a community of almost 20,000 that has sprung to life in just seven years, tailor-made for the tastes and aspirations of the Middle-Class Millionaire.

Nearly everything that is special about Ladera Ranch—from its child-friendly neighborhoods to its profusion of clubs and activities to its walkable access to shops, schools, houses, and parks—either fulfills some primary value in the middle-class hierarchy of values or corresponds to one of our four points of Millionaire Intelligence. Ladera has a culture that exalts children, family, education, and quality of life—all the values our Middle-Class Millionaire survey respondents ranked highly with near unanimity. Activities that foster networking and self-betterment—essential to Millionaire Intelligence—are not only encouraged at Ladera Ranch but actually staffed and subsidized by a community tax on home sales.

On top of all this, the sheer uniqueness of Ladera Ranch in Orange County, a place more often identified with cookie-cutter Spanish-style tract housing, has made the town a magnet of sorts for affluent Early Adopters who bring with them a taste for novelty and risk. The result is a sociological experiment in what happens when a Middle-Class Millionaire ethos takes hold in a town with no traditions to confine it, no social problems to speak of, and, because it's so new, no local government.

Even in the midst of a national real estate slump in 2006 and 2007, home sales in Ladera Ranch remained fairly strong, thanks in part to homeowners who want to stay in the community. Forty percent of Ladera Ranch homebuyers are move-ups like the Murthas, giving the community one of the highest move-up rates in the county. These are people who keep increasing their bets on the community by buying bigger and bigger homes as they become available in the newer "villages" within Ladera Ranch. Far from being just a place for expressing affluence, Ladera Ranch has helped many of its residents achieve affluence through their investment in their homes. Ladera Ranch is so attractive to Middle-Class Millionaires that those who got in early enough have become Middle-Class Millionaires if they weren't already.

Although the land beneath Ladera Ranch was indeed once part of a vast cattle ranch and wheat farm, the name is, like so much of the community itself, a charming re-creation. For the past 120 years, the rolling pastureland surrounding the dry Horno Creek bed was owned by descendants of a cattleman named Richard O'Neill. In 1964, as Orange County's sprawl crept ever closer to their ranchlands, O'Neill family members started a development company, Rancho Mission Viejo (RMV), to manage the process of suburbanizing portions of their holdings. Their first project was Mission Viejo, where Darren Murtha grew up, an 11,000-acre planned community that is now a city of 95,000 residents. Two smaller planned communities followed in the 1980s and 1990s. The stage was set for development of the 4,000-acre parcel southeast of Mission Viejo, a place ranch hands had long called "El Horno"—the oven.

For all its warm and fuzzy appeal, Ladera Ranch is the product of careful consumer research and a hardheaded drive to maximize El Horno's profit potential. Surveys conducted by RMV and its development partners had detected a growing dissatisfaction with the quality of neighborhoods in southern California—including those developed by RMV. Particularly in Orange County, as prices continued to spiral upward, homebuyers were getting fed up with nearly identical houses lined up on sterile cul-de-sacs. A joke went around that residents needed to drive down the street clicking their garage door remotes just to find their homes. The question facing RMV was whether it could afford to take on the considerable expense of providing a more distinctive, village-like development at Ladera. Would homebuyers be ready to pay a large enough premium to make the risk and trouble worthwhile? If not, the joke would be on RMV.

To gain inspiration for how El Horno might be transformed into a premier "value-added" community called Ladera Ranch, planners working with RMV scouted out some of the older neighborhoods in southern California that had held up well over the years. Two of the towns they visited were Pasadena and Laguna Beach—communities that have come under the kind of teardown pressures from Middle-Class Millionaires that we detailed in Chapter 3. What the planners found in these places was a pleasant jumble of varied home styles, porches in the front, garages in the back, and people walking down tree-lined sidewalks. The challenge would be to reinterpret these architectural and design features for new construction in a new era. Right from the start, the design DNA for Ladera Ranch was identified in part by following the home-buying tracks left by Middle-Class Millionaires.

The 962 houses of Oak Knoll represented a toe-in-the-water test of the value-added approach for developing Ladera Ranch. On a per-square-foot basis, it is more costly to build architecturally varied homes with different floor plans than it is to create multiples of the same design, so each home was built a little smaller to keep within a certain targeted price point. Setting aside land for a pocket park every few blocks required the sacrifice of a lucrative homesite, so all the houses on the block had to be crowded a little closer to the street and closer to one another, also to contain costs. These little parks were often set aside on prime lots that offered the best views. "Other developers would say, 'You're crazy,'" recalls Paul Johnson, RMV's vice president of community development. "But you know, you can stick another house on the hilltop, or you can have a hilltop park that everyone can enjoy."

The design of Oak Knoll still owed as much to balance-sheet accounting as it did to planning and landscape architecture. Steve Kellenberg, leader of Ladera Ranch's master planning group, remembers hashing out with Johnson and other RMV officials just how far they wanted to go at every step of the process. For Oak Knoll, total development costs ended up budgeted at only 2 or 3 percent above what cranked-out tract housing on the same acreage might have cost. The difference, however, was that instead of a sunbaked garage-door-dominated bedroom community, Oak Knoll looked and felt like an authentic small town where children would feel safe to play in the streets and neighbors could interact spontaneously on the sidewalks.

Physical design was only half the story as the Oak Knoll phase of Ladera Ranch was readied for an August 1999 opening. The balance of Ladera's special appeal would come from a "community-building" organization, a professionally staffed community council run by RMV's chief development partner, the Arizona-based DMB Associates. A handful of paid administrators would run regular seasonal events at Ladera and assist with organizing activity clubs and community projects such as fund-raisers to help the schools. At the height of the Internet boom, Oak Knoll would also be advertised as Orange County's first "wired community." All the homes were provided with high-speed Internet access, and a special residents-only intranet system called LaderaLife would help new homeowners with similar interests find one another. The hoped-for result, said an RMV official, was "hastening the development of social institutions" in Ladera. DMB had already tested these ideas at one of their very-high-end planned communities in Arizona. Now they were scaling the community council idea for the first time in a community of homes priced below $1 million.

About 22,000 people came through Oak Knoll during its grand opening weekend. Closings came fast, spurred in part by low interest rates and a booming demand for new houses in Orange County. At one point 300 families entered a lottery for nine houses. The average household income of the first new homebuyers was close to $100,000, ranking them in the top 12 percent of income nationally. IRS records show that about one-quarter of them filed as either full-time or part-time sole proprietors of businesses—a rate nearly ten percentage points higher than the national average. Overwhelmingly, the buyers were under forty-five years old and either had young children or were in the process of starting families, a pattern that would continue throughout the community's build-out. A 2005 *Orange County Register* article recounted how, when a couple new to Ladera Ranch held an impromptu housewarming party on their block, seven of the ten women who attended were visibly pregnant. For the newcomer it brought to mind a certain movie about a mythical 1950s small town. "It really feels like we're living in Pleasantville," she told the paper.

As new villages were developed, RMV took bigger risks with the design. Ladera's Township District is a classic example of genial New Urbanism, with schools, parks, houses, apartments, shops, and restaurants all within walking distance of one another. It meets the "Popsicle test" for livability set out by New Urbanist guru Andrés Duany, who believes that every residential neighborhood should be designed so an eight-year-old can ride a bike to the nearest ice cream shop without needing to cross a single dangerous street.

To serve some of Ladera's entrepreneurial work-at-home population, the company experimented with Front Street, a subtle twenty-two-home business plaza tucked away inside one of the residential villages. The innovative design of the buildings allows a realtor, a hairdresser, and a day-care provider, among others, to bring employees and customers through one door and use another door to enter their living quarters. It was such a breakthrough for suburban design that one impressed urban historian told the *Los Angeles Times,* "This will be in the architecture history books in 20 years."

In 2004, RMV's work with market researchers revealed an affluent and underserved population of "cultural creatives," defined as educated, socially aware people who craved nest-like homes fronted by cozy courtyards. The result was a unique "green village" within Ladera called Terramor. Most of the 1,200 residences have garages in the back and front doors facing each other across landscaped pedestrian lanes leading to the wide, car-free Central Paseo Trail. Sixty percent of the detached homes in Terramor were built with rooftop solar panels, making it instantly one of the largest solar communities in the nation. Prices for very small homes in Terramor started at $350,000 and went all the way up to $1 million as RMV, according to plan, kept pushing land prices to get an improved return on all the community investments it had made up to that point.

By the time Ladera Ranch began its final phase in 2006, a 1,006-home gated community called Covenant Hills, RMV was able to command prices of $1 million or more just for vacant homesites—prices more commonly seen in Beverly Hills or Orange County building sites offering clear blue-ocean views. One Ladera Ranch move-up couple spent $1.2 million for a lot in Covenant Hills so they could build a $5 million home with an apartment for the husband's parents. The family had considered moving to a home at the exclusive Nellie Gail Ranch in Laguna Hills, but they decided that Ladera, with all its activities, would be a better place for their grade-school son to grow up in.

There is a large plaque inside the foyer of the Craftsman-styled Oak Knoll clubhouse emblazoned with a stirring quote from the southern author Hodding Carter. Under the title "Roots and Wings," it says: "There are only two lasting bequests we can hope to give our children. One is roots; the other wings."

"Roots and Wings" is an aspirational sentiment that appears often in Ladera Ranch literature. Read a certain way, it can lend a double meaning to the phrase "value-added." Much of the "value-added" content of Ladera Ranch—what sets it apart, for instance, from the previous community RMV developed just a few miles away—reflects an investment in very specific personal values. As we've shown throughout this book, values-driven spending can be an effective sorting mechanism for Middle-Class Millionaires. Whether it's for concierge health care or vacation clubs, values-based spending is one of the surest ways of bringing people together who put a high value on the same things in life.

In earlier chapters, we've pointed out that while Middle-Class Millionaires assign about the same high value to educating their children as the middle class do, Middle-Class Millionaires are more apt to apply that value in deciding where they choose to live. "The school system" was cited as a very important or extremely important reason for choosing a community by 78 percent of Middle-Class Millionaires, compared to 57 percent of the middle class. The members of the middle class were almost as likely to cite the importance of "convenience to work" (53 percent), which was deemed important by just 8.5 percent of the Middle-Class Millionaires.

At first it wasn't possible to select Ladera Ranch for its schools, because they were still under construction when the first families moved into Oak Knoll. On the other hand, Ladera Ranch is located in the Capistrano United School District, one of Orange County's more highly regarded districts. And perhaps just as important, anyone could see by the nature of the community that the schools would be well supported—which has turned out to be true. The PTA for Ladera Ranch Elementary School has no fewer than nineteen different committees, and an education foundation sprang up almost immediately to fund supplemental programs at Ladera's schools. After only three years in operation, Ladera Ranch Middle School won a State Distinguished School award, one of just 171 out of 2,400 California schools.

Perhaps the only thing conspicuously missing from the community that has everything is government. Except for the schools, the library, and occasional traffic enforcement by the Orange County sheriff's department, there aren't too many signs of a governmental presence in Ladera Ranch. Although Ladera has its own zip code, it exists legally as an unincorporated area of Orange County and has no municipal government. Most routine municipal functions—outdoor lighting, trash pickup, street cleaning, park maintenance—are handled by private contractors under the direction of Ladera Ranch's homeowners' association. The Orange County sheriff investigates crimes in Ladera, but routine patrols are manned by a private security firm. Even fire protection requires the community to enter into a contractual relationship with the Orange County Fire Authority.

In some little ways, Orange County's government has always had the potential to hold Ladera back. The whole physical layout of Ladera Ranch would have been impossible if Kellenberg and RMV hadn't made a strong case for dozens of variances to the zoning code, involving everything from the design of streetlights, to how close together the houses can be built, to how wide the sidewalks and streets needed to be. One reason why so many newer suburban streets feel barren and needlessly broad is that fire companies routinely insist that every street provide a comfortable turning radius for their largest fire trucks. Kellenberg's planning team would have liked to make most of Ladera Ranch's streets even narrower and more intimate than they are. Instead, the team persuaded the county government to allow landscaped medians in certain places and tapered street widths near the crosswalks.

Similar road regulations initially stymied efforts to get more Terramor residents to use neighborhood electric vehicles—those little "golf-carty" things that Tesla Motors founder Martin Eberhard found so objectionable in Chapter 4. Each of the 1,200 residences in Terramor has an electrical hookup to charge the vehicles, but they are illegal for operation on any road with a speed limit above 35 mph—and all of Ladera's main through roads were posted originally at 40 mph. Orange County traffic engineers balked at requests to compromise their methods for establishing speed limits, but a concerted effort by a group of residents, formed as the "transportation club" with the help of DMB's community-building organization, managed to change the engineers' minds.

Aside from occasional complaints that the sheriff's department should do more about speeding and unsafe driving, there's very little sense in Ladera that government is something they need. It matches up fairly well with our survey of Middle-Class Millionaires, which shows a sharp split between the way they and the middle class regard the reliability of government institutions. Fifty-four percent of the middle class told us they are "highly confident of the government's ability to help them in case of a natural disaster or terrorist attack." Just 14 percent of the Middle-Class Millionaires made the same claim. On the other hand, 62 percent of Middle-Class Millionaires say they are "taking significant precautions to take care of themselves and their loved ones in case of a natural disaster or terrorist attack." Only 19.5 percent of the middle-class survey respondents said they were taking similar precautions.

Our survey found, on the other hand, that Middle-Class Millionaires remain interested in politics, even if their view of government has grown jaundiced. About 92 percent of them have voted in a national or local election in the last three years, compared with just 70.5 percent of middle-class individuals. Middle-Class Millionaires hold back, however, on direct political involvement. Only 6 percent of them have run for or held public office, compared with 24 percent of the middle class. And while they are almost three times as likely to have donated money to support a politician or candidate (57 percent vs. 23 percent), just 2 or 3 percent say they have volunteered for a political campaign or with a political party, compared with about 24 percent of the middle class. In other words, if the choice is between donating money and donating time, Middle-Class Millionaires choose to write a check. Perhaps this makes sense considering their seventy-hour workweeks.

Middle-Class Millionaires are more likely to be Republicans in their political affiliation (57 percent vs. 31 percent Democrat), while our middle-class sample was almost evenly split. But Middle-Class Millionaires are more likely to have crossed party lines when voting in the past three years (82 percent vs. 63 percent for those in the middle class).

Issue by issue, Middle-Class Millionaires like their politics the way they like most things—customized and à la carte. Given the choice between being treated as customers or citizens, Middle-Class Millionaires would almost always prefer to be customers. As the concierge health care phenomenon showed us in Chapter 5, Middle-Class Millionaires are more likely to trust the profit motive in others than altruism or civic duty, because that's how they've attained their own position in life. Even the best-run city halls don't treat their citizens as well as a well-run bank or restaurant treats its preferred customers.

Take, for instance, the simple problem of dog droppings in the park. In most cities, failing to pick up after one's dog is punishable by a fine, but the laws are rarely, if ever, enforced. The result? Violators go unpunished, and the dog mess is still a problem. In Ladera Ranch, there is no law against leaving your dog's droppings in the park because there's no government to pass such a law. Instead, Ladera's management puts up signs requesting that you pick up after your dog, and it distributes disposable plastic "mutt mitts" for dog owners who forget to bring baggies on their own. But most important, Ladera contracts with an Orange County company called EntreManure to come and pick up after the negligent dog owners twice a week. The contract costs Ladera $120 per week, and EntreManure estimates it bags up about 240 pounds of pooch poop from Ladera every year.

This is a style of municipal management that seems to hold a great deal of appeal for Middle-Class Millionaires. LARMAC, the homeowners' association that oversees Ladera's day-to-day activities, draws its funding from monthly assessments that range from about $170 to $400 per month, depending on the value of the properties assessed. Addresses with special benefits pay special-benefits fees. For instance, houses along hillsides pay extra for their privileged views with a fee to landscape the slopes below their houses. It's government à la carte.

Funding for the community council's activities—the LaderaLife intranet and all the special events, club support, and other "soft" initiatives—comes from a different source, one that residents hardly feel at all. Ladera Ranch, like other planned communities, funds its community council with a fraction of a percent of each home sale. Thus excluded from regular assessments, these activities are safe from cost-conscious homeowners looking for a tax break.

"I like to say that the homeowners' association is like Darth Vader and the community council is Yoda," says Terry Randall, the DMB Associates vice president who serves as a liaison with Ladera. While the homeowners' association deals with difficult issues such as contractors and non-compliant residents, he says, "Yoda is looking to elevate the community."

Ladera Ranch's staff of six event planners spends tens of thousands of dollars per year putting on a Harvest Festival, a Spring Festival, and the biggest blowout of all each year, the Fourth of July. Yoda, it turns out, can come through when government fails. In 2006, some nearby towns were feeling a budget pinch and decided to cut back on their Fourth of July festivities, leaving their residents with no place to see fireworks. Many wound up in Ladera Ranch. It was a crowd the likes of which the community had never seen before. Some said there must have been 10,000 people in Founders Park. The food started to run out, and the event coordinator had to send some of his people to find an open supermarket so they could reprovision the concession stands.

All this built-in connectedness at Ladera Ranch has inevitably worked in the developer's favor. It builds community, and happy residents can form volunteer legions of sales representatives. In our own survey we saw that Middle-Class Millionaires are much more likely than the middle class to recommend their communities to other people. Ladera Ranch's real estate office estimates that two-thirds of sales prospects come from referrals generated by residents eager to get their friends and family to join them. The Influence of Affluence no doubt had a hand in the rapid build-out of Ladera Ranch.

On the other hand, Paul Johnson of RMV says he knew all along there was a risk involved in helping the residents get organized. "In giving them tools to organize," he says with a smile, "we realized that they might organize against *us*." Developers at many planned communities have avoided setting up intranets like LaderaLife for just that reason and also to avoid any thorny issues surrounding freedom of speech. In 2006,

Johnson and the DMB staff that moderates LaderaLife had to issue a six-month suspension to one Ladera Ranch resident, a professional Web designer, for what they determined was a lack of civility in his postings. The irate Web designer set up a competing Web site, LaderaPortal.com, and started using it to hammer away at the management of the community council and the operating costs of LaderaLife. In October 2006, during a rancorous election dispute over resident control of the council, LaderaPortal provided Ladera Ranch residents more detailed blow-by-blow coverage than either the local newspapers or LaderaLife.

In general, Johnson says he's never seen residents take such a strong hand in the life and management of a young planned community as quickly as they have at Ladera Ranch. "I've never seen them ignite at that speed before," Johnson says with an air of wonder about him. "We're way ahead of the timeline." Previous RMV communities, for instance, had taken eight to ten years to transition slowly from developer-run homeowner association boards to resident-run boards. Ladera Ranch residents have made the transition inside of two years. Johnson's intensive surveys and psychographic buyer research—which helped him create a planned community naturally appealing to Middle-Class Millionaires—did not prepare him for the cumulative effect of all that Millionaire Intelligence in one place.

At 1:10 P.M. on May 4, 2007, thirty-seven-year-old Lori Coble of Oak Knoll was driving toward home just a few miles north of Interstate 5 with her mother in the passenger seat beside her and her three small children in the backseat of her Chrysler Town & Country. A jam-up ahead suddenly caused traffic in Coble's lane to slow almost to a halt, but the driver of an eighteen-wheel tractor trailer behind her didn't react fast enough. The cab of the truck slammed into the back of the Coble minivan, shoving it forward into a Chevy Tahoe in front of it.

Lori Coble and her mother were seriously injured, but by the following morning, all three children—Katie, 2; Emma, 4; and Kyle, 5—had died.

It was a tragedy the likes of which the young community had never experienced, and expressions of grief and efforts at fund-raising to support the family began almost immediately. The trees throughout Ladera's neighborhoods were bedecked with pink and blue ribbons. One Ladera Ranch woman designed and printed up memorial windshield stickers to raise money for the family. A Ladera Ranch motorcycle enthusiast pulled together a 400-bike memorial ride that raised $16,000. All the merchants in Ladera set aside a day when the proceeds of their sales went to the family. Neighbors in Oak Knoll made arrangements for a memorial to the children to be placed in the village's park.

It was as though Ladera Ranch residents, with all their connections and business acumen, could not do enough to support Lori Coble and her husband, Chris, who lost their entire family in a single day. All of Orange County marveled at Ladera Ranch's response, and the *Orange County Register,* in a short notice, asked, "What do you think is behind the outpouring? Do you feel the community's response is unique, and why?" It is a question that we have been attempting to answer throughout this book. Oak Knoll resident Bo Kelleher wrote a response that indicates they do feel it's unique. "Ladera Ranch has somewhat of an island mentality," he explained. "When something happens on the island, it affects the whole tribe. We're all connected in a way that other communities might not understand."

The lessons of Ladera Ranch are almost too many to count, and they reveal themselves in a vast variety of ways, whether it's at those informal neighborhood Friday evening happy hours, during a Sunday morning brunch in a Township District restaurant, or at one of the community council's big events in Founders Park. The developers of Ladera Ranch had detected through their research that a craving for this kind of smaller-scale connectedness existed. But they could hardly have guessed that the new residents attracted to such a community would, in a sense, partner with the developers as though they were together on a mission to grow the community. These homebuyers would embody the concept of "Roots and Wings" so fully that they would tell their friends about Ladera Ranch and, in some cases, move in their extended families and create a true multigenerational community where a few years earlier there had only been arid pastureland. Ladera Ranch proved that if community planners go to the added expense and trouble of providing walkable streets, interconnected neighborhoods, clubs, activities, and family-oriented events, there is a breed of people—most of them Middle-Class Millionaires—willing to help them succeed and to pay extra for the privilege of living that way.

In 2006, the Urban Land Institute honored Ladera Ranch with its Award for Excellence, which is given each year for "creativity, vision and best practices in land use." It is not just an award for clever and interesting design or architecture. An important qualifying factor is financial success. Winners of the Award for Excellence are held up as examples to be learned from and followed because they make money. With its Terramor development, for instance, Ladera Ranch broke new ground by providing an entirely new neighborhood with energy-efficient homes built from eco-friendly building materials and topped by hundreds of solar roof panels. A subsequent survey of Terramor residents showed that nearly 9 out of 10 had been willing to pay as much as $124 per month for "green-oriented features" in their homes.

Terramor proved to the development community the potency of values-based spending in the "green" niche of the homebuilding industry. It showed that hundreds of homeowners were willing to spend on average $4 extra per square foot for what they considered a healthy home for themselves and their families. That's $12,000 of pure profit for the developer of any 3,000-square-foot house who figures out how to build green efficiently, which guarantees that Terramor will be studied and tried again. It will be further developed as an idea and inevitably scaled downward to meet the needs of the broader market.

Over the ridge, to the south and east of Ladera Ranch, is the last developable piece of the old O'Neill Ranch. In January 2007, Orange County gave the final okay to develop 16,000 homes there, a planned community twice the size of Ladera Ranch. It's one of the last open spaces available for development in the entire county, which continues to add 28,000 people per year. The same team that built Ladera—RMV, DMB Associates, and Steve Kellenberg's planning firm, EDAW—are in the beginning stages of laying out the streets and neighborhoods, and figuring out how to profit further from the lessons that Ladera offers.

But an encore for Ladera Ranch's community-building approach doesn't have to wait until ground breaks on the final frontier of the O'Neill family land. In a patch of desert twenty-five miles west of Phoenix, DMB Associates is well into the second phase of a planned community called Verrado.

If you've seen Ladera Ranch, Verrado has a very familiar feel, which shouldn't be too surprising since Steve Kellenberg leads Verrado's master planning team. There are porches on the houses, broad manicured parks, and sidewalks and trails everywhere. In many respects, the promotional materials could have been lifted right from Ladera Ranch's brochures: "Top 5 reasons why we love Verrado: 1. Never had so many people I'd trust with my house key. 2. Running into my friends on Main Street. 3. Going back in time to a real hometown. 4. Hosting porch parties with my neighbors. 5. I love walking. Everywhere!"

And as with Ladera Ranch, Verrado broke some rules that made the local development community think that DMB Associates was crazy. While the average home price in the Phoenix area is around $220,000, dropping as you move farther away from the center of town, prices at Verrado start at about $260,000 and range upward to $575,000. One homebuilder told a construction trade magazine, "DMB told us to expect large crowds at the opening, but we thought, 'How can that be? We're in a new area that's so far west and the prices are going to be so high.'" During the first weekend at Verrado, 40,000 people came through. Real estate refugees from California are moving to Verrado to take advantage of the comparably low prices.

One small difference between Verrado and Ladera Ranch is that Verrado falls within the town of Buckeye, whose center is a few miles away. During the first few years, Buckeye and Verrado each held their own Fourth of July celebrations—the Fourth is as big in Verrado as it is in Ladera Ranch—which was awkward, because it seemed to confirm the suspicion that Verrado was somehow a place apart from the rest of the town. In 2007, the celebrations merged. Thousands of people from all over Buckeye celebrated the Fourth with fireworks—on the field at Verrado High School.

CHAPTER NINE

THE NEW RULES OF THE NEW RICH

There were already plenty of worries about the U.S. economy in late August 2005 when Hurricane Katrina struck the Gulf Coast states and submerged much of New Orleans. The Iraq war and the previous year's hurricanes had already pushed up gasoline prices across the nation. After Katrina knocked out much of Louisiana's oil production capacity, crude oil prices hit a record $71 per barrel and gasoline reached $3 per gallon for the first time ever. Economists assumed that the pain felt by motorists at the pumps would put a squeeze on consumer spending, so many started downgrading their estimates for that year's economic growth. The Congressional Budget Office projected that the gross domestic product might grow at a rate of just 2.5 percent for the second half of 2005, a full point lower than previously predicted.

But the economy didn't stall in 2005. All of the statistical measures that might have foretold a slowdown even before Katrina—depressed household savings rates, a high foreign trade imbalance, tepid consumer confidence—proved unreliable at year's end. By the fourth quarter of 2005, economic growth and consumer spending for the year had met most forecasters' prior expectations. Then there was a strong rebound in the first quarter of 2006. One year after Katrina, twelve out of thirteen economists polled by ABC News gave the U.S. economy either an A or a B-plus for its surprisingly strong, if uneven, rate of expansion following the storm.

In October of 2005, a group of young equity analysts at Citigroup had all but predicted this would be the case. Citigroup's global equity strategy team had already been analyzing the way most economists had overestimated the probable effects of gas prices on the economy in 2005. Maybe, they wondered, there was something fundamentally wrong with the traditional assumptions used to make such economic projections. Ajay Kapur, then Citigroup's head of global equity strategy, authored an influential research paper, dated October 16, 2005, that pointed to recent trends in household income distribution as a more logical explanation for why the economy would continue to hold up so well. Kapur's group proposed that since the top 10 percent of U.S. households collected 43 percent of annual income in 2004 and controlled 57 percent of household wealth, the spending behavior of the vast majority of Americans—the other 90 percent—no longer matters very much.

Kapur boldly declared that the United States is now a "plutonomy," an economy in which the behavior of the wealthiest 10 percent drives economic growth, no matter how tough the economy is for everyone else. Consumer spending among the highest-income households remained so strong through 2005 that when rising gasoline prices and credit rate hikes put a dent in spending by most Americans, the economy kept chugging along without them. "There is no such thing as 'the U.S. consumer,'" Kapur told one interviewer. "There are a few rich who own a disproportionate and gigantic slice of total income and consumption, and there are the rest, the 'non-rich,' the multitudinous many, who account for surprisingly small bites of the national pie."

The trend can be seen most clearly in the way Wal-Mart's sales growth at its U.S. stores has lagged for several years behind that of luxury retailers such as Nordstrom and Neiman Marcus. Kapur's research paper concluded that the rich are getting richer every year, that they will increasingly dominate consumer spending, and that both trends are unlikely to end anytime soon. His recommendation: "Buy shares in companies that make the toys that plutonomists enjoy."

Citigroup developed a "Plutonomy Basket" of stocks that included Bulgari, Burberry, Richemont, and the homebuilder Toll Brothers. Someone who invested in these stocks back in 1985 would have averaged an enviable 17.8 percent annual rate of return since then. Following Citigroup's lead, one New York hedge fund has taken up the strategy of investing in a similar mix of luxury stocks while systematically short-selling the stocks of mass-market U.S. retailers such as Liz Claiborne and T. J. Maxx. Betting against the middle-class consumer is now just another way to grow rich with the rich.

If the Citigroup plutonomy theory is correct, then most people reading this are living in a substantially different society from the one in which they grew up. For decades the vast middle-class majority controlled so much consumer spending that economic decisions made in Washington and influenced by Wall Street naturally sought solutions that would address the needs of the typical American household. What was good for the middle class was good for America. The plutonomy theory suggests that the "typical U.S. consumer" either no longer exists or is no longer relevant. The wealthiest 10 percent—populated by the super-rich, Middle-Class Millionaires, and some Middle-Class Half-Millionaires—have taken the driver's seat in the twenty-first-century consumer economy.

American society has been moving in this direction for a while. The recovery from the 1982 recession marked the first time since the 1920s that income gains of the richest households exceeded those of the middle class. Incomes at the top have been on a general upward trajectory ever since. In 1982, the top 1 percent of households accounted for 12.8 percent of national income, while the top 10 percent took home 36 percent. In 2005, the top 1 percent collected 21.8 percent of all income, and the total for the top 10 percent had risen to 48.5 percent. Total U.S. income rose by 9 percent in 2005, but the average income of the bottom 90 percent of tax filers actually fell by 0.6 percent—a loss of about $172. The graph of income distribution among U.S. households is losing the traditional bell-shaped curve that placed the greatest number of American families in the middle-income range. Now the shape of income distribution has begun to look more like a sideways hourglass or a barbell. The poor are at one end, the prosperous are at the other, and together they threaten to outnumber the thinning ranks in the middle.

Outsized gains in executive compensation, small-business profits, stock market returns, real estate, and other investments have all contributed to making the rich richer these past twenty-five years. Automation and globalization have permitted incomes and investment returns to accumulate in ways that were uncommon or unheard-of ten or twenty years ago. Information technology, for instance, allows companies to track employee performance more closely. The practice of paying on the basis of performance has increased in the corporate world as a result. One study of performance-based pay has found that 44.5 percent of workers at Fortune 1000 companies received such compensation in 2003, up from 34.7 percent just seven years earlier. Other data cited in the study suggest that just 30 percent of jobs offered some form of performance-based pay in the 1970s.

The same forces of globalization and automation have decimated the higher-wage manufacturing jobs that once formed the backbone of America's blue-collar middle class. Low-wage foreign labor—first in Mexico and then in China—led to the closure of thousands of U.S. factories and undermined trade union bargaining positions. The most commonly prescribed antidote for displaced workers is to supply them with job training and higher education opportunities, since income is tied more closely than ever to educational attainment. The latest census data show that an average college degree holder made $51,554 in 2004, about $23,000 more than the average high school graduate.

What the census data obscure, however, is that a wide gap in income continues to grow among all those college graduates as well. Robert H. Frank's 1996 bestseller *The Winner-Take-All Society* was probably the first book to point out that a rise in average white-collar incomes didn't necessarily mean that most white-collar professionals were better off. Upon closer inspection, average incomes for many white-collar job descriptions were going up mainly due to enormous gains enjoyed by a small minority at the top of their respective fields. For many other white-collar workers, incomes had been either stagnating or even falling.

Frank, a Cornell economics professor, studied the shifts in income trends within a number of professions between 1979 and 1989. He found that, in general, the number of professionals with moderately strong earnings had gone down, while the number of higher and lower earners had increased dramatically. Income distribution within each profession has been developing a barbell shape of its own. For instance, the number of dentists making more than $120,000 in 1989 was 78 percent higher (when adjusted for inflation) than in 1979. However, the total number of dentists in the "moderately high" range of $60,000 to $120,000 declined during that period. The numbers of dentists in the income groups below this middle range had also increased sharply.

In Frank's view, this is an income pattern that has begun to imitate the one we've seen for many years in competitive winner-take-all fields such as sports and entertainment. Advances in computing, telecommunications, and other business innovations have created multimillion-dollar superstar salaries among business CEOs and, more recently, hedge fund managers. But, as Frank points out, the most profound source of growing income inequality in America is "the escalating earnings of the near-rich—the salespeople, administrators, accountants, physicians and millions of [others] who dominate the smaller niche markets of everyday life." He called these people "minor league superstars," but we know them as the working rich: the Middle-Class Millionaires.

To explain the way dentistry has become a winner-take-all field,

Frank outlined how new technologies have helped bring about strong growth in the cosmetic end of the field in particular and more specialization in general. Dentists who invest in these technologies have the opportunity to develop a highly valued area of expertise. In a success-breeds-success fashion, they command higher salaries as their reputation in their niche grows over time. In describing this self-reinforcing process, Frank takes pains to point out that this is how someone who is not necessarily the best dentist in town can become the best-paid dentist in town.

Frank also makes a hypothetical comparison between two clinical psychologists of equal training and talent who experience very different financial outcomes. One manages to build a successful private practice based on referrals from physicians and other therapists, while the other psychologist is not as well-connected, fails to sustain his private practice, and quits to take a modest-paying job at a health clinic. Frank's point is that while winners in the winner-take-all society are generally selected from among the most able, "the distribution of earnings within a group of experienced [professionals] reflects the vagaries of chance along the career path." His point seems to be that the best-paid dentists and psychologists get rich through luck instead of professional merit.

What's missing in Frank's analysis, of course, is the impact of Millionaire Intelligence. There are no "vagaries of chance" in the decision of a dentist to invest in expensive advanced technology and take the risk of developing a narrow field of expertise in hope of greater financial gain down the road. For a dentist to put his practice "in the flow of money," as we discussed in Chapter 2, it requires hard work and a willingness to take risks. Similarly, in Frank's tale of the two psychologists, he suggests that one was simply fortunate to have better referrals than the other. To be sure, luck plays some role in most success stories, but the real lesson of the two psychologists is this: In today's economy, the most financially successful professionals are likely to be the ones best able to focus on achieving financial success. They exercise Millionaire Intelligence. The first psychologist exhibited the persistence and networking ability necessary to garner enough referrals so that she could fill her calendar and raise her rates. The other psychologist had a rougher time of it and gave up rather than work at developing the referral base he needed to succeed.

Which of Frank's psychologists reminds you most of yourself? Where do you fit in a two-tiered, winner-take-all society? Do you want to become a Middle-Class Millionaire? If you're already one, are you ready to raise your game?

Whatever your place in today's economy, we have created a list of ten questions about Millionaire Intelligence that may help you determine what the likelihood is of your achieving your financial dreams.

Just as emotional intelligence is the discipline of behaving in ways that signify emotional maturity, Millionaire Intelligence is the discipline of acting in ways that contribute to wealth-making maturity. Someone with a high degree of Millionaire Intelligence tends to make financial achievement and success a primary focus in his or her work life.

Financial success is a middle-class value for all of our respondents—those who are millionaires and those who are not. More than 60 percent of the people in both groups agreed that "money is essential to lead a full life," and about 90 percent agreed that "anyone can become a millionaire if he or she works hard enough." Very few believed the statement "Money can't buy happiness." It seems that if money can't buy happiness, a vast majority of the middle class would like the chance to find out for themselves!

1. Are You Ready to Become a Millionaire?

When we first compared the results from our survey of middle-class people and Middle-Class Millionaires, we were struck by how Middle-Class Millionaires put their middle-class values into action with a consistency that was lacking among much of the middle-class sample.

Among Middle-Class Millionaires there is an almost unanimously high value assigned to both career and financial independence. Generating a good income through devotion to career is the chief way in which the typical Middle-Class Millionaire reaches the goal of financial independence.

With those who are middle class, more than 67 percent also consider "being financially independent" very or extremely important. But far fewer attach the same weight to their careers. Less than 44 percent consider career a very or extremely important value. In other words, at least one out of four members of the middle class thinks financial success is important but doesn't think much of his or her own career prospects. In fact, 66 percent of the middle-class survey respondents assigned a higher degree of importance to their own "interests and hobbies" than to their careers.

It's certainly possible to achieve financial independence while punching a clock at a job you don't care for. One of us, Lewis Schiff, wrote a book about the subject, *The Armchair Millionaire*, in which he advised people to spend less, save more, and invest the savings. No matter how you feel about your work, if your income and savings are sufficient, you can accumulate a very nice nest egg.

But consider for a moment the trends we've cited in the opening of this chapter: the growing use of pay-for-performance salary incentives, the winner-take-all effect in more and more white-collar fields, and the gradual loss of middle incomes among the middle class. It seems to us that placing a low value on your career is dangerously inconsistent with the goal of financial independence.

The newspapers have been filled for twenty years or more with tales of middle-aged, middle-income employees unceremoniously tossed out of their jobs through corporate mergers, takeovers, and reorganizations. Middle-Class Millionaires seem to understand that true financial independence comes from having a distinguished career, a unique set of talents and skills you can take from one position to another. It's a bad thing to be jobless and looking for work. It's much worse when all you have to offer your next employer is a set of qualifications in a career you personally don't hold in very high esteem.

Middle-Class Millionaires like to maximize their earnings. It's one of those things that set them apart. By a margin of 83 to 67 percent, they are more likely than the middle class to agree that "money is important to your personal happiness." For the most part, though, their perspective on money is reliably middle-class. About 92 percent of both groups agree that "good health is more important than money," and about 85 percent agree that the love of someone special is more important than money. It's not that their priorities are very different from the rest of the middle class. It is, as we've said, a matter of consistency. They go after what they want.

We know that this approach to life isn't for everyone. About one-third of the middle-class survey respondents don't assign a very high value to money or career. In this respect they are at least consistent in their values and beliefs. For the other 67 percent of the middle class who acknowledge that money is important to their happiness, they might ask themselves, "If that's really true, how hard am I willing to work to develop my Millionaire Intelligence to bring more money and happiness into my life?"

2. Are You Willing to Work Hard to Find Your Best Opportunities?

More than half of our middle-class respondents agreed with the old chestnut "Do what you love and the money will follow." Less than 2 percent of the Middle-Class Millionaires agreed.

A good number of the middle-class sample, those with household incomes under $80,000, have succeeded fairly well in life by pursuing what they enjoy. They naturally assume that doing more of the same will eventually provide them with the success they desire. Middle-Class Millionaires, on the other hand, make no such assumption. Having achieved a higher level of success, they know that it took more than allowing the money to follow from whatever they like doing.

Yes, it's important to know what you love to do. That kind of knowledge can be an important ingredient in anyone's success. But our survey tells us that most people who achieve true financial success in today's economy haven't used it as the chief criterion for selecting their livelihoods. More than 73 percent of Middle-Class Millionaires say that "choosing a career for its prospective financial rewards" is very or extremely important in achieving financial success. Just 28 percent of the middle class made the same assessment. Perhaps the Middle-Class Millionaires realize that starting with the thing you love is like looking through the wrong end of the telescope. If the goal is financial independence, it's wiser to determine first which occupations offer the greatest opportunities before deciding which path to take.

Greg Hund, the Mail Boxes Etc. franchise owner in Chapter 2, gives us an excellent snapshot of how a Middle-Class Millionaire matches his talents with his passions. Hund started out as a gifted account executive on Wall Street. He won awards and bonuses for the business he generated for his company. But he left Wall Street because he was sure he'd be more successful—and therefore happier—working for himself. When he purchased a Mail Boxes Etc. franchise in Manhattan, it wasn't because he had any particular interest in the company itself. Running an MBE wasn't a dream of his, and shipping other people's stuff is not what you'd call a glamour job. And yet he worked long and hard at it, until his store was one of the highest-performing MBEs in the nation.

The passion Hund brought to his MBE store came from the opportunity to make a lot of money if he could build a loyal clientele and boost the sales of store products with the highest profit margins.

There's no question that you're more likely to do well at something you love. But what if chasing after the work you love the most has undercut your ability to achieve the level of financial success you'd like to achieve? When was the last time you seriously considered pursuing another job—perhaps in a specialty or a subdiscipline within your field of expertise—that doesn't exactly entail doing what you love, but offers a far greater opportunity to see your hard work financially rewarded? A Middle-Class Millionaire might tell you that once you learn to love the opportunity itself, the money will follow.

3. Where in Your Work Could You Tap into the Flow of Money?

In August 2005, an article appeared in the *Chronicle of Higher Education* called "Missed Chances." It told the life story of an eighty-six-year-old cancer researcher who had spent a lifetime finding cures for disease and not worrying too much about who got the credit.

Jerome P. Horwitz exercised Millionaire Intelligence in every important aspect but one: For all his hard work, persistence, and avid networking with funding sources and other researchers, Horwitz rarely, if ever, negotiated patents and royalties on his own behalf. Now retired, Horwitz was a brilliant, dogged, gifted researcher who never put himself first when it came to his personal finances. As a result, he never received any royalties for three drug compounds he pioneered in the 1960s that have since gone on to become famous AIDS-fighting drugs. The best-known and most lucrative one, AZT, was patented by Glaxo-Wellcome and has earned the company more than $1.7 billion in sales.

Whether they work for themselves or for others, two out of three Middle-Class Millionaires say that "obtaining an ownership stake" in their work is important to their financial success. Less than 28 percent of our middle-class sample said the same. For Middle-Class Millionaires, having a piece of whatever they do eclipses even formal education as a key factor in success. This is why we believe they are so well suited to prosper in an economy that runs increasingly on a winner-take-all basis.

Among businesses eager to squeeze the best out of employees, incentives, commissions, and performance pay are all proliferating. Management is willing to share the wealth with those workers who contribute value to the company. Much of this book has been dedicated to the inspiring stories of entrepreneurs motivated by the prospect of great rewards and poised to revolutionize major sectors of the U.S. economy as a result.

Not all fields offer top performers financial incentives, of course. There are legions of civil servants, nonprofit workers, and professionals in valuable middle-class occupations such as teaching, nursing, and law enforcement who are all doing important jobs outside the world of profit-and-loss balance sheets. Their ability to find the flow of money is limited by the very nature of their jobs.

Or is it? In recent years, merit pay and performance bonuses for schoolteachers have become valuable tools for helping keep the best teachers in schools where they are needed most. Outside the classroom, there are also some great teachers who have extended their reach and influence into the business side of education, leveraging their expertise to achieve an ownership stake in their work. They write books. They consult with for-profit educational companies. They've started charter schools in the dozens of troubled school districts that are relying on academic entrepreneurship to boost their standardized-testing results. These teachers are making more money and making a bigger difference in the world. The two are not mutually exclusive.

Who knows what other advances Jerome Horwitz could have discovered in his long career if along the way he'd bargained for a little more personal financial security? AZT has saved thousands of lives, and Horwitz told the *Chronicle* that this fact is a source of personal pride for him. But all he has to show for it today is the needlepoint decoration his wife made for him in the design of the AZT chemical compound. "It's hanging in our den," he told the *Chronicle*, "a constant reminder of what I did and what I didn't do."

4. Do You Look for Ways to Focus and Concentrate Your Energies Where Your Opportunities Are Strongest?

More than 53 percent of the middle-class individuals we surveyed believe that "diversifying the ways you make money" is important to their financial success. This view is shared by only about 15 percent of

Middle-Class Millionaires, who are far more likely to extol the virtues of "concentrating all your efforts on one moneymaking endeavor."

In other words, Middle-Class Millionaires focus; middle-class people hedge. To a certain extent, this makes a lot of sense. Diversification provides safety, and much of middle-class financial success relies on reducing risk. Middle-Class Millionaires, on the other hand, are more apt to be entrepreneurs and executives, occupations that require very intense periods of focused attention.

However, there is a difference between diversifying your assets and diffusing your interests and activities. Having picked a career based on its prospective financial rewards, a Middle-Class Millionaire is likely to nurture that career with long working hours, networking with people who can assist that career, and making investments in coaching, training, and other self-betterment activities.

Our survey shows that such focus is often lacking among our respondents in the middle class. They work on average about thirty hours per week less than Middle-Class Millionaires. They take more and longer vacations. They network less frequently, and even among those who participate in networking, they're not as proficient at recruiting new members. Middle-class people rarely hire life coaches or professional coaches. When they do invest in self-betterment courses or programs, they enroll overwhelmingly for personal reasons, not professional ones. Just over 50 percent of the middle-class people we surveyed believe in "cutting back on little luxuries" as an important step toward achieving financial success. About 5 percent of Middle-Class Millionaires think the same way.

The only thing wrong with this picture is that more than two-thirds of our middle-class respondents say that money is important to their personal happiness. They may believe that, but judging from our survey results, most of them simply don't act on it. Instead, we see a propensity among the middle class to engage in what could only be called "magical thinking." Among the many factors they consider very important or extremely important to their financial success, 73 percent of the middle class cited "thinking like a millionaire." Just 2 percent of Middle-Class Millionaires saw any merit in that idea.

Persistence or "not giving up" is a value that more than three-quarters of both Middle-Class Millionaires and the middle-class agree is a key to financial success. But in the absence of hard work and preparation, it's as though many of the middle class have a magical-thinking notion of what it means not to give up. A Middle-Class Millionaire might tell you that persistence is something that happens as a by-product of focus. You settle on a goal, refine it through hard work, and come to believe in it so deeply that you can't give up on it. It's not about banging your head against a wall, and it's certainly not about "thinking like a millionaire."

5. Are You Playing to Win?

Dan Sullivan, the super-coach to entrepreneurs, told us that the one character trait he has found in common among his clients is that "they're all killers." Sullivan's Strategic Coach program attracts some of the best, most talented entrepreneurs in North America. We're not saying that having a killer instinct is necessary to become a Middle-Class Millionaire. Our survey, however, did reflect Sullivan's observation that highly successful people show a more pronounced instinct for going for the jugular in their business dealings.

More than 80 percent of Middle-Class Millionaires ranked such practices as "coming out a winner" in negotiations and "coming out on top in business dealings" as important to financial success. Among the middle class, only 60 percent were in agreement. About half of Middle-Class Millionaires chalked up financial success to "believing you have to be Machiavellian to succeed" and "taking advantage of weaknesses in others." A little more than 20 percent of middle-class individuals said the same.

This is the somewhat dark side of Millionaire Intelligence. Self-interest—looking out for yourself—demands keeping an eye on others, too. The need to take advantage of other people's weaknesses, for instance, is more understandable when you realize that in competitive situations someone else is ready to take advantage of *your* weaknesses—especially as you near the top of a field.

An ability to negotiate is essential for success in any competitive field—even if you're negotiating for a raise. More than 65 percent of Middle-Class Millionaires describe their negotiating approach as "do whatever you need to do to win"; only 32 percent said that "it should always be win-win." Among the middle class, "win-win" was slightly more popular. The biggest difference between the two groups was their attitude toward losing. Almost 25 percent of the middle class agreed that "losing is acceptable if you doubted your chances to win in the first place." Less than 3 percent of Middle-Class Millionaires felt the same way.

Middle-Class Millionaires tend to be very disciplined when it comes to their commitment to success. They put themselves first and don't indulge the idea that they deserve to lose. In sports we call it mental toughness, and it's another essential ingredient in persistence. It's vital to keep your wits about you and see everything clearly in a competitive situation, but at the same time you need to block out the notion that you deserve to lose. If you don't, there are just too many temptations to take the path of least resistance and quit.

6. Where Do You Need to Adjust Your Attitude Toward Risk?

As far back as the 1830s, French observer Alexis de Tocqueville saw risk-taking as an essential attribute of the American character. Tocqueville remarked how bankruptcy was a source of great shame in Europe, but it didn't bother Americans nearly as much and was regarded as the natural, inevitable result of taking business risks. "In Europe," Tocqueville wrote, "we habitually regard a restless spirit, a moderate desire for wealth and an extreme love of independence as great social dangers, but precisely these things assure a long and peaceful future in the American republics."

Similarly, by a margin of 55 to 33 percent, Middle-Class Millionaires were more apt than the middle class to say that "choosing projects with greater risk and greater prospective reward" was important to their financial success. The bigger difference between the two groups showed up in how they are likely to manage the risks they take. Almost 53 percent of the middle-class sample said that "putting your own capital at risk" is a key to succeeding financially, an idea that less than 18 percent of Middle-Class Millionaires agreed with. On the other hand, almost 57 percent of the Middle-Class Millionaires said that "persuading others to invest with you" was a recipe for financial success. Just under 15 percent of the middle-class sample said the same.

In other words, Middle-Class Millionaires focus their bets, but they hedge their risks. Middle-class people seem to do exactly the opposite. They are more likely to say that they should diversify their financial interests and put their own capital at risk in the process. Part of this explanation, no doubt, is that those in the middle class lack the same opportunities to bring others in on investment deals with them. But the overwhelming preference of Middle-Class Millionaires not to put their own capital at risk should tell us all something about what it takes to make it in today's economy. Risk-taking is not thrill-seeking. A calculated risk taken with the help of other people's money means that even if something goes wrong, you won't face ruin. You'll survive to take more risks tomorrow.

Objectively speaking, it's easy to say that Middle-Class Millionaires have succeeded to the point where they now live with less risk. On average, most of them estimate they could maintain their current lifestyle for more than a year if they were to lose their current income. By contrast, middle-class survey respondents figure they would be tapped out in just three or four months. Nonetheless, as we mentioned earlier in the book, about 78 percent of Middle-Class Millionaires still say they are "very or extremely concerned about their ability to maintain their current financial position."

Risk is a way of life for Middle-Class Millionaires. Every day they use it aggressively to compound the financial gains they've already made. Perhaps this is how they have managed to take an ever-larger share of the national income and are beginning to exert a dominant influence on the rest of society.

7. How Do You View Failure?

About 90 percent of all our survey respondents report having made a "major career or business decision that had a very bad outcome." But Middle-Class Millionaires fail approximately twice as often as the middle class. On average, Middle-Class Millionaires reported 3.1 such bad outcomes in their careers, while middle-class respondents averaged just 1.6. Surprisingly, successful people fail more often than less successful people do.

Averages, however, don't begin to tell the whole story when it comes to Middle-Class Millionaires. Nearly 20 percent of them reported more than four bad business or career decisions. The champion had six. Remember, this is an individual who still has a net worth over $1 million, despite failing six times.

Even more eye-opening were the results when we asked the respondents to describe their "most common course of action following a bad outcome." Nearly 77 percent of Middle-Class Millionaires checked off "tried again in the same field," while just 2 percent said they "gave up and focused on other projects." For the middle class, the response was almost completely the opposite. Only about 14 percent responded to a bad outcome by trying again in the same field. More than half—51.5 percent—responded to failure by giving up and trying something else.

When we relayed these findings to Steve Dering, the originator of fractionally owned ski vacation homes, he gasped. If you give up after the first try, he said, "then you don't get any of the benefits of learning from what went wrong." To Dering, this is as obvious as the snows in Park City, Utah. As you'll recall, Dering suffered through two unsuccessful attempts at fractionally owned developments before he got it right. Now he's the foremost expert in the field.

It's hard to overstate how highly Middle-Class Millionaires regard the importance of learning from their mistakes. More than 72 percent of them say that "learning from bad business or career decisions" is very or extremely important in achieving financial success. This was mentioned more frequently as a key to success than having a good formal education, obtaining an ownership stake in your work, or even building rapport with people. For Middle-Class Millionaires, learning from failure was ranked on a level of importance with "choosing a career for its prospective financial rewards."

It is a lesson, however, that seems lost on most of the middle class. Just 36 percent of our middle-class respondents said that it's important to learn from bad business or career decisions. More than 51 percent said it was important to "accept failure as a sign that you're doing your best."

Middle-Class Millionaires behave in a way that is more consistent with their stated values and beliefs. They don't simply assert the importance of persistence. They *are* persistent.

8. Do You Network with Your Financial Goals in Mind?

Middle-Class Millionaires not only network more often than other members of the middle class but also do it with their careers in mind. Almost two out of three Middle-Class Millionaires we surveyed said that they either belong to a formal or informal networking group or plan to join one in the next three years. This was true for only 25 percent of the middle-class respondents.

Overwhelmingly, Middle-Class Millionaires said that networking is important "to connect with people you can turn to for information."

But a very small minority of the middle-class networkers, about 26 percent, expressed the same belief. For about 40 percent of these middle-class networkers, it was more important to use networking to meet people who "can help you personally (outside your career)."

Even the relatively few members of the middle class who see any value in joining a networking group neglect to use the network to connect with others, to find information useful in their work. Networking seems to play a negligible role in achieving the financial goals the middle class set for themselves.

Roughly half of the middle-class and Middle-Class Millionaire survey respondents are involved in charities, and both survey groups express almost identical values as their reasons for joining. About 83 percent of both groups say they "believe in the cause" and "it's the right thing to do."

But about one-third of the Middle-Class Millionaires say they have another important reason for charitable activity—networking. Almost 37 percent say charity work is a way "to connect with people you can turn to for information." Less than 1 percent of the middle-class survey respondents cited this as important to their charity work.

Charity work brings like-minded people together, people with shared concerns and shared values. It can be an excellent way to get to know people outside the workplace who can nonetheless be helpful to you in your career. And if you make a useful connection in your charity work, wouldn't that charity be among the first beneficiaries of your new success?

9. Are You Willing to Invest in a Coach to Further Your Career?

One fairly common way Middle-Class Millionaires focus their disparate energies is by hiring a life coach or business coach to help them manage their professional lives. As Chapter 6 described, Middle-Class Millionaires use coaches to help them adhere to their long-term career goals amid the grind and distractions of their daily activities. Coaches also help them balance their personal lives with the demands of their work.

Our survey showed that about half of Middle-Class Millionaires have hired a business or life coach in the past three years, and another 20 percent or so say they intend to hire one in the next few years. The primary purposes they cite for hiring a life coach are help with career skills (90 percent) and connecting with other people (71 percent). In other words, Middle-Class Millionaires invest in their own self-efficacy, through coaching and any number of other self-betterment regimes.

The middle class, as a rule, do not. About 51 percent of the middle-class individuals we surveyed say that "cutting back on little luxuries" is an important way to achieve financial success. They believe in saving up rather than investing in themselves. About 2 percent of Middle-Class Millionaires think that's a good strategy. Yet 92 percent of the middle-class respondents say that "anyone can become a millionaire if he or she works hard enough." And over 81 percent believe that "a person can change his or her personality if he or she makes the commitment to do so."

That's a tall order, however, for even the most self-directed individual. Career coach Anne Bachrach says that for any busy, active person, it's very difficult to rearrange your daily behavior if you don't have help in keeping your eye on your highest long-term goals. The counsel of friends and spouses isn't enough. Bachrach points out that everyone else in your life has his or her own agenda. Only a coach can help you identify the goals you find most meaningful in your life and then challenge you to stretch to fulfill them.

The secret here is that the high achievers out there aren't doing it alone. They invest in themselves rather than cut back on little luxuries. This is useful advice for anyone determined to get ahead.

10. Who Are the Middle-Class Millionaires in Your Life?

In the 1920s, the last time that the top 10 percent of households controlled about half the nation's income, income came from very different sources than it does today. Among the wealthiest 1 percent, for instance, the overwhelming majority of income in 1926 was earned in interest, rents, and dividends. Today, most of the income of the top 1 percent comes in the form of wages—compensation for work. Even the richest in America today tend to be the working rich. "The rich," Ajay Kapur wrote, "went from coupon-clipping, dividend-receiving rentiers to a Managerial Aristocracy indulged by their shareholders."

Located somewhere between this aristocracy and the average wage earner are the Middle-Class Millionaires. They possess all the same values, wishes, and worries of the debt-laden, mortgage-holding members of the middle class. The edge they possess is that their talents and aptitudes are extremely well suited to the changing rules of our new economy. But the Middle-Class Millionaires succeed by helping other people succeed. Is there a Middle-Class Millionaire somewhere in your life who could help you become one too?

We suspect that everyone reading this book knows a half-dozen Middle-Class Millionaires. The reason you know them is that it's their business to be known, to be available, to be in touch, to help others. Reach out to them. Chat them up. Middle-Class Millionaires are not shy, and they appreciate people who aren't afraid to ask questions. Even if becoming a Middle-Class Millionaire doesn't appeal to you, there is much to be said for being in their orbit, working in their company, and allowing yourself to be inspired by their attitudes, their abilities, and their aspirations. We believe that this book has shown how they are the future, the ones to watch. The rest of this nation and this world is going in their direction anyway. You'll enjoy the ride more, we feel certain, if you take it in the company of Middle-Class Millionaires.

NOTES

CHAPTER ONE: THE INFLUENCE OF AFFLUENCE

4 *John Hutchins is one of the many entrepreneurs* . . . A fine article about how and why hospitals seek out international patients appeared in the January 18, 1999, issue of *Medicine & Health*.

5 *With a staff of a hundred, Hutchins set about* . . . More details about Marburg Pavilion's conception and design can be found in the *Baltimore Sun* of January 20, 1996, and the *Washington Post* of February 10, 1996.

8 *This book examines the pivotal role* . . . The estimated number of Middle-Class Millionaire households in America is drawn from the triennial Federal Reserve Board Survey of Consumer Finance of 2004. The Fed will publish results of the 2007 survey in early 2009. Estimates of the rate of growth in Middle-Class Millionaire households come from the Capgemini World Wealth Report and our own extrapolations of the Federal Reserve data.

13 *Our staff of professional researchers surveyed* . . . We assume that most Middle-Class Millionaires have annual household incomes above $200,000. We decided, however, not to use income as a qualifier in developing our Middle-Class Millionaire survey sample because small-business proprietors and partners in professional corporations (about two-thirds of the Middle-Class Millionaire sample) have too many ways of obscuring their real income by deferring it for tax purposes and other maneuvers. Since we were also interested only in surveying *self-made* Middle-Class Millionaires, we excluded from the survey anyone who had been given more than $50,000 by their families, including the cost of their educations.

14 *Upon its introduction in 1996, OnStar cost* . . . A General Motors news release of August 22, 1996, billed OnStar as "Peace of Mind for $22.50 a Month." For an opposing view, see www.onstarprivacy.com.

CHAPTER TWO: MILLIONAIRE INTELLIGENCE

20 *Franklin's practical nature* . . . Besides *The First American*, a good short biography is *Benjamin Franklin* by Edmund S. Morgan. Blaine McCormick's book *Ben Franklin: America's Original Entrepreneur* claims that the print-shop

partnerships Franklin set up in towns outside Philadelphia also qualify him as the nation's first franchiser.

20 *In November 2005, ICR Research* . . . The survey documenting the Wobegon Effect was commissioned by the *Washington Post* and appeared in the paper's February 8, 2006, edition.

21 *This familiar phenomenon in survey research* . . . Justin Kruger, a social psychologist at New York University, is a leading authority on the Wobegon Effect. He is also co-author with David Dunning of "Unskilled and Unaware of It: How Difficulties in Recognizing One's Own Incompetence Lead to Inflated Self-Assessments," which appeared in the *Journal of Personality and Social Psychology* (December 1999). The Dunning-Kruger Effect describes the tendency of people who are incompetent at a particular task to overestimate their own abilities and to also express the belief that they know more than those who have demonstrated competence at the same skill. . . . Swedish researcher Ola Svenson found that 76 percent of motorists believe they drive more safely than the average driver, and 65 percent believe they are more skillful. The humorous title of Svenson's 1981 paper was "Are we all less risky and more skillful than our fellow drivers?"

25 *Americans, in general, work longer hours* . . . In "Workers Feel Burn of Long Hours, Less Leisure," *USA Today* reported on December 18, 2003, that "American workers put in an average of 1,815 hours in 2002. In major European economies, hours worked ranged from 1,300 to 1,800, according to the International Labor Organization. Hours were about the same in the USA as in Japan." . . . For the full story of New York's expanding commuter train schedules, see "Expanding Workday Makes Its Mark on Transit," which appeared in the March 26, 2006, edition of the *New York Times*.

25 *Both Middle-Class Millionaires and the members of our middle-class survey sample* . . . For the sake of readability in the text of this book, we have taken the numerical results and rounded down any decimals of .4 or below, and rounded up decimals of .6 or above.

31 *When we talk to Middle-Class Millionaires about networking* . . . "See Daddy Make a Deal," *New York Times*, October 16, 2005, includes several amusing accounts of networking behavior taken a little too far.

33 *Failure in the case of someone with Robert Levitan's high profile* . . . CNET's ranking of "Top 10 Dot-Com Flops" included Pets.com and GovWorks.com.

34 *Among the most important differences* . . . Psychologist Angela Lee Duckworth at the University of Pennsylvania has studied the relationship between success and what she calls "grit"—a mix of tenacity and perseverance in the

pursuit of difficult goals. Her survey of 1,223 West Point freshmen showed that their rankings on her gauge of "grit" more accurately predicted who would complete a difficult training program than other measures, including intelligence, prior achievements, and faculty assessments.

38 *Ping Fu had gone through enormous hardships* . . . For more on Ping Fu's odyssey of accomplishment, see *Inc.* magazine's December 2005 article, "Entrepreneur of the Year: The Dimensions of Ping Fu" by John Brant, and *Business Leader* magazine, January 2005, in which Ping Fu was named "Entrebizneur™ of the Year."

CHAPTER THREE: MIDDLE CLASS BUT MILLIONAIRES

46 *Unfortunately for the Martins* . . . The travails of the Martin family getting their dream home approved can be found in the *Chicago Tribune,* April 14, 2006, and in coverage by Sheila Ahern in *The Daily Record*.

47 *In recent years, during the latest run-up in nationwide housing values* . . . The National Trust's resources on teardowns can be found at www.nationaltrust.org/teardowns/.

48 *As with the Martin family project in Arlington Heights* . . . According to the *Atlanta Journal-Constitution* of January 4, 2007, the vandalized garage in Decatur belonged to a house that was about four times as large as the 1,450-square-foot brick bungalow it replaced. For an interesting take on the Chevy Chase egging incident, see John Tierney's "The Mansion Wars," *New York Times*, November 15, 2005. What one newcomer Middle-Class Millionaire sees as a matter of practical home design ("I feel I should be embarrassed that I need a mud room"), an old-timer interprets as a values divide ("It's conspicuous consumption, meaning in a sense their values are all out of proportion").

49 *Despite the objections of preservationists* . . . "Teardowns: Costs, Benefits and Public Policy" by Daniel P. McMillen, an economist at the University of Illinois at Chicago, provides a balanced and highly readable look at teardowns. It appeared in the July 2006 edition of *Land Lines*, the publication of the Lincoln Institute of Land Policy. *The Two-Income Trap*, by Elizabeth Warren and Amelia Warren Tyagi, provides a nice summary of how perceptions of school district quality can drive up suburban housing prices: "As parents increasingly believe that the differences among schools will translate into differences in lifetime chances, they are doing everything they can to buy their way into the best public schools." The authors point out that although the schools are "public" in nature, families end up paying a kind of tuition in the form of inflated housing prices in select school districts.

51 *Does this mean that people who live above and below the middle-class social stratum . . .* University of Maryland sociologist Annette Lareau uses the term "concerted cultivation" to describe the process by which middle-class parents, more often than poor and working-class parents, expend time, effort, and money to draw out the skills and talents of their children. She is the author of *Unequal Childhoods: Class, Race, and Family Life*.

52 *If values are difficult to define . . .* Paul Fussell's book, *Class*, is the most entertaining available exegesis of the American class system.

52 *Contradictions such as this one and others . . .* A survey by Visa Signature, released on February 8, 2005, showed that 72 percent of "New Affluent" consumers "are embarrassed by or dislike being identified by terms such as 'wealthy' or 'well off,' while acknowledging these terms accurately describe their situation." The survey identified "New Affluents" as adults with household incomes exceeding $125,000. Nine out of ten identified themselves as either "middle-class" or "upper-middle-class." Just 7 percent considered themselves "affluent."

56 *"That's what fueled the teardown activity," Hickey says . . .* Real estate agents who specialize in selling expensive new houses on teardown sites say that their business relies not on status-seeking but on satisfying common middle-class desires. "The buyers zero in on the towns they want," one told the *Chicago Tribune* of August 12, 2006. "Their requirements are remarkably similar: 'Close to schools, the swimming pool, parks, the train and Starbucks.'"

63 *Westport is a historic river town of 26,000 . . .* According to the TVLand.com synopsis of *I Love Lucy* episode number 167, "Lucy decides that it would be nice to move to the country and prevails on Ricky to place a comfortable deposit on a big house. Ricky agrees and puts a down payment on a house in Westport, Connecticut." In later episodes, Lucy joined the Westport PTA. . . . The Westport Historical Society proudly notes that an alternative name considered for *Bewitched* was *The Witch of Westport.*

63 *The* New York Times *reported in 1985 . . .* The archives of the *New York Times* since 1985 have recorded the decline and rise of Westport's education fortunes. As with Hollywood, the *Times* has employed Westport over the years as a kind of suburban bellwether.

66 *Evidence of how much Westport had changed . . . WestportNow.com* and the *Westport News* provided ample coverage of the Westport election of 2001 and the controversies surrounding the design of the addition to Staples High School.

67 *In April 2004, the* Wall Street Journal *studied . . .* The *Wall Street Journal*'s look at the freshman classes of elite colleges was part of an April 2, 2004, col-

lege planning package called "The Price of Admission." An accompanying item called "Your Tuition Dollars at Work" asked rhetorically, "Do costly private high schools have an edge on public schools? See which schools delivered the most value in the college-admissions sweepstakes, and see how we ranked the schools."

CHAPTER FOUR: THE RICH WORK FOR THE POOR

70 *For the past ten years or so, a growing number of parents* . . . The Independent Education Consultants Association estimated that 22 percent of private college freshmen had paid for admissions counseling, according to *BusinessWeek,* June 19, 2006.

72 *Selling into a market of parents* . . . Michele Hernandez's admissions counseling could cost $36,000 if she advises your child from eighth grade through college acceptance, the *Hartford Courant* reported on March 20, 2006. That's still just a fraction of the $160,000-plus price of four years of private college tuition. According to the *Courant*, Hernandez claims that "clients have told her that, everything considered, her fee is a drop in the bucket. 'Some people don't think anything of spending that much for a Lexus,' she says."

73 *Many of Cohen's students are the offspring of Middle-Class Millionaires . . . The Financial Times* of October 21, 2001, called IvyWise clients "a monied mix of bankers, entertainers, politicians and lawyers."

74 *When it comes to making spending choices* . . . The "rich work for the poor" quotation by Milton Friedman appears in the book *Miracle Cure: How to Solve America's Health Care Crisis and Why Canada Isn't the Answer,* by Sally C. Pipes, who in turn attributes the quote to a speech that Friedman made at the Club for Growth in San Francisco in July 2001. We can't independently verify the quotation's accuracy, but Friedman expressed the same sentiment less pithily in a written defense of school vouchers: "One function played by the rich is to finance innovation. They bought the initial cars and TVs at high prices and thereby supported production while the cost was being brought down, until what started out as a luxury good for the rich became a necessity for the poor." The article, "School Vouchers Turn 50," is available from the Milton and Rose D. Friedman Foundation.

79 *In 1941, two Iowa State University researchers* . . . A full account of the hybrid seed corn study appears in *Diffusion of Innovations* by Everett Rogers. It is a remarkable book, peppered with colorful stories, not all of which celebrate the advance of progress. One particularly poignant tale recounts how the diffusion of snowmobile technology in northern Finland devastated the fragile reindeer-herding culture of the Skolt Lapps.

81 *Between September 2004 and October 2005, Florida was hit with three hurricanes . . .* The trade publication *Gas Daily* reported on September 1, 2006, that after some parts of South Florida suffered power outages of up to eight weeks, Florida City Gas had to ramp up its rate of residential standby generator installations from 10 or 12 a month to about 200 a month.

83 *In a very brief period of time, the home standby generator . . .* The *Christian Science Monitor* of August 11, 2006, stated, "The standby power generator, like an iPod, is the latest must-have gizmo." It quoted Ron Gholston, president of Houston-area Gold Star Custom Builders, as saying that "one in five customers asks for standby generators as part of their building plans, something seldom seen a few years ago." The same article told of a New Orleans–area business consultant with a standby generator in his home who had to evacuate in advance of Hurricane Katrina: "When he returned a few days later, his four-bedroom home was not only standing, it was air conditioned."

86 *In this light, it's fairly easy to see no electric car has ever . . .* The $10,000 buglike Xebra, manufactured in China for Zap Motors of Santa Rosa, California, has three wheels and even though it seats four, it is classified in many states as a motorcycle. . . . The $69,000 electric Scion xB, dubbed the eBox, is built by AC Propulsion, the same California company that supplies the electric drive system for the Tesla Roadster. According to *Vanity Fair*, Elon Musk sighed at the prospect of buying a slightly less-expensive eBox when AC Propulsion wouldn't agree to custom-electrify his Porsche. "Who wants to take an ugly $20,000 car and buy it for $65,000?" Musk asked. "That's not a very viable strategy. I wouldn't want to drive it. My wife certainly wouldn't want to drive it."

90 *Even more important to Eberhard, the Roadster also promises to change . . .* On June 11, 2006, Martin Eberhard told the business magazine *Red Herring,* "There have been tons and tons of companies, for the last 40 years, that have tried to make little commuter electric cars. The trouble is that, for the most part, it requires the buyer of such a car to change his or her nature. You're buying a car that is not as good as an equivalent gas car at all—slower, uglier, with not as much range—and they're trying to compete on price, where they can't win. None of these cars were built for people who really like to drive. I get the feeling they're for people who don't really think you should be driving, but think if you do have to drive, it should be an electric car. I think if you build a car for people as they are, not requiring them to change their nature, it's much more likely for you to succeed. And I think our investors agree."

91 *There are signs other electric-car makers are catching on . . .* In early 2007, Zap announced it was partnering with Lotus Engineering to develop the

ZAP-X Crossover, a luxury electric sedan priced at about $60,000 that will presumably compete with Tesla's White Star. Zap promises the ZAP-X Crossover will have a superior 350-mile range and rapid-charge technology that can recharge the batteries in ten minutes. Both claims have been greeted with skepticism in the electric-vehicle world.... Tesla Motors received a $561,000 grant from the Alternative Fuel Incentive Program of the California Air Resources Board. The Tesla Motors news release of May 25, 2007, quoted the grant proposal solicitation as stating, "Electric fuel vehicles have the largest potential to reduce climate change emissions and petroleum dependency relative to any other alternative fuel vehicle under consideration."

92 *With California already subsidizing the construction* ... Former CIA director James Woolsey, writing in the December 20, 2006, *Wall Street Journal* ("Gentlemen, Start Your Plug-ins"), argues that innovations in lithium-ion batteries (the type used by Tesla Motors) will soon make it possible to replace foreign oil with cheap, off-peak electricity by plugging in hybrid gasoline-electric cars overnight. Since the cars would power-up during low-demand nighttime hours, Woolsey cited estimates that 84 percent of all U.S. vehicles could switch to plug-ins before any new power plants would be needed to be built. During hot summer days when power demand peaks, any electric cars plugged in with their batteries fully charged could actually return power to the grid. That would help take the strain off the electric system and help avert the risk of costly brownouts and blackouts—a case of the rich working for *everyone*.

CHAPTER FIVE: THE DOCTOR WILL SEE YOU WHENEVER YOU'D LIKE

95 *The term* concierge *has seeped into common parlance in America* . . . Glenn Withiam authored the paper "Concierges Set Service Standards," which appeared in the *Cornell Hotel & Restaurant Administration Quarterly*, August 1993.

98 *Based on the success of the Cierge program* ... Facts about the Centurion card are gleaned from various news accounts. American Express is very circumspect about discussing qualifications for the "black card," or how many people actually carry it.

99 *The size of Circles' clientele means the firm has leverage* . . . The estimate of Circles' stature as a major buyer of flowers was made by American Demographics way back in 2000, in "The End of Leisure—Teleshopping at Work," July 2000. Circles will neither confirm nor deny its ranking in the flower-buying business.

99 *For a concierge company to have attracted such scale* . . . The *Wall Street Journal* published "Undivided Attention: How PepsiCo Gets Work Out of People—It Has Hired a 'Concierge' to Do Helpful Personal Chores That Can Be So Distracting" on April 1, 1993. The article reported that PepsiCo's in-house concierge was willing to try to do "any useful thing that isn't illegal or sponsored by Coca-Cola."

100 *As the concierge economy has been steadily expanding* . . . On July 20, 2006, the *Wall Street Journal* tested Andrea Herbert Lifestyle of New York, Prominent Concierge of Atlanta, Gofer Girls of Los Angeles, Upon Your Request of Dallas, and Envy Concierge of San Francisco. All charged between $25 and $50 per hour for tasks that included picking up dry cleaning, pet-sitting, gift-buying, and finding an event caterer. The *Journal*'s writer deemed all of them to be valuable services well worth the money during stressful times and emergencies.

100 *This decline in exclusivity has led to some chafing* . . . Houston-based Everest Funeral Package, LLC, offers what it claims to be "the first nationwide funeral planning and concierge service." For an annual fee ranging from $48 to $68, Everest is on call for when your time comes, and will research local prices and negotiate on your survivors' behalf with the funeral home of their choice. The company made the *Entrepreneur* magazine "2007 Hot List." . . . In the Oct. 2005 issue of *Travel & Leisure*, author Michael Gross tested out a high-end personal concierge service in Manhattan called Quintessentially. Gross and his party of six were seated immediately at a hopelessly crowded and popular restaurant, thanks to a call from his Quintessentially concierge to the maître d'. "The restaurant's managing partner later denied that any of this had happened, insisting that nobody ever gets preferential treatment," Gross wrote, "which goes to show that Quintessentially can make the impossible happen."

103 *A 2005 study by the Government Accountability Office (GAO)* . . . The most comprehensive government study of concierge care is *Physician Services: Concierge Care Characteristics and Considerations for Medicare,* GAO Report GAO-05-929, August 2005.

103 *Concierge medical practices remain a rarity in most communities* . . . There is a shortage of primary care physicians in the United States, but not in the metropolitan regions where concierge physicians are typically found. Some 56 million Americans live in areas with insufficient numbers of primary care physicians, according to a 2007 report by the National Association of Community Health Centers called "Access Denied: A Look at America's Medically Disenfranchised." A map produced for the study shows that primary

care physician shortages are most acute in rural counties, particularly in the deep South and the prairie states, usually hundreds of miles from the nearest concierge practice.

104 *Middle-Class Millionaires, it appears, have both the inclination and the means . . .* Adults receive recommended levels of medical care only about half the time, according to a Rand Corporation study, "The Quality of Health Care Delivered to Adults in the United States," which appeared in *The New England Journal of Medicine* on June 26, 2003. Rand surveyed 13,000 adults in the largest and most comprehensive health care survey ever conducted in the United States. The study's authors concluded that "the deficits we have identified in adherence to recommended processes for basic care pose serious threats to the health of the American public." . . . The Disney World quote is from "How to Set Up a Concierge Practice," by Wayne J. Guglielmo, in *Medical Economics*, August 22, 2003. . . . In "Deluxe Doctors," *Fortune Small Business*, July 1, 2004, Steve Geller is described as MDVIP's first customer and subsequent CEO.

111 *With physicians' incomes flat and their workloads growing . . .* The American Medical Association has asked for state and federal regulators to investigate retail health clinics for possible conflicts of interest, *Medical News Today* reported on June 26, 2007. The store-based clinics have appeared in supermarkets, pharmacies, and "big-box" retailers including Wal-Mart. There are an estimated 200 open today, with plans in the works for another 1,000.

115 *From its inception, concierge medicine has been treated with almost universal disdain . . .* Richard Roberts' criticism of concierge care appeared in "Doctors' New Practices Offer Deluxe Service for Deluxe Fee," *New York Times*, January 15, 2002. Waxman's bill, H.R. 4752, introduced on May 16, 2002, never made it to a vote in the 107th Congress. Uwe Reinhardt's critique appeared in "McDocs for the Rich," *Forbes,* August 6, 2001.

115 *Since concierge medicine originated . . .* In "Dr. Levine's Dilemma," *New York Times Magazine*, May 5, 2002, Dr. John D. Goodson, a primary care physician and associate professor at Harvard Medical School, called concierge medicine a "slow-developing apocalypse" for the entire medical system. "These guys are going to have to spend a significant percentage of their time marketing themselves, creating a perception that they offer more," Goodson said. "That's where a lot of their extra time will go." The truth is that, thanks to the Influence of Affluence, concierge physicians often have wait lists of prospective clients referred to them by their Middle-Class Millionaire patients.

116 *Marketing has also proven not to be a problem . . . The St. Louis Business Journal* of June 28, 2007, reported that MDVIP has already spawned a concierge-

care imitator in pediatrics—the exact service Bradley Tavel wished he could provide for his daughter. Dr. Natalie Hodge charges her patients $1,500 per year and told the *Journal* she intends to grow Personal Pediatrics, Inc., as a national network, along the lines of MDVIP.

116 *Former Wisconsin governor Tommy Thompson* . . . Tommy Thompson expressed his support for concierge care in general and for MDVIP in particular on the *NBC Nightly News*, December 26, 2005.

121 *Prior to 2005, the Society for Innovative Medical Practice Design* . . . Dr. John Blanchard, then-president of the American Society of Concierge Physicians, was quoted in the April 2004 issue of *Physician News Digest* as saying, "We're going to be changing our name . . . to try to describe the more personalized nature of the services that we offer." He suggested "retainer-based medicine" and "patient-driven healthcare," but neither seems to have the resonance of "concierge medicine."

CHAPTER SIX: THE BEST ADVICE MONEY CAN BUY

124 *It wasn't until 1995 that coaches had a credentialing association* . . . The International Coaching Federation study was done by the research firm PriceWaterhouseCoopers. Nearly 6,000 coaches in seventy-four countries were surveyed between September and December 2006. The average coach is forty-six to fifty-five years old and has coached for between five and ten years; more than half of those surveyed had attained at least a master's degree.

125 *As a marketing concept, coaching has caught fire* . . . In "Personal Life Coaches Seek Advice from Other Coaches," the *Wall Street Journal* on Nov. 2, 2002, estimated at the time that there were 25,000 people in the United States calling themselves life coaches or work coaches—double the number three years earlier.

128 *Enrollees in the basic three-year program* . . . "A Well-Balanced Life: Got Game?" appeared in the February 2004 issue of *Inc.* magazine.

138 *Ben Franklin wrote, "Leisure is the time for doing something useful . . ." The Arizona Daily Star* reported on September 14, 2006, that Miraval had taken the "triple crown" for spa ratings in major travel magazine reader polls. It was top-ranked in North America by SpaFinder and *Conde Nast Traveler,* and rated best in the world by *Travel & Leisure.*

139 *Miraval's latest move is to open a 350-unit "inspired living residence"* . . . The *New York Sun* sent a real estate writer to look at Miraval's Manhattan home. "There are simple renovations in the condo business, and then there is what they're doing to this place, which is nothing short of spectacular," he wrote on November 16, 2006. "Everyone moving into this place seems young,

hip, and rich. They've been to Miraval spas before and are willing to pay beyond the $3 million it costs for some of the three-bedroom apartments to get those premium spa services. This is Manhattan. Everything costs extra."

CHAPTER SEVEN: THE OWNERSHIP EXPERIENCE

147 *When Case's name—with an AOL e-mail address . . .* Revolution LLC, Steve Case's private holding company, also owns Miraval, the spa we wrote about in Chapter 6. Regarding Revolution's business approach, Case told *Newsweek* in its October 2, 2006, edition, "The goal is to find early-stage companies with an idea we think has the potential to be a multibillion-dollar business . . . built around the idea that there's a better way." Other Revolution-controlled companies include Flexcar, which extends the time-share concept to automobiles, and RediClinic, which offers fee-for-service routine health care in retail stores, including Wal-Mart.

148 *It all helps explain why fractionally owned residence clubs . . .* The latest estimates on the fractional ownership industry are from the executive summary of the Ragatz and Associates report "The Shared-Ownership Resort Real Estate Industry in North America: 2007." The report struggles with the nomenclature and various ownership-status differences among "fractional interests," "private residence clubs," and "destination clubs." The main thing all three groups have in common is their appeal among Middle-Class Millionaires. Ragatz assumes the potential market is made up of about four million households with incomes exceeding $200,000. Exclusive Resorts officials have in the past considered their market to be households with a net worth of $2.7 million and above—just about the median for our Middle-Class Millionaires.

150 *In an interview with* Brandweek *magazine in 2006 . . .* In "Marketers of the Next Generation," *Brandweek*, April 17, 2006, a vice president for Exclusive Resorts' advertising agency claimed that ad campaigns for Exclusive Resorts sought "to connect bad experiences with solutions. . . . If someone says, 'We're going to Hawaii with two families and a nanny and there's no room in our hotel,' we have the solution. We had to sell the category and the brand."

152 *The whole notion of owning just a piece of something great . . .* "Always on Your Mind: The Burning Issues Business Owners Are Thinking About." *Entrepreneur*, December 2005, opined that "in the gotta-have-it social world we live in today, offering consumers a piece of the pie could be a sweet deal for you."

152 Forbes *magazine's rundown of seven luxury trends . . .* "Seven Trends in Luxury," *Forbes*, June 2005, asked, "Why own and maintain a yacht, luxury auto, jewelry or even big-name art when membership in an elite club will allow you to use the stuff just about anytime?" *Forbes* thought membership

makes better business sense than ownership, too: "It cuts your cost and reduces risk." . . . Milton Pedraza of the Luxury Institute predicted in late 2006 that the small entrepreneurial pioneers of fractional ownership "will merge, consolidate, or disappear, due to lack of resources, flawed business models, or worse." In Pedraza's view, the more established luxury brands will inevitably use their vast resources to legitimize fractional ownership "for the mainstream affluent and wealthy."

155 *If the Deer Valley Club sounds to you like little more* . . . No one but developers seems to make money on time-shares. Ray Jacobs, editor of *TimeSharing Today*, an independent specialty magazine, told the *New York Times* on August 19, 2006, that when an owner sells a time-share property bought new from a developer, he or she is likely to get only about half the purchase price. He added that owners who manage to buy from other individuals are more likely to break even when they sell.

159 *The rapid growth of fractional ownership clubs* . . . Richard Keith of Private Escapes is quoted in "Destination Clubs Become Popular Way to Experience Dream Vacations," *Hartford Courant*, July 5, 2005. . . . In "What Is Luxury Without Variety?" *Harvard Business Review,* April 2006, Milton Pedraza and coauthor Eric Bonabeau ask, "In an age when consumers crave variety, luxury items pose a bit of a problem. How do you satisfy affluent people's yen for a range of goods that are simply too pricey to buy in multiples?"

159 *That question is now being asked every day in a wide range of luxury businesses.* . . . For news, reviews, and buyer's guides, *Helium Report* at heliumreport.com is an essential and objective source of information about all things fractionally owned—real estate, jets, yachts, and cars.

165 *Even with 250,000 members, the Seattle company* . . . In June 2007, Bag Borrow or Steal launched "America's Ultimate Bagaholic Contest," a search for the country's most handbag-obsessed woman. Said a company spokesperson, "We're constantly looking for creative ways to actively engage our members and also introduce the concept of 'borrowed luxury' to bagaholics everywhere."

CHAPTER EIGHT: "ROOTS AND WINGS"

173 *About 22,000 people came through Oak Knoll* . . . IRS data for the Ladera Ranch zip code shows remarkable stability in household income during the first four years of the development. As it grew from just 1,493 filings in 2000 to 6,978 in 2004 (the most recent year available), the average gross adjusted income each year varied only slightly in the $95,000-to-$101,000 range. The number of small-business filings remained around 25 percent. To lend some

perspective, the most famous zip code in the world, 90210, Beverly Hills, had about 28 percent small-business filings.

174 *As new villages were developed, RMV took bigger risks* . . . The ten principles of New Urbanism, as detailed on the New Urbanism Web site, www.newurbanism.org, are walkability, connectivity, mixed-used and diversity, mixed housing, quality architecture and design, traditional neighborhood structure, increased density, smart transportation, environmental sustainability, and quality of life. Ladera Ranch lives up to these principles with two notable exceptions—diversity and transit. The desirability of the community has made it unaffordable to homebuyers who are not Middle-Class Millionaires, and there is no public transit connecting the community to the rest of Orange County—a failing of government, not Ladera Ranch.

174 *Psychology Today* took a long look at Ladera in its September/October 2005 issue with "Backlash in the Burbs: There's a new movement that uses intelligent design to cure America's soulless subdivisions. Is it possible to make people the moving force in suburban life?" Writer Sarah Elizabeth Richards concludes, "Ultimately, what makes New Urbanist communities like Ladera most exciting may be their willingness to experiment with a revised balance of community and individual interests. For many Americans they may be the homiest way to curb the isolating excesses of individualism."

174 *To serve some of Ladera's entrepreneurial work-at-home population* . . . The *Los Angeles Times* profiled Ladera Ranch's Front Street on December 28, 2003, with "It's a Make-a-Living Room: A California Neighborhood Truly Mixes Business and Residential Use." The *Times* hailed Front Street as representing "the leading edge in the transformation of the American suburb from residential refugees into modest centers of commerce." The story quoted a National Association of Homebuilders estimate at the time that nearly a quarter of homes are being built with home offices—spaces exclusively designed for work

174 *In 2004, RMV's work with market researchers* . . . Covenant Hills and Terramor are partly products of RMV-commissioned psychographic research done by a firm called American Lives. The process is described with a somewhat jaundiced eye in the *Washington Post* of April 16, 2006: "Redefining Property Values: By Design, Status Seekers and Tree-Huggers Don't Have to Commune."

184 *And as with Ladera Ranch, Verrado broke some rules* . . . In November 2004, the *Arizona Republic* published an extraordinary five-part account of Verrado's early development. In its edition of November 28, 2004, a 4,500-word article entitled "Phoenix's Growth Driven by Insatiable Demand," followed independent businessman Kevin Johnson and his wife, Holly, as

they make the typical Middle-Class Millionaire choice of a desirable community that is also in the flow of money: "The Johnsons liked their home in Phoenix. But after seeing Verrado's town center, home designs and, most importantly, the crowds rushing to buy, they knew buying early would mean a healthy profit in the future."

CHAPTER NINE: THE NEW RULES OF THE NEW RICH

186 *There were already plenty of worries about the U.S. economy . . .* "Shares Slip as Investors Fear Oil Prices Will Slow Growth," *New York Times,* August 27, 2005, told of how Wal-Mart's worries about oil prices affecting its sales might reflect a wider pullback in consumer spending. "Mixed Signals," *National Journal*, September 17, 2005, offers a snapshot of the confusion in government and financial circles following Katrina.

186 *But the economy didn't stall in 2005 . . .* From "Katrina's Economic Impact: One Year Later," ABC News, August 25, 2006. "The majority of economists surveyed by the ABC News Business Unit said the storm had only a short-term impact on the nation's economy. 'It's amazing how large and resilient the economy is,' said Bill Dunkelberg, economist for the National Federation of Independent Businesses."

187 *In October of 2005, a group of young equity analysts at Citigroup . . .* Citigroup issued two "industry notes" on Plutonomy within about six months. The first, "Plutonomy: Buying Luxury, Explaining Global Imbalances," was issued on October 16, 2005. A follow-up, "Revisiting Plutonomy: The Rich Getting Richer," issued on March 5, 2006, took a second look at the theories advanced in the first paper in light of the just-released Survey of Consumer Finances for 2004.

187 The Citigroup paper of October 16, 2005, pointed to the high-earning, high-spending habits of Middle-Class Millionaires and the distorting effects those habits may be having on traditional economic forecasting: "Outlandish it may sound, but examined through the prism of plutonomy, some of the great mysteries of the economic world seem to look less mystifying. As we showed, there is a clear relationship between income inequality and low savings rates: the rich are happy to run low or negative savings given their growing pool of wealth."

187 Every year the *Wall Street Journal* runs a competition among economic forecasters, and for 2005, the winner of the competition was the one forecaster who took his eye off the econometric models. Sung Won Sohn, an economist and chief executive of Hanmi Financial Corporation in Los Angeles, made a rosier prediction for economic growth than almost all his

competitors, and he turned out to be right. In "Pricey Jeans Give Hanmi CEO Leg Up to Top Rank of Forecasters," January 3, 2006, Sohn explained in the *Journal* that a clothing manufacturer had told him they were having trouble meeting the demand for $250 jeans: "He figured 'there must be money out there if people are willing to pay that much' for blue jeans." Like a real Middle-Class Millionaire, the Korean-born Sohn likes to lunch with clients and visit their workplaces to get a firsthand sense of what's going on. "I talk to people on the ground," he told the *Journal*.

187 *Kapur boldly declared that the United States is now a "plutonomy"* . . . By Ajay Kapur's analysis, not all advanced economies have become plutonomies—it's mainly just the English-speaking ones. The United States, United Kingdom, and Canada are "world leaders in plutonomy," but with the single exception of Italy, none of the nations of continental Europe are plutonomies. Japan is not a plutonomy, either.

187 The "Top 100 Retailer" report in *Stores* magazine, July 2007, showed that Wal-Mart's profits grew by just 0.5 percent in 2006. Nordstrom's profits grew by 23 percent, and Saks' profits grew by 140.5 percent. Saks' same-store sales grew by 14.4 percent in the first quarter, the highest rate of growth the company CEO claimed he could remember.

187 *The trend can be seen most clearly in the way Wal-Mart's sales growth* . . . The Associated Press reported on July 23, 2007, that Wal-Mart's same-store sales—a key indicator of any retailer's health—actually fell in April 2007 compared with the same period in the previous year. It was "the weakest performance since [Wal-Mart] began publishing monthly sales in 1980." The economy during the same period showed moderate growth.

188 *Citigroup developed a "Plutonomy Basket" of stocks* . . . "Citigroup's Kapur Says the Rich Keep World Afloat," *Bloomberg News,* March 20, 2006, describes how Drawbridge Global Macro Advisors has taken up short-selling mass-market retailer stocks. In the same article, Gerard Lane, an investment strategist at Morley Fund Management in London, says that the plutonomy theory helps explain "why so many of us have been wrong about the U.S. consumer over the last five years."

188 *American society has been moving in this direction* . . . Economists Emmanuel Saez of the University of California at Berkeley and Thomas Piketty of the Paris School of Economics have continued to update their November 2004 paper, "Income Inequality in the United States, 1913–2002." Their work is cited in the Citigroup Kapur paper, and their most recent update was covered by David Cay Johnston in the *New York Times*, March 29, 2007, "Income Gap Is Widening, Data Shows."

189 *Outsized gains in executive compensation* . . . The growth of performance pay was studied in a National Bureau of Economic Research working paper, "Performance Pay and Wage Inequality," by Thomas Lemieux, W. Bentley Macleod, and Daniel Parent, issued May 2007. "Income Inequality, Writ Larger," a Daniel Gross column in the *New York Times*, June 10, 2007, quotes Lemieux as saying that beyond performance pay in corporate jobs, "when you look at the self-employed and contractors, inequality is much higher." Entrepreneurship is a bigger winner-take-all game than most.

193 *But consider for a moment the trends we've cited* . . . Other recent books that have addressed the growing instability of middle-class incomes include *The Great Risk Shift,* by Jacob S. Hacker, and *The Disposable American,* by Louis Uchitelle.

196 *In August 2005, an article appeared in the* Chronicle of Higher Education . . . For researcher Jerome P. Horwitz's full story, see "Missed Chances," by Goldie Blumenstyk, in *The Chronicle of Higher Education,* August 12, 2005.

196 *Among businesses eager to squeeze the best out of employees* . . . In his most recent book, *Falling Behind: How Rising Inequality Hurts the Middle Class,* Robert H. Frank says the winner-take-all trend in the economy has remained strong since his 1992 bestseller was published. "No matter how you slice the data, the pattern of inequality growth is the same," he writes. "If you look only at college graduates, for example, the basic pattern is that those at the bottom of the earnings ladder have gained almost no ground since 1980, those in the middle have gained only slightly and those at the top have experienced extremely rapid earnings growth. The same is true of authors, real-estate agents and physics majors. Within almost every group, the pattern is the same as the one we see for the economy as a whole." An alternative way of interpreting Frank's findings is to note that also within almost every group, within every profession, the twenty-first-century economy continues to expand the opportunities for people to become Middle-Class Millionaires.

INDEX

Courtesy of the author

RUSS ALAN PRINCE is president of the market research and consulting firm Prince & Associates, Inc. (russalanprince.com), and a founder of *Private Wealth* magazine. He is a columnist for *Elite Traveler* and the author or coauthor of more than forty professional development books. He lives in Redding, Connecticut.

© Emile Wamsteker

LEWIS SCHIFF leads a team of private wealth experts specializing in the needs of high-net-worth clients for Advanced Planning Group (advancedplanning.org). He is a regular contributor to Inc.com and TheStreet.com, as well as a columnist for *Investment Advisor* magazine. He wrote the popular investment book *The Armchair Millionaire*. He lives in New York City.